D0948543

MARGUERITE DURAS

WRITING ON THE BODY

MARGUERITE DURAS

WRITING ON THE BODY

Sharon Willis

UNIVERSITY OF ILLINOIS PRESS
Urbana and Chicago

Publication of this work was made possible by
a grant from the Andrew W. Mellon Foundation.

This book is printed on acid-free paper.

Library of Congress Cataloging-in-Publication Data

Willis, Sharon, 1955–
  Marguerite Duras : writing on the body.

  Bibliography: p.
  1. Duras, Marguerite—Criticism and interpretation.
2. Body, Human, in literature.   3. Narration (Rhetoric)
4. Feminism and literature.   I. Title.
PQ2607.U8245Z94 1987   843'.912   86-4289
ISBN 0-252-01335-2 (alk. paper)

Contents

Acknowledgments

No work has a punctual genesis. Since it is the conjunction of intellectual legacies and a set of subjective passions, obsessions, and projects expressed through a specific historical discursive field, the work is a process. That being said, I want to acknowledge those who encouraged and sustained this project, and me along with it. My teachers at Cornell University, Nelly Furman, Richard Klein, and David Grossvogel, who read its earliest versions, provided me with the encouragement and direction without which this work could not have continued. Particular thanks are due David Grossvogel. Without his guidance through the details and frustrations of this writing, it might never have ended.

I also wish to thank my friends and colleagues in the Department of French and Italian at Miami University: James Creech, Marie-Claire Vallois, Mitchell Greenberg, Peggy Kamuf, Paul Sandro, Jesse Dickson and Nat Wing. Together, they have provided the best possible working conditions for this project: an arena of daily exchanges that are both generous and uncompromising. I would especially like to thank Janet Mercer; she may not have realized that *I* realized she was providing me with much more than technical support and assistance during my more frantic days at the word processor. I would also like to express my appreciation to Miami University for a generous grant in support of the publication of this book.

My thanks to those friends and colleagues who continue to sustain and transform my intellectual life, and my feminist projects in particular: Fran Bartkowski, Elissa Marder, Linda Singer, Jane Dickinson, Lynn

Enterline, Frances Kuffel, and Jackye Zimmerman. My thanks also to Ann Lowry Weir of the University of Illinois Press, for her sustained work on behalf of the manuscript, and her most intelligent suggestions, and to Lee Erwin for her thoughtful and thorough editing.

Finally, I want to acknowledge Len Green's participation (sometimes voluntary, at other times imposed) in this project. He was there at the beginning, and he has had an incalculable impact on my thinking about gender, desire, pleasure, and politics. It is through my exchanges with him, my most formidable and most forgiving critic, that I continually reposition my thinking, and myself, in the world.

Introduction

Long a respected figure on the French literary scene, Marguerite Duras eludes any effort to situate her work in a fixed area. In the over forty years she has been publishing, her work has always resisted easy classification, in part because she produces novels, plays, and films simultaneously. To date, she has produced over twenty novels, nearly as many plays, numerous essays in the lively exchanges of French journals, and a number of films, her filmic production having evolved from early scriptwriting and collaborative efforts on *Hiroshima mon amour* and *Moderato cantabile* to her more recent work as a director executing her own concepts. Occupying several fields at once, Duras' work sets up a series of exchanges among them, particularly because it often produces narrative, theatrical and filmic incarnations of the same themes and scenes.

Duras' texts resist generic convention: films without narration *(La Femme du Gange, Nathalie Granger)*, novels composed of visual figures *(Le Ravissement de Lol V. Stein, India Song, L'Homme atlantique)*, film scenarios that read like novels *(India Song, Hiroshima mon amour, Aurélia Steiner)*, theater and films in which the actors read, rather than perform, their roles *(Le Camion, La Maladie de la mort)*. Her significance in the French literary scene no doubt derives in part from that position—between novels, theater, and film—as if no medium could convey a final version of a story. Significantly, most of her titles carry a generic label as well, as if we would not be able to determine the status of the object without it.

Duras disappoints—or perhaps deceives? French has an admirable

1

double meaning for the word *décevoir,* which can mean either disappoint or deceive. In their invariable display that something is missing, her fictions are about expectations unfulfilled. Perhaps it is this potential for deception and withholding that makes her fiction alluring. This is not a passive disappointment, for Duras' force lies in her active subversion of expectation and demand. Her novels, films, and theater effectively defy generic bounds because they are inevitably rewritings or restagings of scenes that persist throughout her work. But even as repetition, they fail to satisfy *that* expectation entirely—the repetition is never quite the same. Something similar might be said of the writer herself, as a figure on the literary scene. The elusiveness of her texts is replicated in the mobility of her own position; as film producer, playwright and novelist, she is difficult to situate. As such, she may figure the subterranean contradictions and exchanges that ground literary production as a political and historical field as well. Reading her work may be a means of reading certain shifts and contradictions that make literary production what it is today in France, a complex exchange between theoretical and artistic production that yields perpetual efforts to explore and transform the encoding of literary and cinematic practice. Along with the constant repositioning that characterizes her work, Duras' elusiveness as a literary figure is no doubt one of the sources of fascination for readers—the artist exploring a variety of practices that contest and criticize one another.

Part of the task of situating Duras as a figure is to explore the sources and effects of the fascination she exercises upon the reader. Her obsessional method yields a variety of effects, not the least of which is a curious tension between familiarity and estrangement produced by the reappearance of figures in a series of texts, since these repeated figures inscribe an obsession that has all the features of a private, personal drama, despite its near-anonymous character, its feeling of authorlessness. The sense of uncanny familiarity then extends to figurations of the author within the work, as the origin of their obsessions. It becomes difficult to separate the figure of the author from her work, the life story from the emblems it inscribes in the obscurity of its textual references. That is, part of the reader's fascination depends on the effort to locate the author's traces in the work, to follow the clues, reconstruct *her* figure.

Duras' earliest narratives, beginning with *Les Impudents* (1943), and including her better-known *Un barrage contre le Pacifique* (1950) (which has just appeared in English as *The Sea Wall* [London: Hamish Hamilton, 1985]), *Le Marin de Gibraltar* (1952), and *Moderato cantabile* (1958), all present a linear narrative development, even though they bear the traces of the later textual obsession with memory and desire, locked together in repetition, which will become the performance of repetition that characterizes the later texts, from the 1960s onward—*Dix heures et demie du soir en été, L'Après-midi de Monsieur Andesmas*, and the Lol V. Stein cycle. These texts perform the repetition they thematize, reducing narrative movement to a minimum. Increasingly, each text recalls previous ones, isolating fragments, scenes, details, and figures that appeared in a larger context in an earlier text. Duras' work, taken as a whole, appears based on fragmentation and dispersion. This serial focus on the fragment is consistent with a certain "postmodern" concern for the broken piece, for the shattered totality and for serial repetition of a minimal set of elements. However, in their refusal of textual boundaries—their intertextual recall and perpetual rewriting—the texts from the 1960s to the present resemble more one long narrative than a series. They constitute a sort of inverted *A la recherche du temps perdu*, substituting dispersal for recollection. It is this feature that establishes Duras' difficulty of access. Beginning with the Lol V. Stein texts—*Le Ravissement de Lol V. Stein, Le Vice-consul, L'Amour* and *India Song* and *La Femme du Gange*—it is difficult to read one Duras text without the support of the others. To read *one* is to become caught in a cycle of repetition and to know it, so that the reader follows a set of relays through other texts in a search that parallels the texts' own obsessive repetition. While it is possible to read a text in isolation, one only feels the force of the narrative mechanism, or strategy, through retroaction, a retroaction that develops after several readings, producing a sense that what one reads was "already read."

As such, Duras' texts exemplify a resistance to consumption and disposability. Instead, they demand perpetual rereadings; they do not consolidate a singular message that, once received, is finished off in the act of consumption. These are not books to consume and throw away. Rather, they offer an apprenticeship in another form of reading, based on repetition and intertextual circulation. At the same time, however, they demand an engagement, a commitment on the part of the reader, a willingness not to finish, not to advance, but to return, to repeat, to read

3

the entire corpus, since the legibility of a given text is dependent upon the others. Such repetition then calls into question and reframes literary reception as being itself a process of inscription.

This picture of Duras' work has just taken yet another shape, and with it, the picture of Duras herself. The publication of *L'Amant* (1984) and its nearly immediate translation into English as *The Lover* (translation Barbara Bray [New York: Pantheon, 1985]) marks Duras' first really popular success. Heretofore, as a novelist, she has not had such popular success in France, although her plays have been produced with regularity in the past few years. In the United States, her work is virtually unknown, and is considered rather inaccessible, at best. With the publication of *L'Amant,* which won the Prix Goncourt and subsequently sold over 700,000 copies within six months of its publication in France, I find myself wanting to account for such an unexpected phenomenon. Once again, Duras disappoints, deceives?

It's not just a compulsion to account for literary phenomena, to situate them in fixed and irrevocable categories, that motivates my explorations here, but rather the desire to take into account the fact that Duras' work is again crossing boundaries and thereby throwing them into question. In this case, the work questions the boundaries between "high" and "low" culture, between academic and popular, or mass-reception, literature, which may be emblematic of certain conjunctions and certain shifts in literary production and reception.

While Duras' most recent text is structured according to a more familiar and legible narrative order, it also displays the ambivalences that characterize her more difficult work. The June 9, 1985, issue of the *New York Times Book Review* carried a full-page advertisement for *The Lover* which highlights, unconsciously, the text's doubleness. First, there is the contrast between the external face of the text—its cover, or, more figuratively, the publishers' and critics' discourse surrounding it, as a sort of packaging within which it is offered to the public—and the contradiction it strikes with the text's inner face—the content, the letter of the text. The ad announces "Duras' incandescent novel of first love," and includes a *Saturday Review* comment that "this exotic, erotic autobiographical confession will deservedly become one of the summer's hottest books." Catchy as that sounds, one is most struck by the doubleness and the contradiction within the ad, between "novel of first love" and "autobiographical confession," a contradiction never resolved. One might argue that this is more than an oversight; in its groping way, this superficial, perfectly ordinary copy has hit the mark: *The Lover* is profoundly ambivalent, undecided. In its narrative vacillation between "I" and "she," this mostly linear textual organization will not be pinned to the conventional confessional or fictional modes.

Indeed, one suspects that part of the appeal of this text lies in its duplicity, its pretense to confession coupled with its refusal to swear to truthfulness (thereby replicating a standard feminine icon, the woman who seduces by her duplicity). The reader's pleasure is that of hearing the private "exotic and erotic" confession, these qualifiers not to be taken at all lightly. Clearly, despite the third person narrative intervention, many will want to read this text as strict autobiography, taking pleasure in its erotic side (this is the story of a sexual initiation and a first love affair), and its exotic side (set in Indochina in the 1930s, it recounts a "forbidden," or at least socially proscribed, affair between a Chinese man and a European woman). Not only does the text contain many parallels with Duras' own life (she was born in Cochin China, a part of what was then Indochina and is now Vietnam, in 1914), but it opens with a lyrical but brutal description of the narrator's/author's face. It is that description that has prompted critics to turn to Duras' face, to images from her youth and contemporary ones, in focusing their comments. Diane Johnson concludes her review of *The Lover* (*New York Times Book Review*, June 25, 1985) with a reference to its author's beauty. And Michel Tournier, in *Vanity Fair*, July, 1985, devotes most of his article on *The Lover* to scrutiny of Duras' face, study of her image, speculation on her ethnic origins. A text that begins with the face of its author, although it contains no images, and that elaborates a prolonged description of the author as a subtext to the love story, is, in a sense, a book about shaping a figure. The disfiguration of the face (figura) may be its real subject.

At the same time, as a result of a particular coincidence with the literary market, Duras is cutting a figure in the commercial scene, cutting a figure that cuts across literary boundaries—between popular and high culture, between the novel and autobiography, between the figure and the face. And, I think, her new success is in part due to her capacity to be a figure, and the coincidence of that capacity with readers' desire for a fascinating woman author-figure. Like her book, it seems, she is an erotic and exotic figure.

But what is this figure, exactly? What is singular about Duras is her resistance to a single reading or appropriation, immobilization in a fixed frame. Similarly, the complex configurations of her texts raise hard questions about the connections between eroticism, pleasure, and power, sometimes in violent forms. Therefore, we must see the figure of prostitution in *The Lover* as having several faces, or registers. It might be read as the literalization of a persistent metaphor for the marginal economic status of literary production in Western culture: the author as prostituted to the literary market. In that case, *The Lover* is an ironic figure for the writer's ambivalence about her insertion into market relations, or for the public's discomfort with that insertion, a discomfort based, on the one hand, on a false separation between art and the profane matter of making a living, and, on the other hand, on a resistance to the appropriation of all artistic practice as an object of consumption. As readers and consumers, then, we can't escape certain reflections on our own position.

But *The Lover* is also a figure of transgression, and not just in the common way, as a woman writing her erotic memoirs, "telling all" about an affair. Rather, Duras the author can be linked to the woman of her story—the alcoholic woman, parading her devastation and her survival, and recounting her past as an "exotic" seductress. She was raised in Indochina, and grew up bilingual, although she spoke Vietnamese everywhere but at home until age eighteen, when she departed to study in France. She is thus the "Other" within, a strangely familiar, or familiarly estranged, figure—a "non-Western" Western woman. In this double-faced figure of Duras, we might then read our own anxiety about the Other, as well as our desire to incorporate the other, to reduce difference. However, given the text's strategy of veiling and unveiling, where "I" veils herself as "she," but where "she" just as frequently masquerades as "I," we cannot maintain a rigid and secure separation of same and other, interior and exterior. Nor can we as readers determine and fortify a fixed vantage point, and the reassuring distance that that would entail. We are implicated in the issues the text raises and refuses to put to rest.

It is not accidental that it is with a novel that is explicitly erotic that Duras gains popular recognition. No doubt this is one of the pleasures of the text—the woman represented here passes from virgin to prostitute, a passage motivated by transports of passion unleashed by the appeal of the forbidden. But what differentiates this text from a pornographic scenario is precisely its attentiveness to the complex of erotic impulses that motivate both the affair and the narcissistic confessional enterprise. This text explores with subtlety the subtext of a passionate affair, a subtext filled with violence and brutality, since it takes up the problems of separation and loss, power and domination, within a social and familial scene, as well as the private space of the two lovers. The text displays the complex connections of sexual pleasure and violence, and sexual pleasure and economics, as the woman more or less prostitutes herself to the man, allows herself to be kept, and uses her power over him to extort money for her brothers' entertainment.

Like some other recent Duras texts *(L'Homme assis dans le couloir, Agatha, La Maladie de la mort),* this is a text whose erotically appealing passages are linked to a devastating violence and negativity. Traces of this effect appear in most of her love stories, and the conjunction of domination and desire appears in better-known early texts like *Hiroshima mon amour* and *Moderato cantabile,* and even as early as the short story "Whole Days in the Trees" (1954). Until *The Lover,* however, these earlier narratives seemed to be the form in which these configurations could be most easily tolerated; the violent fragmentation of their more recent embodiments render them too disturbing. This version, in fact, retroactively facilitates our access to the earlier texts of the 1980s, since it repeats the scenes they offer. Consequently, to read them in view of *The Lover,* and to read *The Lover* as part of a series of narratives rooted in erotic fantasies and exploring their lability, clarifies the stakes of this form of representation.

The figure of an exhibitionist female subject should have special force for feminist readers. Duras has long been a central figure for feminist readers and critics, in both the United States and France, in part because she is one of the most prominent contemporary French woman writers. More important, her work centers on issues of concern to most feminist theoretical enterprises: desire and sexuality, gender and biology, the relation of the body to language.

The Lover reinscribes the exhibitionist scenario in a woman's active self-display, a presentation of her life as spectacle—active, that is, as opposed to the passive form of woman as object of/spectacle for a mastering gaze, that of reader or spectator. As such, the text is a complex structure: an erotic tale which is not based on representation of a woman as object, but which constitutes a narcissistic parade. Its seductive effects operate not only within the narrated scenes, but also, and perhaps most powerfully, in the autobiographical register, as the "I" veils itself in "she," giving us a new version of the seductive intermittence of erotic spectacle. Duras evades us, as she attracts us, in an alternating play of veiling and unveiling.

A similar ambivalence is central to readings of the sadistic edge to eroticism, as it is depicted in *The Lover* and, even more powerfully, in texts like *La Maladie de la mort, Agatha, Détruire, dit-elle,* and *L'Homme assis dans le couloir.* And this ambivalence is crucial, since it firmly links pleasure and violence, demanding that the reader confront their imbrication in desire and sexuality. Duras' transgressive impulse extends to an area of particular concern for feminist thought at the moment: the politics of pleasure, the relation between pleasure and power. Where her texts raise the question of how pleasure and power, desire and violence, are related, they invite us to imagine other forms in which these terms might be configured. In order to do so, we must give up our impulse to maintain a rigid separation between pleasure and power, desire and violence, just as we recognize the complex construction of gender identification as part of a process, a social articulation of the body. For these reasons, Duras is not only a compelling figure for feminist critics, but a crucial site of interrogation for theoretical enterprises concerned with the articulation of pleasure and power in representation and sexuality.

Finally, the transgressive nature of this text operates on another level as well; transgressing the conventions of erotic literature, and crossing the boundary between "difficult" and popular fiction, this text allows us to explore the complexity and ambivalence entailed in representing feminine sexuality within a more popularly available form than her previous texts. It may allow us to map the effects of such representation within the framework of popular consumption. Certainly, feminist theory has long debated the historical significance of these boundaries and their effects on women's production and reception of art and literature. Does one betray a feminist project, origins, or goals by becoming popular? Or by refusing to be popularly accessible? And here, my own position is uncertain, as I try to render Duras more accessible. Do I mislead by proposing that the uninitiated reader explore her work? Do I subvert the force of her project by trying to make it more available, more legible; do

I situate it within a false framework of interest? These final questions, significant for a literary critic and a feminist, indicate the range and scope of the terrain Duras' textual transgressions open for us, since they demand nothing less than the reconsideration of our operative categories of literary production and reception.

CHAPTER

1

Preliminary Mappings

From her earliest narratives, Marguerite Duras' work has concerned itself with borders. One of her first novels, *Un barrage contre le Pacifique* (1950), thematizes relations of power and desire in maternity, and figures the violence of separation and loss within a metaphoric network centered on the image of an intractable, engulfing tidal flood that repeatedly destroys all barriers. A marginal figure in this text is that of cinema, for the mother in the story once earned her living playing the piano in a movie house. Almost thirty years later, Duras takes up the same family scene: the moment when a brother and sister, whose relationship is highly incestuous, are at the threshold of permanent separation from a deranged and overbearing mother. This time, however, the narrative has become theater. *L'Eden cinéma* (1977) is theater called by the name of cinema, theater haunted by its other, the other form of spectacle just beyond its boundaries, just behind the scene, just offstage, since the cinema is no more than a metaphor for the illusory utopic past, prior to any separations, and before the family's move to the tidal plain which is constantly threatened with inundation.

In a sense, the configuration produced by *Un barrage contre le Pacifique* and *L'Eden cinéma* is emblematic of Duras' entire project. Her production is equally prolific in narrative, theater, and film; often a single narrative or scene generates a separate work in each of the three genres. Scenes and figures—of trauma, loss, separation—are perpetually transformed, from the earliest narratives to the most recent theatrical and filmic productions.

Thematically, all of Duras' work is concerned with desire and representation, desire in representation, and with the impossibility of adequate translation, or perfect coincidence, between desire, the body itself, and language. But this project has a performative aspect as well, since, taken altogether, it constitutes a continual translation and reconstruction of the same configurations, formations, scenes. It is a continual reframing that forces us, as readers/spectators, to confront the very contradictions the work thematizes: between body and language, image and voice, reading and acting, writing and producing images. This work refuses to stay centered in frame. Instead, it continually repositions us as its readers/spectators, rewriting itself in ever more complex and contradictory ways. Beginning with narrative texts that refuse closure through the radical instability of their narrating agency, and, concomitantly, of the reader position they invoke, Duras' work eventually translates the issues of framing and address into theater and films that question the limits of their own generic structures. Her recent theater operates on the border between reading or recitation and acting; her cinema renders explosive the contradictions between voice off- and image onscreen. In each case, her work pits the genre against its own rules, exploring the contradictions of each representational formation, while it uses different generic configurations—translations—of the same scene to call into question any stable frame.

In their overt focus on feminine figures, perpetually transformed, deconstructed and reconstructed in "repetitions" of the same scenes, Duras' texts raise the issue of gender in representation as well. Because of their obsessive concern with maternity and feminine desire within a perpetual reframing, these texts explore the non-coincidence of body and language, a particularly crucial issue for a feminist reader, critic, or theorist.

In a recently published debate, Peggy Kamuf and Nancy K. Miller stage a dialogue, grounded at two opposing theoretical poles, concerning the status of feminist criticism. In the course of this discussion, they adumbrate a contradiction that presently conditions feminist literary inquiry and that finds a condensed embodiment in the debate surrounding terms like *écriture féminine* and "inscription of the body." This debate questions the relationship of writing to the body, of language and the referent, as part of a larger examination of the possibility of posing any feminine specificity.

This particular debate is but one instance among many recent performances that work within the same frame and upon the same contradictions. I therefore put it forward as *exemplary*. I do not wish to privilege it, since its exemplary status resides precisely in the overdetermined relationship that example and rule always maintain: the example always works to question and displace the rule it might be imagined to "illustrate." Beyond its explicit sense of its own frame, even as it attempts to frame the major issues of feminist theory, this debate has the advantage of a particularly rich metaphoric relay, whose close examination reveals certain implicit conflicts at work within the general theoretical field. Finally, the written form of the originally oral performance *momentarily* fixes, in a generally accessible location, the terms of a debate that repeats itself, albeit always with differences, as well as with delays, in most discussions of feminist theory—discussions which, because of their situation in oral exchange, are not so generally available for examination.

For Nancy Miller, it is necessary to maintain a concern for the status of the woman writing, in the interest of producing connections with the woman reading, with women in the world. Her objection to theory that wants to leave aside as "essentialist" the question of the gendered body is the following: "By glossing 'woman' as an archaic signifier, it glosses over the referential suffering of women. Moreover and implicitly, to code as 'cosmetic,' and to foreclose as untimely, discussions of the author as sexually gendered subject in a socially gendered exchange . . . is to be too confident that non-discursive practices will respond correctly to the correct theory of discursive practice."[1] For Peggy Kamuf, however, to lay too much stress on the referent is to hypostatize a category of "woman" to place over against masculine discourse, and thereby to remain within its humanist boundaries. For her, the decision that "criticism should aim to rectify an omission from the institutional mainstream, producing a knowledge about women which has been excluded there by a masculine dominated ideology," carries the danger of being merely "cosmetic modifications on the face of humanism and its institutions," thereby reproducing "the structure of women's exclusion in the same code which has been extended to include her."[2]

I find myself snared in a similar contradiction in my choice of a project. Why a woman writer? It is clearly not a matter of indifference to me. If I choose the oeuvre of Marguerite Duras as a field within which to analyze something like "feminine representation," it is because her narratives inscribe the form of this contradiction. At stake in Duras' texts is the problem of feminine representation and discourse, and of a relationship to the referent—the body, gender, history—as that which discourse approaches asymptotically. Indeed, the same must be said of my own text's approach to what I refer to as "the feminine."

The problem is surely not to "isolate" what is specifically feminine in Duras' production, for, I want to argue first of all, the "feminine" here is not at all punctual or unified. Furthermore, any attempt to isolate the feminine as a critical object necessarily reinforces a subject-object split that coincides with the false separation of theory from practice—literary or representational. Instead, I want to pose as clearly and as critically as possible a set of questions taken up by these texts in their elaborations of a desire that may be feminine.

My own position here clearly demands examination. To present Duras' texts as "feminist" texts, feminist writing, would be to betray my whole project by presuming to consolidate a feminist identity and, further, by producing a facile linkage between a feminine thematics and a feminine-gendered author as its referent. It would also be a reduction of the complexity of Duras' texts to the level of illustration. Instead, I take these texts as pre-texts which engage, in a noncontingent way, the most pressing concerns of my own position as a feminist reader, so that my critical writing, along with my reading of Duras' work, forms a sort of parallel project, a coincidence with her textual enterprise. This is, to say the least, a situational intervention which grounds itself in a series of texts that raise issues of a feminine discourse and its situation in a social field.

For a feminist criticism grounded in or propped upon literary practices that confront the issue of "women" in writing, the problem is as inevitable as it is insoluble. Not to broach the question of the body and writing is impossible, but to find a stable relation of determination between the two is unproductive. Here I find my text in the same aporia as Duras' with respect to the infinitely displaced, but never entirely disappeared, referent.

To ask, "Is this writing feminine?" is suspiciously close to asking "What is a woman?" (or to the hysteric's asking, "Am I a man or a woman?"). However, to pose a question without anticipating an *answer*, but instead a reply, a continuing displacement, may be different. My aim is to provide a point of reference, while also examining the status of such questions. What raises the interrogation in my own discourse is the suspicion that my fascination with these texts is related to an appeal, a pull or solicitation, that is mapped in them, and that, correspondingly, maps a position for the reader which I find it hard not to occupy.

Where might we find a feminine economy in these texts? Is it grounded in the textual syntax, as Duras seems to suggest at times? In *Les Parleuses*, when asked by Xavière Gauthier if the linguistic organization of her texts is in some way different from that governing men's texts, Duras gives the following extended reply:

> I never concern myself with the meaning, the signification. If there is a meaning, it emerges afterwards. . . . The word counts more than the syntax. Before anything else, it's the words, even without articles, that come and impose themselves. . . . Grammatical tense follows, rather far behind. . . . It is the blanks, if you will, that are pressing. It happens like that: I am telling you how it happens, the blanks are what appear, perhaps without the stroke of a violent syntactic expulsion, yes, I think I recognize something there.[3]

However, at Gauthier's insistence that the feminine be localized there, in the blanks, the rupture of syntax (as she puts it: "If there is a blank inside, wouldn't it be there that the woman would be?"), Duras will only ask, "Who knows?" (12).

Duras confronts the questions of desire and feminine writing more directly in an interview with Michelle Porte in *Les Lieux de Marguerite Duras*. Referring to her own literary production, she comments: "We don't write at all in the same place as men. And when women don't write in the place of their desire, they don't write, they are plagiarizing."[4] Duras repeats this conception of feminine writing in an interview published in *Signs*, where she associates women's writing with translation: "I think 'feminine literature' is an organic, translated writing . . . translated from blackness, from darkness." The issue of translation is connected to "plagiarism," as Duras formulates it: "The writing of women is really translated from the unknown, like a new way of communicating rather than an already formed language. But to achieve that, we have to turn away from plagiarism."[5]

Although these statements imply a belief in an essential femininity, their juxtaposition with Duras' literary practice, which expresses quite a different impulse, adumbrates an impasse that conditions feminist critical theory in general. In its concern for feminine specificity and its awareness that the feminine always resides in a relation to discourse, which, however structuring, also transcends gender in forming part of the social field, Duras' literary practice concerns itself with representation as translation. Translation here must be considered along the lines of Mary Lydon's complex reflections on the process, as embodying a "difference within," exploding relations of priority, the fixity of the original, which must instead be seen as forever lost in, to, and through the translation.[6]

Translation seems a particularly useful metaphor for a feminist theory of textuality. As Jane Gallop formulates it, translation can serve as a metaphor for the relation discourse maintains with the body:

> Translation, like metaphor, is imbued with the difference within, for it is never simply itself, but must represent another text and thus includes another within its identity. Not only is literature at the heart of sexual difference, but sexual difference is at the heart of literature as the absent original to which the translation must refer. I would attempt the statement that literature is a translation of sexuality if I could add that we have no direct access to the original, that the best we ever have available is a good translation.[7]

In "Woman's Stake: Filming the Female Body,"[8] Mary Ann Doane traces the contours of this ideological impasse through critical readings of several feminist theorists. In one of the most incisive treatments yet of this issue, she outlines the debate as organized around the two poles of "essentialist" and "anti-essentialist" readings of femininity. The essentialist position tends toward an idealist and utopian assumption that there is a fundamental feminine *nature* to be disclosed, demystified; the anti-essentialist position, contrarily, tends to consider any representation of the feminine in relation to the body necessarily a "naturalization" of a discursively produced feminine specificity.

The article addresses the issue of sexual difference as it both conditions and is conditioned by a differing relation to discourse and representation. Doane begins with the work of Parveen Adams, for whom the "phallus represents lack for both boys and girls. But the boy in having a penis has that which lends itself to the phallic symbol. The girl does not have a penis. What she lacks is not a penis as such, but the means to represent lack" (28). In other words, the woman "lacks lack," or as Michèle Montrelay, a theorist to whose critical analysis Doane devotes considerable space, puts it: "For want of a stake, representation is not worth anything" (29). The "point" here is that the little girl has no means to represent lack and no anatomical/visible site subject to symbolic threat, the paternal prohibition. According to this theory, the girl's relation to language would then be conditioned by her "having nothing to lose." Indeed, for Montrelay, the feminine is "capable of remaining on the edge of all repression,"[9] and, hence, of representation, which, in her view, depends on repression, as well as on the loss of the object, since the woman herself becomes the lost object when she repeats her mother's maternity. All of this, however, comes suspiciously close to simply substituting the "lack" for the "phallus," and thus merely leaving in place the opposition to have/to have not as the stake of sexual difference. In this effort to specify a feminine imaginary associated with its particular form of maternal relation, Montrelay's theoretical position indeed supplements the psychoanalytic (Freudian) refusal to recognize that sexual difference operates even in the imaginary region of the maternal dyad, a refusal accomplished to the profit of a theory of sexual difference that situates an essential, preverbal/presocial "feminine" as a kind of nature.

In this respect, many feminist theorists find Julia Kristeva's work on the maternal dyad more fruitful, since, through the notion of the drive or pulsion, it allows for a conception of this pre-Oedipal space, the semiotic chora, as already symbolized and symbolizing. Kristeva takes the *pre*-symbolic to be precisely that—prior to, but already in relation to, the symbolic. In the Kristevan affiliation of the feminine with the presymbolic—because of the woman's negative entry into the symbolic—the risk is the permanent marginalization of the woman with respect to symbolic discourse, as the irruption within it of the "semiotic."[10]

In a discussion of "feminist" theory, or rather, theories of/and the feminine, in France, Alice Jardine situates Kristeva's most contemporary work in a larger frame of theoretical modernism, in order to show that its stress on the semiotic constitutes a complex reading of the semiotic as the site of the primary mappings which later support discourse.

> Henceforth, theorists of/in modernity will begin a search for the potential spaces of a "truth" which would be neither true nor false, for a truth which would be *in-vrai-semblable*. . . . This approach involves, first and foremost, a relinquishing of mastery—indeed a valorization of non-mastery. Secondly, the *true,* to be isolated in those processes as anterior to, or in some cases, beyond the truth as produced by the *Technè,* is that which can never be seen, which

never presents itself as such, but rather, captures, points, withdraws, hides itself in veils; and that true is "woman"—the "non-truth" or "partial true" of Truth. Or, for others, "woman" is precisely that element which disturbs even *that* presumption (Truth as castrated).[11]

The impact and importance of these developments, as Jardine outlines them, is in their ability to take into account that the category of the feminine is something to which our best access may be its discursive effects. However, it is also possible that the field of discursive exploration may shift, so that woman would only make sense as a discursive category. More important, as Jardine argues, the risk is that woman as metaphor of the Truth may be treated as *only* a discursive effect, leading to the possibility of its appropriation into theoretical and philosophical currents that finally evaporate the materiality of the body and the world in which it works.

Confronting the contradictions of contemporary feminist theory, Mary Ann Doane returns quite productively to the work of Laplanche, in *Life and Death in Psychoanalysis,* using it to link the two opposing tendencies. For her, the pivotal notion is expressed in Laplanche's elaboration of the Freudian concept of anaclisis, propping, to explain how sexuality peels off from the vital functions, through displacement and metaphorization. When the drive moves beyond the object of function and satisfaction, for instance nourishment, to a hallucinated object—the breast as part object—this latter object is derived from, and displaced in relation to, the object of vital function.

> The drive, properly speaking, in the one sense faithful to Freud's discovery, *is* sexuality. Now sexuality, in its entirety, in the human infant, lies *in a movement which deflects the instinct, metaphorizes its aim and internalizes its object, and concentrates its source on what is ultimately a minimal zone, the erotogenic zone.* . . . This zone of exchange is also a zone for care, namely the particular and attentive care provided by the mother. These zones, then, attract the first erotogenic maneuvers from the adult. An even more significant factor, if we introduce the subjectivity of the first "partner": these zones focalize parental fantasies and above all *maternal fantasies,* so that we may say, in what is barely a metaphor, that they are points through which is introduced into the child *that alien internal entity* which is, properly speaking, the sexual excitation.[12]

Laplanche's refusal of a split between the somatic processes and their psychical "representatives" finds the two always already inserted in a social, intersubjective, discursive structure, as body *invested* with sexuality by the parental speech, gestures, and fantasies that constitute the discourse of the family romance within which the child's place is already inscribed. In other words, it is the material care and the stimulation it causes which map these zones as eroticized. At the same time, however, the actions involved in caretaking are themselves saturated with meaning, so that what passes through the zones of exchange in the body is inevitably both matter and meaning.

For Laplanche, the meaning exchange is based in the family discourse, the complete Oedipal structure, which is "present from the beginning," both "in itself" ("in the objectivity of the family configuration"), and, above all, "in the other," outside the child (45). The path through which that entity "in itself" is appropriated "passes initially through a confused and, in a sense, monstrous apprehension of the complex in a primordial other" (44). In other words, the Oedipal structure is built into the family, as both contemporary and historical, since the parents reconstruct it in a social organization and through the mediation of their own relations to *their* parents, as in a series of interlocking triangles. It is this family discourse that invests the body with sexuality and gender.

This is the gesture that interests Doane most intensely and that she uses to set up a "zone of exchange" between the conflicting currents of feminist theoretical practice. In addition, Doane wants to introduce into feminist theorization of the body the concept of propping articulated by Laplanche, and according to which sexuality is, precisely, propped on the body's vital processes, from which it deviates continually. She effectively extends the figure of anaclisis, with its emphasis on displacement in relation to the object, to the relationship of discourse and the body. "Sexuality can only take form in a dissociation of subjectivity from bodily function, but the concept of bodily function is necessarily in the explanation as, precisely, a support" (27). By analogy, for Doane the discourse of feminine theory (and feminist film practice) then may, and perhaps *must*, see itself as "propped on" the body. This fundamental imbrication of body and language through metonymic and metaphoric displacement is what allows us to see the body as metaphorized by language, and language as grounded in the body, which is sexed in its earliest contacts with another body.

Moreover, the theory of propping locates the zone of exchange in a social field, where the child takes in discourse along with food, where sexual difference is invested through the discourse of the parents. To think sexuality as propped on a family discourse, as a mapping of investments, allows us to imagine sexual difference as a function of a relation to the mother. That is, the child's shift from being or not being the phallus, to having it or not, must involve considering for *whom* one is or has the phallus.

This insistence on a relation to the mother allows us to begin to conceive the production of or access to sexuality as already at work in the acquisition of language and subjectivity, since the maternal body, which is also propped on the child's, recognizes and acts in function of sexual difference. For Kristeva, moreover, the moment of anaclisis in the subject's history is related to the menace of death, as well as of castration: "Incest prohibition throws a veil over primary narcissism and the almost always ambivalent threats with which it menaces subjective identity. It cuts short the temptation to return, with abjection and jouissance, to that passive status within the symbolic function, where the subject, fluctuating between inside and outside, pleasure and pain, word and deed, would find death, along with nirvana."[13]

The maternal dyad always poses to the subject the risk of "being swamped by the dual relationship, thereby risking the loss not of a part (castration), but of the totality of his living being" (64). Consequently, the incest taboo of which the stake is the phallus, the menace of castration, which imposes the cut, separation from the maternal body, also acts as a safeguard against an engulfing indifferentiation. In that case, the little girl's relation to the cut might be construed as somewhat more difficult and ambiguous than the boy's. For Kristeva, because the woman is always split in her relation to the maternal body, never fully barred from her own mother, and repeating her mother's maternity in her own reproduction, she maintains a privileged relation to the border of the semiotic and the symbolic. "A woman also attains it (and in our society, especially) through the strange form of split symbolization (threshold of language and instinctual drive) of the 'symbolic' and the 'semiotic' of which giving birth consists."[14]

This splitting repeats itself in the loss of the object—the most profoundly lost object—placenta or breast—which is simultaneously, though differently, lost by both mother and child. Thus the woman confronts an unrepresentable on both sides of the specular relation of maternity, as daughter and as mother.

As Michèle Montrelay analyzes it in her essay "The Story of Louise": "To give the hallucinated breast is to live and sustain the anxiety without being able to measure it. In the mother-child relationship there is always this dimension of impotence; there is either acceptance or refusal."[15] Montrelay contends that the experience of giving birth modifies the mother's relationship to the part object (in Lacan's sense), as she repeats her own birth, deferred, where the loss of the placenta reproduces a loss of the breast. Because the mother is a speaking subject, of course, this loss is different; however, both mother and child participate in a loss at this moment: "For the child the trace of a loss of the membranes is the navel. For the mother it is the child's cry when he is born . . . the one and the other lose some life" (85). This is why, as Montrelay puts it, a woman is impotent to say something at the moment of giving birth. We might say that this is also the locus of the unrepresentable, which is grounded in death.

Maintaining this notion of a discourse propped on the body is perhaps as crucial as the notion that sexuality is something acceded to, produced within a set of representations, rather than "given" or natural. If feminist discourse is not to naturalize femininity, to seek an ideal, unmystified, and essential version of itself, and, correspondingly, is not to see sexual specificity as completely inaccessible to representation, it needs to work within this frame. Because sexual difference remains a site of ideological investment, a discursive network that codes accession to specific forms of sexuality and its representation, the notion that the body and language maintain a relation of reciprocal "representivity"—metonymically and metaphorically charged—is essential to theoretical inquiries.

As Stephen Heath poses the problem in "Difference," sexual difference, and the discourses grafted onto it, must be thought of as historical, not essential.

The joining-disjoining overlap of the biological by the mental as the turn of the subject allows a quite radical conception of sexuality, allows the possibility of quite another posing of difference. Sexuality is not given in nature but produced; the individual subject is not constructed from sexuality, sexuality is constructed in the history of the subject, with difference a function of that construction not its cause, a function which is not necessarily single (on the contrary)

21

and which, a fortiori, is not necessarily the holding of that difference to anatomical difference (phallic singularity). Production, construction in the history of the subject, sexuality engages also from the beginning, *and thereby,* the social relations of production, classes, sexes—an engagement which cannot be, the lesson of psychoanalysis, against the effective implications of its theory, cannot be left aside, for later, beyond the enclosure of the analytically defined area.[16]

By setting up the question "otherwise," within the larger social field which subjects must enter and where they must act from their position as sexualized subjects in, and for, ideology, Heath restores to sexual difference its historical dimension and condition, as produced in a material and discursive field.

By virtue of its concern with representing femininity, with the feminine in discourse, feminist theory already entertains an at least tangential relationship to Marxist interrogations of ideological representation. Indeed, it seems that any effort to determine a feminine specificity within discourse or representation is futile if it fails to situate its project within a historical frame; that is, to provide an analysis that questions the field of collective representations that constitute and are constituted by ideology.

Ideology, here, must be understood as "a practice of representation, and a subject constructed for that representation—this being a practice with a specific role and effectivity in the social formation, a practice that acts and is invested in certain material institutions," as Coward and Ellis define it in *Language and Materialism.*[17] With respect to sexuality, they focus on the institutional discourse of the family and its affiliated institutions, and in so doing establish that the relationship of sexuality to institutions and their discursive formations is overdetermined. The process by which the infant comes into both its sexual position and its subjectivity involves a series of identifications already situated within ideology. The access to subjectivity, to agency, also involves a *subjection,* an insertion into a network of power relations. These power relations operate, in part, by means of institutions and discourses addressed to a stable subject, since at the same time that they serve to consolidate this identity, to fix it in place, these discursive formations are also dependent, for their very operation, upon the maintenance of a consistent subjectivity or the illusion thereof.

Because Coward and Ellis attempt to refine an approach to the relationship between material and nonmaterial practices, their work on ideology and subjectivity in ideology seems directly pertinent to the sort of feminist analyses I am proposing, and this, primarily, because their theory allows for a conception of sexuality as produced along with subjectivity, in and for discourse. That is, subjectivity is both produced by and productive of discourse. The relation between sexuality and language is similarly overdetermined, since sexuality is partially structured by discourse while it also *produces* discursive effects.

In order to explore the contradictions that underlie feminist theory through the filter of literary practice, one might consider the complexity of feminine representation. One possible approach to the problem of representing femininity is to consider the "feminine" as a space. For Alice Jardine, the space of internal difference in a narrative, the text's own non-knowledge, the limit of its mastery, is a "space coded as feminine" ("Gynesis," 58). This she articulates, with Lacan, as "the feminine *jouissance* which will be posited as the ultimate limit to any discourse articulated by Man" (61). She situates this limit as follows: "It is, however, only the first of a series of such limits, which, through metonymy, will all be engendered as feminine. For example, the limit of any discourse for Lacan is also the 'true.' . . . The 'True,' like woman, is not All. And this 'true,' inter-dit, located as it is between words, between-the-lines, provides an access to what is perhaps the most important discursive limit for Lacan, the Real" (61).

The feminine, then, is a discursive effect. We might flesh out this argument a bit by imagining that all subjects experience this limit, the "real," insofar as they are subject to discourse, and that women therefore maintain a relation to this "feminine" space as limit also. Feminine *jouissance* is that which escapes discourse, and which may therefore be linked to the real. Jardine situates Lacan's Real as having no ontological foundation: "It is neither Reality, nor History, nor a Text. The Real designates that which is categorically unrepresentable, non-human, at the limits of the known; it is emptiness, the 'zero-point' of death, the proximity of feminine *jouissance*" (62).

I find this stress on the unrepresentable particularly pertinent to the question of a feminine writing. All of those "unrepresentables" constitute limits that may be metonymically linked to the "feminine," to which a female subject establishes a relation that may differ from that of the masculine one, and which would involve a split within that relation. With specific reference to Duras, all of her narratives figure a relation to the feminine, to the border of the unrepresentable, to death. In her textual concern with the unrepresentable, the feminine appears as a kind of limit itself, a limit that is related to spaces—spaces within, gaps within—and spacing, a kind of punctuation that casts a retroactive rhythm through the signifying chain.

Through their insistence on borders, on exploring the limits of their own discursive practice, discursive spacing, and rupture, Duras' narratives approach the unrepresentable. The particular and related *figures* of this unrepresentable: a loss mourned, murder, the dead body, the scream, the hole in speech, all participate in the textual approach, through repetition and displacement, to the real. That is, these texts figure the impossibility of a discursive accession to the real, while simultaneously forcing, through the pattern of breaches, of empty figures, our recognition that discourse is never out-of-relation to that unrepresentable real.

The fascination of Duras' narratives lies in their figuration of the *cut,* separations and boundaries which delimit only ambiguously, and whose torsions abolish a stable distinction between interior and exterior. This textual priority of cutting, *découpage,* and repetition as well, admits the simultaneous operation of an "anterior" linguistic space—the persistence of the semiotic mappings of the body in the maternal space where the subject first emerges in the signifying *coupure,* split in the discourse of the Other. In this sense, the textual relation to the real is analogous to its inscription of the body, the maternal body, the split that inhabits both the body and discourse. This instance of splitting is also the moment of the intersection of the maternal with death, at the point where a cut establishes both a loss and the temporality of before and after.

Hiroshima mon amour crystallizes the problem of narration, telling an impossible story, and of representing collective history (a historical referent, the event of Hiroshima), as well as of figuring femininity within a narrative space. The text's relation to history here is at least double, if not polyvalent, since its historical referential level is imbricated with an investigation of a subject's memories, with the discursive approach to the mastery of a moment of trauma. In this case, the trauma is situated at the intersection of historical and personal past, which throws into question both the public-private split that conditions a major division in our social space and our thinking of history as a set of events collectively produced and retroactively interpreted, narrated, as a story a culture tells itself.

"Elle," the feminine figure in *Hiroshima,* is a woman who suffers from "reminiscences." Moreover, she succeeds in telling her story only in a dialogic mode, recounting past events to a lover, the speaker who utters the "je" to her "tu" address in the discursive memory scene of *Hiroshima.* As such she figures an hysterical discourse.

For Christiane Mawkward, in "Structures du silence/du délire," Duras' discourse may be associated with hysteria because of its textual mutism, which she describes as a kind of systematic blockage or braking of signification, through effects like contradiction, repetition, and memory gaps.[18] Duras' narrative discourse may be linked to hysterical discourse because of its blockages, silences, and gaps, and particularly because her texts are about the overlap of language and the body in their common relation to articulation, segmentation; just as much, however, they are about temporal articulation and segmentation: punctuation, repetition, and succession.

Articulation may be seen as the organizing textual operation, on the level of the signifying chain, the narrative movement, and the textual figures, as well as in the larger frame of Duras' entire corpus. Indeed, the oeuvre itself, in its repetitions and displacements of a minimal repertoire of figures, has a syntax of articulation all its own, which calls into question the integrity of textual boundaries, separate narratives. For Madeleine Borgomano, this peculiar articulation of the corpus of narratives is linked to the "mendiante" figure. She goes so far as to postulate that this figure of the beggar woman, whose multiple maternity has left her barren, and who wanders aimlessly through India, tracing in the process the trajectory of her own movement toward oblivion, is the "generative cell" of the entire narrative project.[19]

This figure emblematizes the narrative enterprise on a variety of levels, condensing the narrative obsession with maternity, loss or abandonment, and death. In its very displacement through Duras' texts, from *Un barrage contre le Pacifique* through *L'Amour,* this imaginary figure of the maternal dyad, mother and daughter, exchanges and loss, perpetually repeating and differentiating itself, reproduces the etymological sense of the word "hysteria"—wandering womb. The mendiante-mother, in all the forms it takes in these narratives, is both a womb and a tomb, maternity and death.

Moreover, the metaphor of hysteria is elaborated most fully in the repeated textual interrogation of the relationship of word and flesh. For hysteria manifests itself as a disturbance of articulation, where the body, so to speak, "enters into the conversation." As such, the hysterical discourse may be characterized as follows: "In the hysterical symptom a part of the body is sacrificed to fill in a gap in the Other, to make him understand or respond. The symptom is signifying. It speaks a reply that the hysteric cannot pronounce—this is because she must await it from another body. When the symptom manifests itself, the hysteric is alienated from a body whose speech is actually addressed to her but in a language that she does not understand."[20]

Hysteria is a particular imbrication of word and flesh—a failure of spoken discourse, and a failure of address. At the same time, it is the word made flesh, the body which speaks in spasms, convulsions, cries, vomit, purgation, and incorporation. Hysteria is also related to a history not accessible to discourse, as Lacan has it: "The unconscious is that chapter of my history which is marked by a blank occupied by a falsehood: it is the censored chapter. But the Truth can be found again; it is most often written down elsewhere . . . in monuments: this is my body—that is to say, the hysterical nucleus of the neurosis where the hysterical symptom reveals the structure of a language."[21] The body appears as a monument displaying an inscription the subject cannot decipher.

Moreover, according to Freud's formulation, "the hysteric suffers from reminiscences." These are, he admits, the memories acted out in the hysterical attack, memories of an anterior space, an insufficiently repressed attachment to the mother, which accounts, he argues, for their fundamentally "bi-sexual" character.[22] So the hysteric presents a tenaciously remembered attachment to the mother, which constitutes a simultaneous refusal/inability to enter the family romance at the place designated for her. By extension, then, troubled in her speech, she troubles the social discourse, the articulations of the social body through the symbolic exchange of women.

Hysteria is intimately concerned with maternity, and in an ambivalent manner, since it is related to the body of the mother as well as to the subject's own maternity. As Moustafa Safouan characterizes it: "Unique condition of the hysteric—a possessed body: a body that spits, vomits, bleeds, grows fat and symptomatizes. Of all that she understands nothing. There is nothing surprising in her understanding, since it is *too much* (she knows too much about maternity), in which resides, not the distance, but the formal hiatus between this knowledge—which however real it may be, is no less marked by denegation—and truth."[23]

Whatever the truth of her discourse, the truth of her own desire, the hysteric approaches it through the question of the meaning of femininity, to which she gives the implicit reply, or interpretation, that it is motherhood. Thus, she puts the mother in the place of the woman, conflating the two to the extent that there is no place for woman. (We might observe that in this, she follows a masculine-dominated ideology of reproduction; however, her relation to it must necessarily be different.)

At the same time, however, if the hysteric keeps the past alive in her own flesh, her body resides at the border where articulation begins, in the indifferentiation of the maternal relation. Where discourse is blocked, where the subject is mute, the body recalls the emergence of the signifier, articulation, the peeling-off of desire from demand. It is surely no accident that the hysteric is characterized as dreaming of the complete coincidence of desire and love, and that, as such, she continually brushes against the space of demand.

We might say, then, that hysteria has to do with relations of language and the body, with the place of speech, and with the question of who speaks, from where, and to whom. For this reason, I can find hysteria a convenient metaphor for the narrative discourse of Duras' texts, particularly since they thematize certain of the symptoms, signifiers, that characterize hysterical discourse: the conflation of love and desire, the cry, the spasm, the fascination with oral functions—the mouth as locus of speech, incorporation and expulsion, acceptance or refusal of food. All of these figurations, in Duras' texts, are related to that maternal zone of oral exchange, where desire and demand (in the Lacanian sense) are bound together, where representation establishes itself in relation to the body, and where articulation imposes itself upon the cry.

For instance, surely the stress Duras' texts place on the cry—pure, unarticulated voice—is related to the hysterical body/discourse, the limit of the subject and discourse. This is the space where the pulsional mapping of the semiotic chora begins to elaborate a spatial mapping, the establishment of the cut. Michèle Montrelay explores the accession of

27

the subject to language, the infant's insertion into discourse in relation to part objects, which coincides with the cut, through the cry that marks an unsatisfied need, and which peels off from biological function, thus installing the subject in the field of the Other through the signifier. But even before the effects of meaning can take hold, there must be in the cry of demand the "*jouissance* of the primal representation," what Montrelay calls the cry as part object, as connected to the hallucinated object ("The Story of Louise," 87).

If the cry-object or the voice is a form of the *jouissance* of primal representation—signifying only itself—we must also connect it with the drives. Lacan clearly relates the part object to the cut, both as separation from the maternal body and within the body itself: "The very delimitation of the 'erogenous zone' that the drive isolates from the metabolism of the function is the result of a cut expressed in the anatomical mark *(trait)* of a margin or border—the lips . . . the rim of the anus . . . the vagina, the slit formed by the eyelids. . . ." The particularity of the part objects is related, by Lacan, to their representing "only partially the function that produces them." Further, Lacan emphasizes the one feature these objects share: "They have no specular image, or, in other words, alterity. It is what enables them to be the 'stuff,' or rather the lining, though not in any sense the reverse, of the very subject that one takes to be the subject of consciousness."[24]

These objects, then, are the unrepresentable, the fallout of representation, that support of representation which has dropped out of it through the agency of the cut. The part objects and drives which inhabit this maternal zone (as described by Lacan) are intimately linked to the problem of representation as Duras' texts explore it, through a perpetual approach to the unrepresentable: separation and death.

Duras' narrative corpus itself figures an hysterical body, in its repetition, a function both temporal and linguistic. If my analysis fails to respect the boundaries imposed by chronological succession in the oeuvre, it is because this body of work itself breaches any linear temporality of development, through the persistent reemergence of the same textual material: figures, words, phrases. The uncanny effect produced by the return of past material operates much like the "alien internal entity" that is sexuality in Laplanche's theory. The "alien internal entity" has the quality of an interior exteriority; it is both in the body and not *of* it, a fold within, something that belongs to the body and doesn't.

Further, its discovery is always dependent on retroaction: a knowledge that arises on the site of something experienced without benefit of a discourse to speak it—known but unknown simultaneously.

We must understand this "alien internal entity," a difference within, as constituting a border, as not fully assimilated. As such, it maintains and marks a limit, a division within the subject. But, just as much, it menaces the possibility of borders, as defining an integrity of the body or the subject. Consequently, we might link this metaphor with the hysteric's vomiting—the expulsion of a "bad" object (in the sense that Melanie Klein determines for it), or the unprocessed matter, food or discourse, that has precisely the effect of menacing the distinction: me/not-me, inside/outside. The undigested remainder of an incorporation, then, remains on the border of inside and outside, designating separation while remaining incompletely separated from the body, as its inside exteriorized, and thus indicates the border of representation and the unrepresentable. This, then, determines the status of the figures Duras' texts repeatedly throw up to us.

Duras' narrative discourse indicates the operation of the drive under representation in another textual obsession as well: the fascination with the voice. The invocatory drive is always toward the Other, according to Lacan, because the ear is, in the field of the unconscious, the only orifice that cannot close.[25] Hence, I think, the privileged status of the cry in Duras' discourse. The appeal, invocation, preempts communication or signification. But it also stresses the function of the drives as related to death, since all of the part objects are merely representatives of the libido as pure life instinct, of that which, paradoxically, the subject loses in its submission to the sexual cycle for its reproduction.

If, in their insistence on the pulsional lining of representation, Duras' texts establish a relationship between sexual difference and death, through a repeated figuration of the maternal, they also maintain another level of approach to death as the limit of speech and subjectivity. And this has everything to do with the effects of punctuation. For Lacan, the analyst's position is that of a scribe who punctuates the subject's discourse in such a way as to confer upon it its truth. That is, he punctuates the subject's question, inverting it for him or her. This discourse is cut up and fixed in function of time—precisely. The operation of punctuation is linked by Lacan to symbolization and to the death drive, through the notion of the compulsion to repeat, which "has in view the historiciz-

29

ing temporality of the transference," as the death instinct "essentially expresses the limit of historical function of the subject" (*The Language of the Self*, 85). The limit of the analytic process is then the subject's attaining his or her being-for-death. This Lacan describes as follows: "When we wish to attain in the subject what was before the serial articulations of the Word and what is primordial to the birth of symbols, we find it in death, from which his existence takes on all the meaning it has. It is in effect as a desire for death that he affirms himself for others; if he identifies himself with the Other, it is by fixing him solidly in the metamorphosis of his essential image, and no being is ever evoked by him except among the shadows of death" (85). Indeed, it is the punctuation, over greater or lesser intervals, that figures the connection of the Word and death, of death and "truth," in Lacan's sense. The interval, and the concern with that which is both before and after the Word, are clearly expressed in Duras' textual mutism as well.

The use of an analytical discursive paradigm here entails another feature that is pertinent both to Duras' narratives and to the question of hysteria and sexual difference. The hysteric's question, "Am I a man or a woman?"[26] would be punctuated by the silence of the response. The analysand's discourse amounts to a form of address, which must be situated: to whom and for whom is one speaking? We might speculate that in the case of the hysteric the question is the mother's—both to the mother and from the mother. Such a formulation relates it to the cry, addressed to the analyst's ear, perpetually open, indeed, in order *not* to hear. We might examine the reader's position with respect to Duras' texts in a similar way, as that which is posed as silent, unhearing, and yet somehow punctuating the question.

In that case, a speculation on the "feminine" in Duras' texts might include the possibility that the gender positions of reader and textual voice are reciprocally determined as discursive effects. As Derrida puts it rather elegantly: "I will even risk affirming this hypothesis, that the very sex of the addressor receives its determination from the other. I mean that it is the other who will perhaps decide who I am, man or woman. And it is not the case that it is decided once and for all; but it can be decided like that some other time."[27] As reader, I am caught in a web of solicitations, questions (not) addressed to me, but which somehow determine an *appeal*, an address that, through my insertion in the text, my punctuations—the ones it evokes and demands from me—determine its speech as feminine, within the perimeters of this historical encounter. Which is to say, an encounter produced in and through a shared discursive terrain of theoretical and literary practices. Which is to say that it could well be decided this way, or not, some other time.

N O T E S

1. Nancy K. Miller, "The Text's Heroine: A Feminist Critic and Her Fictions," *Diacritics* 12, no. 2 (1982): 49–50.

2. Peggy Kamuf, "Replacing Feminist Criticism," *Diacritics* 12, no. 2 (1982): 45.

3. Marguerite Duras and Xavière Gauthier, *Les Parleuses* (Paris: Minuit, 1974), 12, my translation here and in all later citations.

4. Marguerite Duras and Michelle Porte, *Les Lieux de Marguerite Duras* (Paris: Minuit, 1977), 102. All translations from this text are mine.

5. Susan Husserl-Kapit, "An Interview with Marguerite Duras," *Signs* 1 (1975): 425.

6. See Mary Lydon, "Translating Duras: 'The Seated Man in the Passage,'" *Contemporary Literature* 24 (1983): 259–75.

7. Jane Gallop, "Writing and Sexual Difference: The Difference Within," in *Writing and Sexual Difference*, ed. Elizabeth Abel (Chicago: Univ. of Chicago Press, 1982), 289.

8. Mary Ann Doane, "Woman's Stake: Filming the Female Body," *October,* no. 17 (1981): 23–36.

9. Michèle Montrelay, "Inquiry into Femininity," *Semiotext(e)* 4, no. 1 (1981): 229.

10. For a particularly subtle exposition of Kristeva's position and the critique it invites, see the following exchange in *m/f:* Beverley Brown and Parveen Adams, "The Feminine Body and Feminist Politics," *m/f* 3 (1979): 35–50, and Claire Pajaczkowska, "Introduction to Kristeva," *m/f* 5/6 (1981): 149–57. Adams and Brown are critical of Kristeva for construing pre-Oedipal sexuality as "an apolitical autonomy of polymorphous sexuality," which is, for them, "the positing of sexuality as an impossible origin, a state of nature" (39). They want to see sexuality as organized through discourses. Pajaczkowska responds to this critique by suggesting that Kristeva's work on *signifying practices* as constitutive of subjectivity is a necessary corrective to Adams and Brown's insistence on *discourses* without accounting for how they are generated.

11. Alice Jardine, "Gynesis," *Diacritics* 12, no. 2 (1982): 61.

12. Jean Laplanche, *Life and Death in Psychoanalysis,* trans. Jeffrey Mehlman (Baltimore, Md.: Johns Hopkins Univ. Press, 1976), 23.

13. Julia Kristeva, *Powers of Horror: An Essay on Abjection,* trans. Leon S. Roudiez (New York: Columbia Univ. Press, 1982), 63–64.

14. Quoted in Naomi Schor, "Female Paranoia: The Case for a Psychoanalytic Feminist Criticism," *Yale French Studies* 62 (1981): 211.

15. Michèle Montrelay, "The Story of Louise," in *Returning to Freud,* ed. Stuart Schneiderman (New Haven: Yale Univ. Press, 1980), 85.

16. Stephen Heath, "Difference," *Screen* 19, no. 3 (1978): 65–66.

17. Rosalind Coward and John Ellis, *Language and Materialism* (London: Routledge and Kegan Paul, 1977), 71–72.

18. Christiane Mawkward, "Structures du silence/du délire," *Poétique,* no. 25 (1978): 314.

19. See Madeleine Borgomano, "L'Histoire de la mendiante indienne," *Poétique,* no. 48 (1981): 479–94.

20. Stuart Schneiderman, "Lacan's Early Contributions to Psychoanalysis," in *Returning to Freud,* 7.

21. Jacques Lacan, *The Language of the Self,* trans. Anthony Wilden (Baltimore, Md.: Johns Hopkins Univ. Press, 1968), 21.

22. See Freud, "Some General Remarks on Hysterical Attacks," *The Standard Edition of the Complete Psychological Works,* ed. James Strachey (London: Hogarth Press, 1953), 9:227–34. All quotations from the *Standard Edition* will henceforth be cited as *S.E.* followed by volume and page numbers.

23. Moustafa Safouan, "In Praise of Hysteria," in *Returning to Freud,* 57.

24. Jacques Lacan, *Ecrits,* trans. Alan Sheridan (New York: Norton, 1977), 314.

25. See Lacan, *The Four Fundamental Concepts of Psycho-analysis,* ed. Jacques-Alain Miller, trans. Alan Sheridan (New York: Norton, 1978), 200.

26. Cf. Schneiderman, "Lacan's Early Contributions to Psychoanalysis," in *Returning to Freud,* 7–14.

27. Cited in Miller, 48.

CHAPTER

2

Hiroshima Mon Amour: Screen Memories

Hysteria, as Freud originally observes, is a disturbance of narration, of the ability to recount one's history, entailing a failure of translation from image and fantasy to discourse. The symptom, then, is conceived as marking the site of an obstructed translation into words.[1] Now the problem of discursive representation of the unfigurable—death, the trauma of loss, the historical catastrophe of Hiroshima—is a generative issue in *Hiroshima mon amour*. What is the relation between the narrative discourse and hysterical speech? This relation must be characterized here, as in all of Duras' texts, as one of derivation, of drifting from a common site.

In a recent article on *India Song*, Elisabeth Lyon describes the figures of hysteria and the fantasy in that film, in their relation to both psychoanalysis and cinema, in much the same way:

> It is in the *mise en scène* of this impossibility—the desire for an unsatisfied desire—that the structure of fantasy again rejoins the structure of *India Song*. . . . Although it is not here a question of hysteria or of desire and identification in hysteria, it was from a matrix of hysterical fantasies—Lol, Dora—that the question of desire was opened in the film and in psychoanalysis, but it is in their difference that our fascination with *India Song* derives. The film does not pose itself as a corrective to psychoanalysis, but it does take up and interrogate, within the structure of psychoanalytic theory, within the structure of a fantasmatic, the question of desire.[2]

The same may be said of *Hiroshima mon amour*—that it takes up questions of desire and the fantasmatic, in their relation to loss, through its various figurations of hysteria, on both the discursive and structural levels. But these figurations stand in a relation to hysteria as, precisely, a translation does to its "original," introducing difference within the original through that very figuration.

This text leans on hysteria as an organizing figure, through which it also approaches the problem of accounting for a historical event, for its memory as well as its status in the real. At the same time, it also inscribes and enacts certain contradictions at work in the narrative and the cinematic apparatus, as well as in our positions as readers or spectators. The text accomplishes a deconstruction of its own enterprise precisely through its contradictory relation to inscription and to the monument, the tomb as mnemonic device, a concretized inscription of memory, which is simultaneously writing as burial.

The very title of *Hiroshima mon amour* exposes one of the text's principal contradictions. A historical referent and a concrete location are invoked in a phrase that can be read as vocative, a form of address. At the same time, this phrase consists of an appositional structure that renders its reference obscure. The appositive proposes several logical impossibilities: the place or event is personified; the words, *mon amour*, come to qualify it or act as its attribute. Further, the first-person possessive adjective is initially, as well as ultimately, in this text, untethered/unanchored to any localizable "I" subject position. Indeed, this stress on an impossible form of possession only serves to emphasize the utter dispossession the text enacts. But this first textual gesture also encapsulates the central textual problem of subjective access to history, to the historical event. In so doing, it immediately problematizes the text's relation to its referent.

If read in terms of the contradictions it elaborates, the text and the film of *Hiroshima mon amour* propose a critical reading of a theory of history as a series of monumental events which are thoroughly knowable, as well as to a theory of a unified subject for knowledge, for desire, and for history. But this critical stance bears its own risks: that of an endless deferral of the subdiscursive, and of a related collapse into its own fascination with the unknowable and with its own textual practice as an interrogation of sight and narration.

From its beginning, *Hiroshima mon amour* questions the possibility of looking and seeing, as well as the possibility of speaking about an event. The film's opening sequence produces in us an anxiety and a desire to identify a human body as an unmutilated integrity. "All we see are these shoulders—cut off from the body at the height of the head and hips—in an embrace, and as if drenched with ashes, rain, dew or sweat, whichever is preferred. The main thing is that we get the feeling that this dew, this perspiration, has been deposited by the atomic 'mushroom' as it moves away and evaporates. It should produce a violent, conflicting feeling of freshness and desire."[3] The desire in question is a desire to see—but what? First, something identifiable, and, then, a sexual scene. However, the first words of the dialogue create an utterly disjunct convergence: "You saw nothing in Hiroshima" (15). History interrupts the moment of satisfaction that accompanies a mastery of the image through its identification as a recognizable object: However, now that you've seen something, you've seen nothing. This denial of sight, of the having seen, inaugurates the dialogic overture of *Hiroshima mon amour,* which conjoins radical interrogations of seeing and of speaking about Hiroshima. As Duras puts it in her synopsis: "Thus their initial exchange is allegorical. . . . Impossible to talk about Hiroshima. All one can do is talk about the impossibility of talking about Hiroshima. The knowledge of Hiroshima being stated a priori by an exemplary delusion of the mind [comme un leurre exemplaire de l'esprit]" (9).

The highly problematical status of such a notion as an "exemplary lure" already situates the text in a critical relation with respect to the idea of the example as model, proof, or illustration, and to forms of knowledge. This is crucial in a text whose project is to confront an unprecedented and singular event whose enormity emphasizes the limits of discursive practice. But as Duras stresses, the specificity of this inconceivable historical event, which nevertheless occurred, may also act as a lure, in its character as an unknowable experience, a lure, precisely as an instance of individual and collective trauma.

The impossibility of speech generates an obsessional effort to speak precisely that impossibility, to see that event, and to translate that image into words by recounting a story. This impossibility is just as much a lure for us, the readers/viewers, however, and constitutes the site of our absorption in the fantasmatic spaces the text invests.

"Hiroshima will be the common ground (perhaps the only one in the world?) where the universal factors of eroticism, love, and unhappiness

35

will appear in an implacable light. Everywhere except at Hiroshima, guile is an accepted convention. At Hiroshima it cannot exist, or else it will be denounced [sous peine, encore, d'être nié]" (9-10). Hiroshima, then, becomes simultaneously the locale of a love story and the space where nothing comes into being except to be negated.

In fact, the story of Hiroshima itself will be told under the sign of negation. As it is replaced by the substitute story, the *histoire d'amour,* Hiroshima's narrative will emerge only as already negated by that substitution, even foreclosed by it. However, this textual foreclosure is itself complicated. Duras' synopsis of the scenario frames it with negations. She describes the concluding scene of the love story, as well as of the film, as follows: "And in the room, *nothing* happens [rien n'aura lieu]. . . . They will simply call each other again. What? Nevers, Hiroshima. For in fact, in each other's eyes they *are* no one. They are the names of places, names that are not names. It is as though, through them, all of Hiroshima was in love with all of Nevers [le désastre d'une femme tondue à Nevers et le désastre de Hiroshima se répondaient exactement]" (13).

The narrative that displaces Hiroshima itself terminates in a non-event and a stasis (*"Rien n'aura lieu que le lieu"*?), a spatialization of narrative time, immobilized within its own negation. "They are no one." They have no names other than place names, which is to say, non-names, names that are anything but proper ones.

As in all of Duras' texts, however, "nothing" is never quite *nothing;* as we shall see, *The Ravishing of Lol V. Stein,* for example, is a text about a "nothing," precisely, a missing word, a blank space. And in *Hiroshima mon amour,* nothing will happen in the hotel room. Nothing but the constitution of a scene—the staging of an act of failed nomination: the substitution of a false totality, an unattainable place of origin, for the proper name of the subjects.

The possibility that person might become undifferentiated from place constitutes the radical slippage of representation, the collapse of a thetic moment, and, thereby, of a power to designate a distance separating "here-ness" from "there-ness," or inside and outside, which would assure the subject's placement *as* subject. The connection between the proper name and place designation is significant and complex. In her essay "Place Names," Julia Kristeva explores what she calls the "archaeology of nomination," as a movement from spatial references to demonstratives to primitive syntactic structures, and finally to names. This development of linguistic capacity coheres with the consolidation of subjectivity, such that the primary articulations, like the cry, are related to a mapping of spaces, the establishment of "here" and "there," that operates between the infant's body and its mother's satisfaction of its needs. As such, the first spatial designations of "there-ness" are caught up in the semiotic chora, the space without stable inside and outside, where they serve as momentary fixations, relays, before the limits of identity are consolidated. The place name, the concept of place, a spatial reference, then, establishes the site upon which the proper name comes into being.[4]

By the conclusion of this text, we are faced with the contradictory relationship of narrative to its imagined event, effected through narrative time itself: nothing will have taken place. As such, the text constitutes itself upon a failure to perform, a failure to repeat. The problem of discursive apprehension of the event of Hiroshima may be specified as its relation to a profilmic, or protextual, moment. This issue is discussed by Joan Copjec with relation to Duras' later films: "I am also suggesting, however, that all of Duras' films, from *Hiroshima mon amour* to *Le Camion*, display the workings of this compulsion, extend their analyses, like Freud's own, from a recognition of traumatic war neuroses to a theory of the drives, beyond the pleasure principle. Like Freud also, the films displace the trauma from the immediacy of the present, the present unfolding of the film, exteriorize it in some vague profilmic, make of it an event which never takes place."[5] In this sense, the protextual is that which only comes into being in the "repetition" itself, as that which is already *missed*.

The paradoxes of deferral and displacement that inhere in the relationship between the repetition and what it repeats extend even to the text of *Hiroshima mon amour* that Duras published after the film's release. In her preface to the script, Duras explains the chronology of the work's coming to publication: "I have tried to give as faithful an account as possible of the work I did for Alain Resnais on *Hiroshima mon amour*. Readers should not be surprised that Resnais's 'pictorial contribution' is never practically described in this work. My role is limited to describing those elements from which Resnais made his film. The passages on Nevers, which were not included in the original scenario (July, 1958) were annotated before the shooting in France (December, 1958)" (19).

This account of the script's status opens the question of the relationship between written text, conceived as prior to the film, as profilmic, and the utterly false determination of the film as analogous to a theatrical production of a script. As such, this script is caught in the bind it announces, as the film does—the problem of retroaction, memory and forgetting, temporal disturbance and disruption through *après-coup*. As this preface poses the issue, the text-film relation constitutes a reciprocal translation, wherein each deviates from and transforms the other, contradicting it in its very reproduction, repetition.

The scansion of *Hiroshima mon amour* by this compulsion to repeat is an operation clearly manifested in the text's relation to its historical grounding. The narrative of Hiroshima continually produces metaphoric and metonymic precipitates of the non-symbolizable event, which are neither detachable from it nor adequate to it. The missed moment ("I want to have lived through that moment. That incomparable moment" [68]) is described in detail in the dialogic scene that reactivates the machine of memory.

> Little by little he grew cold beneath me. Oh! how long it took him to die! When? I'm not quite sure. I was lying on top of him . . . yes . . . the moment of his death actually escaped me, because . . . because even at that very moment, and even afterward, yes, even afterward, I can say that I couldn't feel the slightest difference between this dead body and mine. All I could find between this body and mine were obvious similarities [des ressemblances hurlantes], do you understand? (*Shouting*). He was my first love. . . . (The Japanese slaps her.) (64–65)

The problem of the non-lived moment, the missed encounter, is described by Lacan as embedded in the death drive, since it establishes the paradoxical connection between chance, trauma, and repetition, in their relation to the real. For Lacan, in *The Four Fundamental Concepts of Psycho-analysis,* the real is that which always lies beyond the "*automaton,* the return, the coming back, the insistence of the signs, by which we see ourselves as governed by the pleasure principle" (54). This status of the real is clearly figured in the trauma: "The function of . . . the real as encounter—the encounter insofar as it may be missed, insofar as it is essentially missed—first presented itself in the history of psycho-analysis in a form that was already enough to arouse our attention, that of the trauma" (55). An absent cause, absent origin of the analytic project, the real appears under the form of the trauma, whose insistence in repetition belies a strict separation of death drive and pleasure principle.

Lacan continues by exploring this contradiction in the child's *fort-da* game, where the trauma of loss and separation from the mother is conjoined with a pleasure of mastery over it through the repeated throw and recuperation of a bobbin—mastery through representation. Because of its structuration according to certain fantasmatic configurations, we may see *Hiroshima mon amour* as an extended exploration and figuration of the drive, the compulsion to repeat.

The return of memory and the possibility of recounting the story arise simultaneously with the disclosure of the "Nevers" scene. Similarly, specular issues are constantly bound up with the narrative halts and turns. The opening sequence of the text is a long argument about sight, a perpetual movement back and forth between affirmation and negation.

> You saw nothing in Hiroshima. Nothing.
> I saw *everything. Everything.*
> The hospital, for instance, I saw it . . .
> You did not see the hospital in Hiroshima. You saw nothing in Hiroshima. . . .
> I didn't make anything up.
> You made it *all* up. (15–19)

Here the problem of truth and fiction, the possibility or impossibility of seeing are interwoven in a structure of extreme contradiction between sight and sound, eye and ear, image and voice.[6] As "Lui" insists that "You saw nothing," we see projected on the screen a series of images of Hiroshima's destruction. Not once do we see the source of the voices (faces we have not yet seen). The possible *destinataire*/addressee of this "you," "tu," remains radically in question, such that, as reader/spectator, we experience a fictive direct address that denies our very act of seeing, even as we engage in it.

On pages 19–20 of the text, we are given the following coincidence of a script instruction with the dialogue: "Just as in love this illusion exists, this illusion of being able never to forget, so I was under the illusion that I would never forget Hiroshima" (19). The script indicates the presence of the following image over/under the dialogue: "Surgical forceps approach an eye to extract it. More newsreel shots" (20). This image of an eye being plucked out, blinded, an annulment of visual reciprocity, destabilizes our position as viewers. The specular connection of our look to this other look, on the point of violent extinction and retroactively perceived as already blind—a "dead" look—profoundly troubles the possible cinematic suture effect here.

In *Questions of Cinema*, Stephen Heath proposes the following concept of cinematic suture. "Cinema as discourse is the production of subject and the subject is the point of that production, constantly missing in and moving along the flow of images, the very assurance of flow, with suture, as it were, the culmination of that assurance."[7] This description of suture is based on a development of the notion of suture in Lacan's theory, with respect to discourse. The suture refers to the subject's relation to its discourse, where the "I" is the site of both lack and availability. In Heath's terms: "The stake is clear: the 'I' is a division that joins all the same, the stand-in is the lack in the structure but nevertheless, simultaneously, the possibility of a coherence, of the *filling in*. At the end of the suturing function is the *ego*, the me: 'it's me!,' the little linguistic scenario of the ego—that *I* am the one who can say, can say insofar as I am one. The ego is not to be confused with the subject: it is the fixed point of imaginary projection and identification, where the subject as such is always on the side of the symbolic . . . : function of the symbolic, suture is always toward the imaginary, the moment of junction—standing-in—a taking place, a something, a some one there" (86).

If the suture is a sewn-together coherence of the subject along the juncture of the imaginary and the symbolic, it is constantly subject to rupture, to breaks. It is on this side precisely that this scene in *Hiroshima* works, both visually and discursively. This instance of punctuation, a break in the film's flow, and perhaps the most radical moment of textual contradiction, where the words repudiate the image before us, is also the moment where the utterance is completely detached from a localizable source. Such a structure, moreover, is repeated throughout the film: in the disclosure of the body under the "mask" of nuclear disfigurement; in "Elle" herself, as an actress in the film within the film. Through this image of the eye, we become aware of a possible radical temporal disjunction between the time of speech and the time of the image. This disjunction is intensified by its occurrence at the moment of direct address and of an annihilation of our look through the specular solicitation of the eye on the screen.

40

I want to link this scene with another scene of specular investment, a scene which, taken together with the image of the eye, serves as a frame for the moment of anamnesis: "Elle," alone in her hotel room, repeats her narrativized memory.

> In Nevers she had a German love when she was young. . . .
> We'll go to Bavaria, my love, and there we'll marry.
> She never went to Bavaria. (*Looking at herself in the mirror.*)
> I dare those who have never gone to Bavaria to speak to her of love.
> You were not quite dead.
> I told our story.
> I was unfaithful to you tonight with this stranger.
> I told our story.
> It was, you see, a story that could be told.
> For fourteen years I hadn't found . . . the taste of an impossible love again.
> Since Nevers.
> Look how I'm forgetting you . . .
> Look how I've forgotten you.
> Look at me.
> (. . . *She suddenly raises her head, sees her wet face in the mirror* . . .) (73–74)

A woman tells herself a story while speaking to her image in the mirror. This structure locates us both as observers and, through the familiar form of the command, "look at me" ("regarde-moi"), as addressees of the monologue. Moreover, filmically, the camera reinforces the monologue's structure, since we see the actress's face only as reflected in the mirror. Textually, however, it is the dialogic shifts that solicit our scrutiny. Pronominally, "Elle" begins to speak of herself in the third person, thereby expanding the scene's space through triangulation. The "je" speaking to herself opens a temporal disunity in the utterance: between the *sujet de l'énoncé* and the *sujet de l'énonciation*. "We'll go to Bavaria, my love," is an utterance of curiously doubled possibility; the source might well be the young German, his voice ventriloquized through "Elle." Following this positional interruption, the monologue/dialogue rotates again through the third-person narrative pole to attain a dialogic "je"-"tu" organization.

From this point, "Elle" repeats a fragmented version of the story she has just recounted to "Lui." "You were not quite dead." Now, it seems, he is. Telling the story is an execution, a putting to death. In addition, the reestablished communicational circuit here is lodged within a purely specular economy. Such an economy produces a particularly unmanageable signifying complex at the point of the following sentences: "Look how I'm forgetting you. . . . Look how I've forgotten you. Look at me."

An injunction to *look* here reinforces the contextual strictures of the utterance. "Look at me," addressed to the mirror, constitutes an impossible demand, that the image *see*. Simultaneously, however, this is the moment that annihilates the image *qua* image. Moreover, to state the demand that the image look at the act of forgetting poses the impossible desire to see the unseeable, to see the moment of disappearance (as Lol V. Stein will look at Anne-Marie Stretter and Michael Richardson in order to witness, by seeing, her own absence).

If we allow momentarily the intrusion of Resnais's camera here (and precisely because it rewrites and doubles the verbal structure of the scene), we must remark that "Elle" 's image in the mirror stops "speaking" at the introduction of the word "tu." We hear her voice, a continuous monologue, in voice-over, but we no longer *see* her speaking. Such a radical interruption of continuity in the image here again punctuates, punctures the scene's coherence, this time along temporal lines. We experience the scene in at least two temporal modes: the image loses the voice. Since *we* become the locus of temporal conjunction, we become, metaphorically, the site of memory, as we *watch* the voice lose itself. Not insignificantly, it is at the moment of the remembering, repeating the resurgence of memory, that we are called upon to look at the forgetting— the unseeable.

Correspondingly, the act of remembering becomes the moment of loss, the death. "You were not quite dead. I told our story." An incomplete death reaches completion when the scene is committed to a narrative unfolding. The possibility of recollection is already fissured by the oblivion that inheres in its very structure.

Temporal play and disturbance of discursive position structure both the opening dialogue of the text and the central recollection scene. In the opening sequence, the dialogic interplay of radically opposing positions is interrupted, cut up by the chiasmus produced in the speakers' reversal of affirmative and negative positions. Initially, it is "Elle" who asserts "I saw everything," and "Lui" who denies it: "You saw nothing." However, at the moment just before the plucked eye arrests us, their enunciative roles have reversed, since she insists, "I didn't make anything up" (19), and his reply asserts, "You made it all up." From this point forward, "Elle" 's utterance insists with increasing intensity upon an identifying gesture: "Like you, I know what it is to forget. Like you, I have a memory" (22–23). As her enunciations begin to prevail, and his to fade, the dialogue culminates in her long recitative speech:

> I meet you.
> I remember you.
> Who are you?
> You destroy me.
> You're so good for me. . . .
> Why not you?
> Why not you in this city and in this night so like the others you
> can't tell the difference? (25)

Such textual maneuvers stress the radical dislodging of the "tu" addressee from the discursive situation. The context then expands, almost evaporating, to culminate in the accentuated reestablishment of pronominal opposition in "elle," "toi" and "lui": "Yes, me. You will have seen me" (25). The obsessional repetition of these shifters through the dialogic movement has amputated their reference from the speaking subjects. Just before the pronouns are spoken in isolation, the text signals the first appearance of faces on the screen: "With exaggerated suddenness the woman's face appears, filled with tenderness, turned towards the man's" (25). In function of this coincidence of image and voice, we encounter a very brutal moment indeed, that of identity's instantiation upon a scene that had heretofore floated freely between the poles of negation and affirmation, you and me. A scene without location, that is, without reference points, dispossessed of the referents of the shifters, is abruptly anchored. To this point, it is the images of Hiroshima that have veiled the scene, constituting its screen. Now the text moves from the fantasmatic scenario to a more localizable narrative pattern—the diegesis of the love story.

If we return to the scene that narrates the moment of trauma, we find the same sort of pronominal slippage at work. The irruption of the past into the present of the diegesis is conditioned by "Lui" 's assumption of the "je" position, as substitute of the dead lover: "When you are in the

43

cellar, am I dead?" (54). Within the textual present of this dialogue, "Lui" is a figure doubled over on the dead lover (a folding prepared by the earlier cinematic superimposition of the dead German's twitching hand upon the hand of the sleeping "Lui"). The "je" becomes an anchor or relay that folds over the past, the "already there," upon the present. We might say, in this connection, that he becomes the screen on which "Elle" projects the remembered images, or the axis around which she effects memory's *mise en scène*. However, just as in the mirror scene, such a superimposition of past on present moment, as a moment already disappearing (into the past, and into memory), constitutes the falsification of memory in its very staging.

In this context, we should recall that the scene turns on the effort to remember a moment that has *not* been lived. Furthermore, this is a moment where differentiation is impossible, "even at that very moment, and even afterward, . . . I couldn't feel the slightest difference between this dead body and mine" (65). In that case, the scene mimes the structure of the fantasy as described by Laplanche and Pontalis, since the fantasy is precisely the effort to dramatize an originary moment, which is always a moment of separation and loss.

As Laplanche and Pontalis describe it, the fantasy originates in the moment of loss; "it is an analytic 'construction,' or fantasy, which tries to cover the moment of *separation* between *before* and *after*, whilst still containing both: a mythical moment of disjunction between the pacification of need (Befriedigung) and the fulfillment of desire (Wunscherfullung), between the two stages represented by real experience and its hallucinatory revival, between the object that satisfies and the sign which describes both the object and its absence."[8] So the fantasy aims at locating and filling the gap between before and after, recuperating the absence inscribed by the sign.

Further, as it concerns subjectivity, the fantasy's "grammatical" structure resists stable subjectivization:

> But the original fantasy, on the other hand, is characterized by the absence of subjectivization, and the subject is present *in* the scene: the child, for instance, is one character amongst many in the fantasy "a child is beaten." . . . And in this sense, the screen memory would have a profound structural relationship with the original fantasies. . . . The indication here of the primary process is not the absence of organization, as is sometimes suggested, but the peculiar character

44

of the structure, in that it is a scenario with multiple entries. (13–14)

Thus the fantasmatic structure constitutes itself on the circulation of positions among subject and objects, and across the *clivage* between before and after, as well as between an imaginary and a real scene.

> Fantasy, however, is not the object of desire, but its setting. In fantasy, the subject does not pursue an object or its sign: he appears caught up himself in a sequence of images. He forms no representation of the desired object, but is himself represented as participating in the scene, although, in the earliest forms of fantasy, he cannot be assigned any fixed place in it. As a result, the subject, although always present in the fantasy, may be so in a desubjectivized form, that is to say, in the very syntax of the sequence. (17)

As spectators of *Hiroshima mon amour,* we find our position caught up in a fantasmatic web through our attendance at a scene that turns on the effort to stage a subject in relation to a lost object, thereby repeating and reinstituting the separation. The scene itself, the narrative unfolding of the past, is overlaid with the projected images of Nevers (the subject's private cinema or theater), thus reinscribing the very gap that has generated it. Our desire to *see,* to observe the moment of loss, thus intersects with "Elle" 's.

If the breast is the paradigm of the object "a," the lost object, we may here connect it with another part object, the look. Lacan characterizes the objects "a" as detachable objects, separated from the body in the constitution of the subject, which then come to stand as the signifiers of loss or lack. Lacan stresses the partialness of the object: breast, excrement, phallus, and, as well, phoneme, look, voice, and what he calls "le rien"—the nothing. That which, once the subject has been separated from it, is nothing for him: this is the "nothing" that the anorexic eats. It is these latter part objects to which I pay particular attention here. These clearly maintain a relation to the body that is traced along both metonymic and metaphoric lines.

Moreover, the part objects are partial in more than one way. Not only are they detached, but they participate in the drive structure, which is itself partial, in that it "merely represents, and partially at that, the curve of fulfillment of sexuality in the living being" (Lacan, *Four Fundamental*

Concepts, 177). The final term of the drive, according to Lacan, in view of which all others are only partial, would be death.

In *The Four Fundamental Concepts of Psycho-analysis,* Lacan describes the gaze as having the privilege of the *objet "a"*: "In the scopic relation the object on which depends the fantasy from which the subject is suspended in an essential vacillation is the gaze" (83). This formulation stresses the radical distinction of the gaze from the eye, and its function as that from which the subject is suspended, as that which sustains his or her desire, *as* suspended. This vacillation in the gaze is related to the inside-out structure of the look, whereby the subject's installation in the visible, the splitting of being in the scopic field, results from the recognition that the look is in the field of the Other and never fully apprehensible. As such, it functions on the level of desire and has to do with the fading of the subject: "From the moment that this gaze appears, the subject tries to adapt himself to it, he becomes that punctiform object, that point of vanishing being with which the subject confuses his own failure" (*Four Fundamental Concepts,* 83). The subject finds himself or herself on the "point" of a lack, a hole in the visual field.

Like all the *objets "a,"* after Lacan, the gaze symbolizes a lack. More important, the structure of the gaze inscribes quite clearly the function of the lure, a term Lacan uses to describe the relation between the gaze and what one "wishes to see": "The subject is presented as other than he is, and what one shows him is not what he wishes to see" (104). The lure is what results from a noncoincidence of the eye and the gaze, since "you never look at me from the place at which I see you," and, similarly, "what I look at is never what I wish to see" (102–3).

On the scopic level, the lack, the cause of desire, is this rupture, the splitting off of the gaze from the eye, of looking from seeing. The look is always elsewhere with respect to seeing. It is this particular inscription of lack that *Hiroshima mon amour* takes as a central obsession that is persistently elaborated from the opening sequence through this scene structured around a gap in memory.

This scene, however, is overdetermined, as a moment of memory, of the resurgence of an event. In *Studies on Hysteria,* Freud describes the problem of memory blockage in hysteria: "Only a single memory at a time can enter ego consciousness. A patient who is occupied in working through such a memory sees nothing of what has already pushed its way through. If there are difficulties in the way of mastering this single path-ogenic memory, as, for instance, if the patient does not relax his resist-ance against it, then the defile is, so to speak, blocked."[9]

Commenting upon this passage, Stephen Heath connects it to the structure of the cinematic apparatus, which is structured to guarantee consistency in the "flow of images, a unity of presentation, a stable memory" (*Questions*, 109). For him, this purpose is doubled in the cin-ematic apparatus by narrativization, that is, by the process of unfolding in a narrative form, which is precisely the form of discourse Freud is privileging in this text. To render as narrative is to constitute a coherent flow of presentation, a stable memory, as opposed to the "stop-go" of image presentation, what Lacan refers to as the "pulsating function of the unconscious."[10] Heath describes the specific operation of narrative in film, as in "narrativization": "The economy of the film's flow in a binding coherence, its remembering, the realization of a single forward time within which multiple times can be given play and held. The system of suture, be it noted, breaks as soon as the time of the scene hesitates beyond the time of its narrative specifications" (*Questions*, 109). The suturing effect, then, has everything to do with time and timing, which guarantees the subject's mirage of coherence through temporal continuity.

Narrativization is also a crucial problem in *Hiroshima*, where the process through which an event *cannot* be told is presented in a narrative development. Something similar happens on the textual level as well, for the central scene attempts to constitute a suture—which appears as a fascinating "dead" point—and then ruptures it with the cry, the slap. In this continuation of the text's pulsating movement, between temporali-ties, the present moment's interruption by the metaphoric or metonymic insertion of memory is continued in the memory's complete absorption into the present space—its enactment.

The text's constant and constitutional play of presence and absence, its pulsation, finds its most surprising expression in two figures—one that appears within the scenario *Hiroshima mon amour*, and a second that arises in the "Appendices," a subtext to guide the staging of the "Nevers" sections of the film. Appropriately enough, these are textual fragments that never made it into the film, at least not explicitly. They are, however, inscribed there, in the cellar scenes, in the underground. At least one of these fragments is the site of emergence, in the textual prolongation, of a figure that has resonated as a determining figure throughout the text "proper."

This is the section entitled: "On the shots of the marble lost by the children," where a lost marble rolls into the cellar in which *She* is incarcerated, precipitating a sort of crisis by reminding her of the outside.

On the shots of the marble lost by the children

I screamed again. And that day I heard a scream. That last time they put me in the cellar. The marble came toward me, taking its time, like an event. . . .

I throw it, but it bounces back toward my hand. I do it again [Je recommence]. It doesn't come back [Elle ne revient pas]. It gets lost.

When it gets lost, something I recognize [reconnais] begins again [recommence]. Fear returns [revient]. A marble can't die. I remember. I look. I find it again [retrouve].

Children's shouts. The marble is in my hand. . . . There it is, captive. I give it back to the children. (91)

I have retained the French verbs here in order to allow the obsessively repetitive quality of the *re-* itself to emerge as it does in the original. The marble figures a textual bobbin, the child's *fort-da* game of repetition and spacing—a play upon presence and absence, first observed by Freud. The *fort-da* game, the casting out and reeling in of an object, is an activity that symbolizes repetition, repetition precisely, according to Lacan, "of the mother's departure as cause of the splitting of the subject—overcome by the alternating game, *fort-da,* which is *here or there,* and whose aim, in its alternation, is simply that of being the *fort* of a *da,* the *da* of a *fort*" (*Four Fundamental Concepts,* 63). This game is the beginning of representation, at the same time that it is a representation itself. The representation is the signifier that marks the subject as subject.

For Lacan, the subject must be designated somehow in the object to which this opposition/alternation is applied. Therefore, the repetition game institutes the space of his or her desire, to bridge the gap it has created around him or her, and also the accession of the subject to the signifier. "The ever open gap introduced by the absence indicated remains the cause of a centrifugal tracing in which that which falls is not the other *qua* face in which the subject is projected, but that cotton-reel linked to itself by the thread that it holds—in which is expressed that which, of itself, detaches itself in this trial, self-mutilation on the basis of which the order of the signifier will be put in perspective" (*Four Fundamental Concepts*, 42). The *objet "a"* is precisely what is in play— the *objet "a*," signifier of an absence, a lack in the subject's being, the gap of desire. Simultaneously, however, the game represents and refers to the mother's absence, so that the splitting, the difference within, grounds the representation and its reference.

That alternation, the rhythmic pulsation that traverses the text, figuring possession and dispossession, is here linked to the problem of reference. The marble belongs to the children and eventually finds its way back to them. But it is also an object "re-found" by "Elle," coinciding with the cry emitted and finally *heard* by her, and with the last day in the cellar. The back-and-forth movement of the marble reproduces the echoing of the voice, the cry that is finally heard, when "Elle"'s voice reaches her own ear. This scene turns on loss and return, and on the word *"recommencer"*: "je recommence," "I do it again"; "quelque chose recommence que je reconnais," "something I recognize begins again." The marble appears as an *event*. And it is indeed a textual event: "I remember." Memory returns in the play of distance and proximity, the here and there, the primary spacing of the pulsion, and of language.

Occurring in the prolongation of *Hiroshima mon amour*, this scene rebounds on the central scene of recollection. That recollection only repeats the "first" return of memory in the cellar. Not surprisingly, in the "Nevers" section, the description of "Elle"'s cure is characterized as follows: "She still calls him, but more and more rarely. The memory of a memory. . . . She's destroying an imaginary universe, overturning objects; looking at the inside out" (100). Here again, it is a question of the interval, and of memory as memory of memory, a radical displacement of the memory's referent, or original object.

We might connect this moment with one of the most arresting of the textual figures: "Like you, I have tried with all my might not to forget. Like you, I forgot. Like you, I wanted to have an inconsolable memory, a memory of shadows and stone" (23). This utterance is followed by the indication, "shot of a shadow, 'photographed' on stone, of someone killed at Hiroshima" (23). Here we are confronted with the impossible image of an image—the false photograph—the traces of light that have reproduced the *shadow* (precisely the image, the afterimage of the flash, the memory of a disappeared object). In effect, this radical cancellation of memory in its very inscription—the shadow on stone as recorded traces of the *passing* of the original and not its memory, the displacement of a lost original—constitutes the graphic trace, the generative hypogram of the textual enterprise.[11] The text poses the permanent mark of the disappearance of what was never there where it "appears." Moreover, this image focalizes the textual inscription of death, the effort to represent death at its center. It then converges with the fantasy of seeing and marking the limit-moment of death as repeatable. In *La Carte postale,* Jacques Derrida addresses the question of the duplicity of all repetition, in its effort to anchor limits within a chronology, in relations of anteriority and succession. "Classically, repetition repeats something which precedes it, it succeeds a first, an originary, a primitive, a precedent, the repeated itself, of which we suppose that it is itself foreign to the repetitiveness or the repeating of the repetition. Just as we imagine that an account reports something anterior or foreign to itself, or in any case, independent of it."[12]

For Derrida, all repetition operates simultaneously as recall and distancing, according to the rhythm of Freud's *fort-da* game, as he reads it in *La Carte postale.* This figure is central to *Hiroshima,* traversing all three of its narrative levels: the historical event of Hiroshima, the love story, and the Nevers memory.

Hiroshima mon amour concludes with the collapse of these three *récits* into one another, across the structure of repetition. The last scene immobilizes narrative motion in a monumental nominalism.

> I'll forget you! I'm forgetting you already! Look how I'm forgetting you! Look at me!
> SHE: Hi-ro-shi-ma.
> Hi-ro-shi-ma. That's your name.
> *(They look at each other without seeing each other. Forever.)*
> HE: That's my name. Yes. Your name is Nevers. Ne-vers-in-France.
> (83)

This last moment engages a possible future which is immediately absorbed in an immobilized present—"I'll forget you! I'm forgetting you already!"—an always already forgotten. Further, this passage superimposes itself, through repetition, on the mirror scene, the first instance of declared forgetting.

Duras has inserted a bracketed passage here, excised from the filmic dialogue, between the last two scenes spoken by "Lui": "They [on] are only just there yet. And they will stay there forever." That is, the future time, already forgotten, coexists with the present and with the "before," which is already dilated into an eternal moment. We are always *before* the event. The story is here suspended *before* its occurrence. Moreover, the collapse of separation among the three *récits*, three temporal modes, coincides with the fragmentation of the names, Hiroshima and Nevers, even as they become stand-ins, indices of the identities of the two figures as *places*, positions.

In her *Territoires du féminin*, Marcelle Marini characterizes this final nomination through the ambiguity of the name Nevers, which has emerged and at times cancelled out Hiroshima itself. Nevers, for her, signifies a-topia, a null space, as the original matrix which generates the negation of both narrative and subject. She unfolds the resonance of the name as follows: Nevers: that toward which one tends, but which one never reaches [ne: negation, not; vers: toward]. This perpetual and failed tending toward, the noncoincidence of name and place, indicates the impossible localization of the subjects as they are "named" in this scene.[13]

Through this explosion of names, the subjects move from position to place. Names have thus *become* the scene. Nothing happens but the establishment of the scene, which returns us to the border of representation, grounded as it is in the primary spatial mappings that characterize the semiotic chora (in Kristeva's terms). In the metaphoric and metonymic culmination of textual lines, the two axes become undifferentiated, and the referential status of places is thereby evaporated.

In a sense, *Hiroshima mon amour* is about establishing a difference between *before* and *after*, about remobilizing temporality, distinguishing past from present. But it is also a text that, while mapping the failure of this differentiation, forecloses a future project. Its last moment, the moment "before," establishes no potential causal or chronological link with a possible future. Instead, the future is already forgotten, already evaporating into the past, across the present. Just as the enunciative moment, "I'm forgetting you already," obliterates the interlocutor's presence in its very acknowledgement of it, the subsumption of pronominal functions under the names of locales obviates all possible identity. This text without a future mode questions the status of stable identity, in its relations to time, over time.

51

Similarly, we might see this ultimate moment as the satisfaction of the epistemological and scopophilic drives that have conditioned, not to say propelled, the textual development: to see/know Hiroshima; to recuperate, see, know the secret of Nevers. Attaching these names to the faces of the figures "Elle" and "Lui" is precisely the annulment of the name through a coincidence with a recognizable identity wholly inadequate to it, a ludicrous synecdoche. Which element is the part, and which the "whole" for which it stands in? This gesture displaces the "proper" reference indefinitely, rendering the nominal function, based as it is on the possibility of repetition over time, obsolete.

Binding identity into narrative temporality, Hiroshima pulsates in an alternation that never restores chronological progression, never orders the series of events into a clearly demarcated before and after which would locate its own origin in a moment of trauma. On this basis, we may even read Hiroshima as structured by a failure of mourning, since where the mourning work is completed, the fantasmatic object is drained of cathexis-significance. In a sense, however, since the ego retains the traces of the passage of all lost or abandoned objects, mourning, by nature, is never completed.[14] The text, then, maps the displacements of a continued mourning, the traces of the lost object that is embodied in the image of shadow photographed on stone.

Marini describes the textual immobilization that conditions *Hiroshima* as a general feature of Duras' narrative oeuvre, and one related to history: "A woman is not the subject of her story [histoire: story or history], women are not subjects of history, and history in progress does not create subjects. The whole world seems immobile" (49). The problem of narrative subjectivity becomes a problem of history, of constructing a subjective history for a subject-in-history. For Marini, however, this issue has a specifically feminine charge in Duras' work and is related to the impossiblity of a feminine subject's becoming a subject-in-history, which is linked to her limited access to the symbolic. Immobilization, in her use, is clearly connected to indifferentiation. Here Marini stresses the textual figure of the triangle. Psychoanalytically, the triangle recalls the Oedipal drama, where the third term intervenes to break the specular-narcissistic circuit in which the feminine subject is caught, introducing separation and absence into this textual mirror space. Without this intervention the subject is caught in a morbid trajectory of repetition.

However, the specific articulations of the representation of the subject and the representation of history remain to be seen. Duras' texts do work over this problem on the site of a subject named as feminine, thereby taking up the crucial issue of sexual difference in representation. It seems to me most important, however, to interrogate the relationships of subject, history, and discourse in *Hiroshima* through the framework of ideology and the imaginary. Specifically, in this case, the text is haunted by the problem of misrecognition [méconnaissance], a function central to both the fantasy and ideology, since both are imaginary representations. For Catherine Clément, the fantasy's relation to the lack-in-being, the unrepresentable moment of separation, is analogous to ideology's relation to history, the "absent cause," the lived relation to the "real."[15]

Operating on figurations of this separation, which is never definitive, but repeated, displaced, and replaced, Duras' text maps a feminine subject's placement in story and history—a placement that is contradictory since it is sometimes mobile, sometimes fixed. The third term ruptures the specular narcissistic dyad, the fantasmatic space, to reinstate temporal, narrative movement. The triangular figure that subtends all of Duras' narrative texts is here inscribed in the three "characters," "Lui," "Elle," and the German soldier, and set in motion by the love story, the *histoire d'amour*, that intervenes between "Elle" and the non-lived, immobilized moment of Nevers. However, this intervention merely constitutes the ground for another loss—the repetition of an impossible loss and recovery.

If we compare "Elle"'s two spoken seductions, the first to "Lui" in the first hotel-room scene, the second a repetition-recall of that speech as interior monologue on the last night in Hiroshima, the structure of repetition is complicated. First of all, both speeches begin with the phrase, "I remember you." The first encounter, therefore, is already marked as a repetition of a remembered one: "I meet you. I remember you" (24).

Both recitations refer to time and distortion. The first has it in this order: "Plenty of time. Take me. Deform me, make me ugly" (25). The second speech, deforming its textual original, reverses the order or priority: "Take me. Deform me to your likeness so that no one, after you, can understand the reason for so much desire" (77). Now this indicates precisely the desire to identify by unicity—a moment, a love, a desire—to differentiate it by rendering it unreadable to anyone else. It is simultaneously, however, a repetition of the consequences of the Nevers affair: the young woman, participant in an impossible, forbidden, and incom-

53

prehensible love story, is literally deformed as a consequence of it (*la tonsure*/the head shaving).

With respect to time, the second speech expands the first. "And a time is going to come. A time will come. When we'll no more know what thing it is that binds us. By slow degrees the word [le nom] will fade from our memory" (77). From "having the time," the text moves through the eternity of time before "Elle" 's anticipated departure (Lui: "All there is to do now is kill time before your departure" [83]), to the eventual restarting of time—"Time will pass. Time will come." It is a question of telling stories to pass the time, and about killing desire in time. Through its deforming repetitions, its grammatical play and imbrication of tenses, and its achronology, *Hiroshima* arrives at its ultimate immobilization of the name-as-monument, marking both suspension and narrative death, the death of narration.

The textual reenactment repeats, in effect, what was never there, except as figure; it refigures and disfigures. In *Fables of Aggression*, Frederic Jameson accounts for the contradiction that conditions the enactment of desire's scenario.

> For Freud and Lacan, desire necessarily emerges in a bound state, that is, inextricably invested in a determinate representation, or fantasy structure. . . . As far back as one can go in the psyche, desire always presents itself as already crystallized or articulated in a particular figuration. This is why the acting out of desire can never be successful: however literal the real-life replay there must always persist a structural, one could even want to say, ontological, incommensurability between the "text" of desire and the "reality" of the subject's enactment of it.[16]

In *Hiroshima,* we see clearly that each enactment is already a reenactment, and the reenactment is a putting to death of the representation in figuration.

In the sense that it causes desire and that it marks the place of a lack, the figure itself plays the role of a part object here. Since the figure here is the trace of a lack, the support of desire, it may be seen as also connected to the structure of the fantasy—which is, precisely, the staging, the lending of figural organization to desire. But, in the sense that the text never exhausts or satisfies desire in the figure, it sustains a perpetual reenactment that resembles the pattern of an insistent, unfinished mourning.

This text, cut up and traversed by detached looks, blind looks, looks belonging to no one,[17] also looks at us. Simultaneously, *ça nous regarde* [in French, the pun is crucial: that looks at us; that concerns us]: across historical referentiality, and across its solicitation of our entry in its polyvalent fantasmatic structure, through the slippage of our address.

The fascination exercised by this look depends on the fundamental fascinatory effect that characterizes the gaze as a part object, in Lacan's view, as rupture or separation that determines the subject. Just as the fantasy, as described by Laplanche and Pontalis, constitutes a scene of circulating grammatical positions, all of which are available to the subject, so it produces multiple and mutually exclusive points of view (views from within and without, from in front of and behind the scene). Thus it can be argued that the source of fascination here is not the object of the gaze, but the gaze itself, as unmastered, mobile, detached from any subject, and hence, as no longer establishing a fixed subject-object relation. In considering this structure, Lacan links fascination to a particular temporality and to death, through the notion of "arrest," of both time and motion. The power of the gaze is a power of immobilization, termination. This is because it is related to the temporality in which the relation to the Other is constructed; on the scopic level, this is the temporality of the terminal moment. Lacan contrasts this temporal point with the temporality of the signifier and the spoken, "the identificatory dialectic," which he characterizes as "haste," the rush or forward thrust of the signifying chain (see *Four Fundamental Concepts*, 118). This contrast is particularly important since it depends on the idea of suture, where suture, in the scopic, is determined as the moment of seeing. Thus, the immobilization or arrest that is risked in the gaze is concealed, sutured in the moment when seeing intervenes.

To elaborate this structure, Lacan uses the example of the gaze scanning a painted surface, such that the gaze is what distinguishes the brush stroke as a movement, by fixing its point of termination, thus constituting it as a gesture through retroaction, at the moment that it marks its terminus. The power of the gaze to arrest, morevoer, is linked to the idea of the evil eye, the *fascinum*, which has the effect of arresting movement, and, literally, killing life. At the moment the subject stops, "suspending his gesture, he is mortified" (*Four Fundamental Concepts,* 118). Lacan describes the dialectical process involved in the gaze in the following way: "The anti-life, anti-movement function of this terminal point is the *fascinum,* and it is precisely one of the dimensions in which the power of the gaze is exercised directly. The moment of seeing can only intervene here as a suture, a conjunction of the imaginary and the symbolic, and it is taken up again in a dialectic, that sort of temporal progress that is called haste, thrust, forward movement, which is concluded in the fascinum" (*Four Fundamental Concepts,* 118).

The moment of arrest is enmeshed in the dialectic of seeing and the gaze, where the asymmetrical reciprocity of the visual presents itself, and in the reinstatement of the suture effect, which then leads to another point of arrest. This dialectical "progress," then, is itself marked by a pulsating effect, arrest and precipitation, where the moments of arrest are a form of punctuation, retroactively conferring signification while also redirecting the flow of images and sight.

In the context of the photographic image, Roland Barthes makes a similar claim about the punctuating effect of an arresting detail that emerges from the texture of a photograph—a detail that arrests the gaze scanning the image. This he calls the *punctum:* "It is this element which rises from the scene, shoots out of it like an arrow, and pierces me. A Latin word exists to designate this wound, this prick, this mark made by a pointed instrument: the word suits me all the better in that it refers to the notion of punctuation . . . for punctum is also: sting, speck, cut, little hole—and also a cast of the dice. A photograph's punctum is the accident which pricks me."[18]

For Barthes, the punctum is the division within a photo, the detail that splits a unitary space, a detail which he also calls a partial object. Moreover, he locates the punctum as a supplementary point, beyond the photo; it is both already there, within the photo, and somehow added to the image by the gaze it arrests and fascinates. Not accidentally, one might suppose, the most general category of the punctum for Barthes is the reminder of death, the trace of the death (inevitable or accomplished) of the subject pictured, which is always inscribed in the image.

If we can apply the concept of suture discursively, in *Hiroshima mon amour,* to our coincidence with the textual movement, its investments and its address, we must feel our falling away from it at this moment of specular fascination where figures and names arrive at the same site and become indistinguishable. Just as the text's temporal connections always disintegrate in repetition or discursive overlap, the moment of conclusion displays the suture's foundation in fascination-immobilization.

The textual lure of "seeing" Hiroshima, as "Elle" articulates it in response to "Lui" 's questions—"Why did you want to see everything at Hiroshima?": "I have my own ideas about it. For instance, I think that looking closely at things [de bien regarder] is something that has to be learned" (28)—is the promise of an *apprentissage de la vue*. *Hiroshima mon amour* ends, however, with our having seen nothing. The moment of our terminal fascination, the death of the image, the death of Hiroshima as screen, is the moment where our fascination recognizes itself as self-fascination, invested upon the figure of "Hiroshima," the figure interceding for that which we can never see. This may be construed as a certain ideological thrust, if we consider Heath's determination that "suture finally names the dual process of multiplication and projection, the conjunction of the spectator as subject with the film—which conjunction is always the terrain of any specific ideological operation of the film" (*Questions*, 110).

The suture effect, then, is inscribed in the film's construction of its form of address. This is why Jean-Louis Baudry proposes the term "cinematic apparatus" to cover the whole system of mechanisms, technical and psychological, that constitute the field of cinematic production and consumption of images. For him, the cinematographic apparatus is directed toward the subject and the subject effects, even before "being directed toward the reproduction of the real."[19] That is to say, it addresses a specific subject position, soliciting the unified and coherent mirage of the "conscious" subject, but doing so only by also engaging the unconscious. As he puts it, this particular structure is what sustains its ideological function: "Instead of considering the cinema as an ideologically neutral apparatus, as an apparatus the impact of which would be entirely determined by the content of the film . . . in order to explain the cinema effect, it is necessary to consider it from the viewpoint of the apparatus that it constitutes, an apparatus which in its totality includes the subject" (119).

The text, then, blocks our pretension to mastery through sight. Does it at the same time evaporate the historical referent? In its radical interrogation of any presumption of totalizing access to the historical referent, its mastery through knowledge, vision, or discourse, this text certainly opens the question of the ideological investments involved in reading history as a series of punctual "events." In its very opening gesture of capitalizing on Hiroshima, evident in the indeterminacy of reference in the title's invocation, the text sets up its subsequent project of exploding the possibility of capitalizing on that investment.

Hiroshima mon amour refuses a translation of memory-image into a smoothly exchangeable communicative discourse or linear narrative. Even the final words of the text, in their fragmentation, are not assimilable; they say nothing, confuse the possibility of thinking the relations of part and whole, figure and ground, past and future. They refuse chronological development in favor of certain punctuations, punctuations that break the flow and insist in the very presentation of the name as precisely not punctual, or of memory and desire as not punctual. The text ends by partially undoing the image of memory inscribed in stone, an exchangeable mediating block, self-contained and legible. Instead, the text writes memory as loss, rather than reserve, and as conditioned by absence and displacement. In effect, if *Hiroshima mon amour* fills the gaps in memory, if it restores our memory of a historical event, it does so in the form of a screen memory.

In fact, the text itself is a screen memory. And this is crucial, for, as Freud reminds us, there is no innocent screen. The screen memory maintains an overdetermined relation to the concealed one, a relation constructed according to both proximity and analogy. In *Hiroshima mon amour*, the relation of superimposed and reversible screenings is the site where the text elaborates its central contradiction. The love story, which initially appears as the screening filter through which the subject may imagine access to Hiroshima, becomes the "originary trauma" for which the historical referent becomes both the name and the screen. At the same time, the historical referent is susceptible of appearing as the wide screen on which the subjective trauma is projected.

In a sense, *Hiroshima mon amour*'s project performs the impossibility of discursive access to the real, of its representability. If we define the real according to Jameson's formulation in *Fables of Aggression*, where his version of the Lacanian notion is applied to a political context, it is that which ultimately resists symbolization. He sees the real as "fundamentally non-representable, non-narrative." "The Real . . . is conceived neither as an unknowable thing-in-itself, nor as a string of events or a set of facts of some 'true' or 'adequate' representation for consciousness. It is rather an asymptotic phenomenon, an outer limit, which the subject approaches in the anxiety of a moment of truth" (12–13). While maintaining a critical stance that conceives the real as inaccessible to the means of representation, *Hiroshima mon amour* runs the risk of amputating the referent completely, and seems to fetishize the site of that amputation, the traumatized region. In so doing, it forecloses history in a specific way—by representing it as a lost object rather than an absent cause. Such a reading then implicitly aligns history with death, setting up an incomplete mourning process—the text's compulsion to repeat. Consequently, the text ends with a monument as the insufficient end of mourning, an immobilization that seems to reinstate the monumentalization of the event.

Such monumentalization is coherent with the textual critique of an impulse to capitalize on Hiroshima. Over against this impulse, the text sets a rhetoric of pure expenditure, of memory as pure loss in repetition, which evaporates history as well. For, indeed, although a text's only approach to the real is asymptotic, there remain its *effects* to be read and analyzed. Likewise, one's failed approach to the real is never without a stake, without investments. In refusing the capitalizing gesture, along with the totalizing gesture of the mastery of history, *Hiroshima mon amour* risks denying its own particular investments, the specific effects of history, and the inescapability of the referent which as much conditions the textual enterprise as does that referent's very inaccessibility.

This risk of erasing historical specificity arises between the incomplete restoration and incomplete disappearance of memory, in a textual figuration of the mourning process, which explores the complexity of the referential gesture. Mourning, like all psychic processes, as they are understood by psychoanalysis, maintains a problematic relationship to its "origin" or source, as well as to representation. The textual problem of historical referentiality, of representing history, is routed through problems of psychic representation, thus engaging referentiality in general. Even displaced and embedded in the figuration of an individual subject's mourning, however, the question of the referent does not disappear. Rather, it becomes central to the textual operations, so that the problem of referentiality is linked to memory, not only the character's memory, but the text's or film's, the reader's, and, finally, one text's memory of another, a feature that persists in Duras' production.

Just as *Hiroshima* returns our look to us from *elsewhere*, rupturing a coherent reciprocal circuit, it restores our memory as irrecuperable loss. The textual screen, like the filmic screen, returns our memory to us *as* screen, as the mark of a noncoincidence of past and present, as the index of an impossible anteriority— impossible because it only takes form in its repetition and deferral.

Deferral, according to Freud, characterizes the relation of the screen memories to the concealed ones; the screen, he writes, "owes its value as a memory not to its own content, but to the relation between that content and some other, which has been suppressed."[20] This structure of deferral, which is, nonetheless, never arbitrary, leads Freud to conclude that we may have no memories at all *from* our childhood; memories relating to our childhood may be all that we possess" (322). Thus, all childhood memories might be seen as screens, insofar as the falsified memory provides no real access to the raw material of which it is formed, but only establishes the mark of a connection, a reference. Such, Freud argues, is also the case in the structure of hysterical symptoms, which are legible neither through resemblance to their source nor through a one-to-one correspondence between a symptom and its cause. Rather, the symptoms, formed by condensation and displacement, operate in relation to each other, but also *mark* the presence of memories that have not become discursive. Hysterical symptoms, then, are like screen memories inscribed on the body.

If there is a matrix from which the figures of *Hiroshima mon amour* are generated, it is located in a textual conjunction of the screen memory, which masks and defers another memory, and mourning, which decathects memories of the lost object, rewriting them through a process of internalization and idealization. Mourning entails a form of identification with the lost object which makes possible its internalization. This basis in identification with a lost object is the common ground between mourning and hysteria. The hysteric's identification maintains the object-cathexis, fails to relinquish the object; even in the mourning work, however, "the shadow of the object falls upon the ego" ("Mourning and Melancholia," 249). Because the ego itself is formed of the precipitates of "abandoned" object-cathexes, which are thus never fully relinquished, we may see it as structured by an incomplete mourning.

It is this figure of mourning which persists in *Hiroshima mon amour*, in its fascination with the trace of the object's passing, and which is further elaborated, repeated, in the later cycle of Duras' texts. Here again, the narration reveals its translation of the hysterical discourse, since, just as the hysteric's symptoms constitute the writing of memory on the body, mark the trace of the irrevocably lost, but not abandoned, objects, the text repeatedly inscribes its own memory, as deferral of the "referent," the originary trauma. In its repetition of fragments and figures from the earliest novels to the most recent, Duras' entire oeuvre figures a pulverized body.

Like *Hiroshima mon amour*, the narrative cycle formed by *The Ravishing of Lol V. Stein*, *The Vice-Consul*, and *L'Amour* catches us up in its fantasmatic networks, captures our investment, and offers us no return on it. Instead, these texts' figures enter into a circulation that traverses all of Duras' narratives, establishing a sort of textual and intertextual memory. In so doing, the later three narratives focalize their repetitive effects on the irrecuperable loss, the inaccessible prediscursive memory of the "originary" trauma of separation—the separation from the maternal body. As such, these texts constitute a simultaneous interrogation of desire and the borders of representation and the body, through an exploration of the emergence of the signifier in the maternal space.

NOTES

1. Cf. Catherine Clément and Hélène Cixous, *La Jeune Née* (Paris: 10/18, 1975), 21.

2. Elisabeth Lyon, "The Cinema of Lol V. Stein," *Camera Obscura*, no. 6 (1980): 37.

3. Marguerite Duras, *Hiroshima mon amour*, trans. Richard Seaver (New York: Grove Press, 1961), 15; in French (Paris: Gallimard, 1960), 21–22. All subsequent references to this work appear in the text. Wherever the resonance of the original is essential to my comments, I have preserved the French in brackets.

4. Julia Kristeva, *Desire in Language*, trans. Leon S. Roudiez (New York: Columbia Univ. Press, 1980), 209.

5. Joan Copjec, "*India Song/Son nom de Venise dans Calcutta désert:* The Compulsion to Repeat," *October*, no. 17 (1981): 45.

6. On this problem in Duras' filmic production see, in particular, Marie-Claire Ropars-Wuilleumier, "The Disembodied Voice: *India Song*," *Yale French Studies* 60 (1980): 241–68.

7. Stephen Heath, *Questions of Cinema* (Bloomington: Indiana Univ. Press, 1981), 88.

8. Jean Laplanche and J.-B. Pontalis, "Fantasy and the Origins of Sexuality," *International Journal of Psychoanalysis* 49 (1968): 15.

9. Sigmund Freud, *S.E.*, 2: 291.

10. Jacques Lacan, *Le Séminaire XI* (Paris: Seuil, 1973), 44.

11. Cf. Michael Riffaterre, *Semiotics of Poetry* (Bloomington: Indiana Univ. Press, 1978).

12. Jacques Derrida, *La Carte postale* (Paris: Flammarion, 1980), 236.

13. Marcelle Marini, *Territoires du féminin avec Marguerite Duras* (Paris: Minuit, 1977), 19. My translation here and following.

14. See Freud, "Mourning and Melancholia," *S.E.*, 14:243–58.

15. See Catherine Clément, "De la méconnaissance: Fantasme, scène, texte," *Langages* 31 (1973): 37–52.

16. Frederic Jameson, *Fables of Aggression: Wyndham Lewis, the Modernist as Fascist* (Berkeley and Los Angeles: Univ. of California Press, 1979), 165.

17. See, for example, the section entitled, "A Cat enters the Nevers cellar," 98, where it is a question of indifferentiation between the cat's stare and the subject's gaze.

18. Roland Barthes, *Camera Lucida,* trans. Richard Howard (New York: Hill and Wang, 1981), 26–27.

19. Jean-Louis Baudry, "The Apparatus," *Camera Obscura,* no. 1 (1976): 119.

20. Sigmund Freud, "Screen Memories," *S.E.*, 2:320.

CHAPTER

3

Le Ravissement de Lol V. Stein:
Something for Nothing

In an intriguing dialogue with Hélène Cixous, Michel Foucault advances the following metaphor to describe the operation of Duras' texts: it is like a game of pass-the-slipper (in which players rapidly pass an object from hand to hand while another player, blindfolded, tries to guess who is holding it at a given moment) in which the slipper may operate autonomously, may leap from one hand to another without the players' being responsible.[1] This metaphor illustrates his point that, in Duras' texts, *ça circule* (it circulates): signifiers, as well as the sources and aims of textual address, are mobile.

From *The Ravishing of Lol V. Stein,* through *The Vice-Consul,* to *L'Amour,* Duras' writing circulates a set of signifiers. Instead of setting up an intertextual exchange, this writing circulates. But this is circulation at a loss. Hélène Cixous describes this textual operation as linked to the passage of the past, and to loss: "The work she accomplishes is a labor of loss; as if loss were unattainable, it's very paradoxical. As if loss were never lost enough, one always stands to lose" (Cixous and Foucault, 11, my translation). This exchange is predicated on and by loss, a loss continually circulating, draining the text of "significance." The object circulating is precisely the letter. And, indeed, as letter, this may be a dead letter.

We might also characterize Duras' narrative as elaborating a split or division in the letter. Metaphorically speaking, we might say that the narrative signifiers, the letters of Duras' text, almost never arrive at their destinations, that things never return to their places. Instead, in place of place, these texts constitute a system of *relays,* of *transfers.* To follow this line of thought, we need only recall the generative textual figure of *L'Amante anglaise,* where the dismembered body of the cousin, Thérèse, is put in circulation through the railway system. "Police pathologists have come to the conclusion that all of these remains belong to the same body. With the exception of the head, which has not been found, a reconstruction of the body has been made in Paris. Analysis of the railway intersections [le recoupement ferroviaire] shows that all the trains concerned, whatever their destination, passed through the same point."[2]

The dismembered body here serves as a metaphor for the dismembered letter, or textual body. *Reconstruit:* The body rejoined, reconstructed, however, is never the same—a headless body. Decapitated, the body is reconstituted in the nation's figurative head, the place through which all trains pass.

It is as if Duras' narratives continually passed through the same posts, relays, constituting the possibility of a *recoupement:* an intersection, or a cross-checking, as of sources of information. But if this is the case, each text transports only a fragment of the body whose parts never add up to a reconstituted totality. The textual "letters" pass through the same relays, switch points, intersections, but they never reach a simple destination.

L'Amour, the last text of the narrative cycle that turns around *The Ravishing of Lol V. Stein,* opens with the repetition of the triangle—a figure inscribed in all three texts, themselves a larger triangulation which "frames" the project.

> The man walking [qui marche] looks at nothing, nothing, other than the sand before him. His pace [marche] is unremitting, regular, distant.
>
> The triangle is closed by the woman with her eyes closed. She is seated against a wall that marks off the square near its limit, the city.
>
> The man who watches is between the woman and the man walking along the shore. Because of the man who is walking, unremittingly, with an even slowness, the triangle is deformed, reformed, without ever breaking up.[3]

Within the unstable narrative borders of these three texts any three points can always be connected; however, such connection never comes to rest within the same contours. The figure's dimensions never repeat themselves exactly, which is to say that no triangle is ever right. The geometric figure that conditions these texts and their intertextual formations presents an unmeasurable hypotenuse. Hypotenuse: hypo + tenin; underlying; to stretch under, subtend.

These texts share a propensity for exploration of what lies under, what is placed under, each ultimately expressing that interest as a concern for a sort of under-placement as well. Things neither hold nor take place in Duras' narrative. Surely it is no accident that the one narrator who holds, albeit intermittently, the position of "je" bears the name that renders explicit the tenuous grip of that figure on the shifter: Jacques *Hold.* In the absence of a determinate source of the narrative discourse, this figure is merely a "place holder."

Another way of characterizing this textual space is as conditional. The narrative movement of *The Ravishing* is entirely inscribed under the absent sign of the conditional.

> I asked her if Lol's subsequent illness [la crise de Lol] was not proof positive that she was wrong. She repeated that it was not, that she, personally, believed that this crisis [crise] and Lol were but one and the same, and always had been [ne faisait qu'une depuis toujours] . . .
> Here then, in full, and all mixed together, is both this false impression which Tatiana Karl tells about and what I have been able to imagine about that night at the Town Beach Casino [casino de T. Beach]. Following which I shall relate my own story of Lol V. Stein.[4]

"Jacques Hold" is repeated and displaced in Peter Morgan, the narrated narrator of the "mendiante's" story in *Le Vice-consul.* Morgan describes his project in much the same terms as Jacques Hold does his.

> I am drunk [je m'exalte] with the sufferings of India. Aren't we all, more or less? It's impossible to talk about such suffering unless one has made it as much a part of oneself as breathing . . . That woman stirs my imagination. I take down my thoughts about her. [Je prends des notes imaginaires sur elle.]
> —Why her, in particular?
> —Because nothing more can happen to her, not even leprosy.
> —There are many different Indias, says Charles Rossett . . . mine, yours, this India, that India. One can, of course, do what you are doing, or so it seems, though I can't be sure because I hardly know you, and that is to put all these different Indias together.[5]

In this case, it is the fundamental story of the *mendiante* that is conditional, hypothetical, and its space, Calcutta, India, which is rendered hypothetical by the narrative movement itself.

The conditional is the mode of the hypothetical, of supposition, conjecture. Hypothesis: that which can be neither affirmed nor denied with certainty; a proposition put forth or stated, without any reference to its correspondence with fact. From the Greek *hypo:* foundation or base, and *thetic:* placing, underlying, the basis of an argument. Etymologically, hypothesis means the same things as supposition—sub-position, under the position, a substitution, that which is less-than-positioned. To return to hypothesis: thesis: such as is placed or fit to be placed; positive, affirmative. Etymologically this term refers to place, position, or affirmation, but also to stress or beat, rhythm.

In Duras' work, it is this latter sense which excavates the former and more commonly accepted one. Her narrative cycle enacts the supplanting of the thetic by the "hypo"-thetic or the non-thetic, shows the work of the non-thetic within the proposition, the thetic itself. This work operates upon the logic of positionality itself, since it is the basis of the logic of the proposition, as constructed in a dialectical movement, through oppositions. Without a structure of opposition, the textual production does not arrive at proposition, at a *setting forth,* so much as it establishes a pulsation, an alternation which poses no stable poles or positions.[6]

In this connection, we may examine Duras' own coments on textual production as repetition and echoing: "I do my books with others. What is a little strange is that transformation it perhaps undergoes, the sound it makes when it passes through me, but that's all. It is a sound that it [ça] makes when it passes through a given person. I am simply, perhaps, an echo chamber" (*Les Parleuses,* 217–18, my translation). Here Duras' reference to the echo chamber is an echo of an earlier remark in this same interview: "Between the auditorium and the stage there is a constant and direct communication. There you have the house and there you have the stage, and you have another space. It is in that other space that things are . . . lived and the stage is only an echo chamber" (*Les Parleuses,* 157, my translation).

The echo is a sound whose reverberation repeats an "original sound." An echo chamber, then, by its very structuration, perpetuates echoes, as echoes of echoes, thereby confounding original with repetition, source with reception. Moreover, the coincidence inscribed here between the scene of writing and the cinematic scene, an echo that describes the contours of another space, between audience and screen, raises the question of linguistic emission and reception, decentering a communicational model of textual practice, precisely by engaging the complexities of the function of repetition. Similarly, we might speculate that the textual *performance* takes place in and through the imbrication of reading and writing as performances. This is another version of the relation of repetition and displacement—of nonrepeatable repetitions—an issue that conditions the narrative instance we "suppose" Duras' texts to pose.

In discussing the figures generated in the textual cycle here in question, Duras repeats the metaphor of the echo chamber obliquely. This is obvious in the following exchange with Michelle Porte, concerning the madman of *La Femme du Gange,* one of Duras' filmic versions of the abstracted and distilled moments of the Lol V. Stein story.

Duras: He keeps the memory, yes. He is without memory and he keeps the memory.

Michelle Porte: I am thinking of the scene where the madman is dancing in the ballroom: you write in the script of *La Femme du Gange,* "the madman, the hollowed form of the madman is traversed by everyone's memory [la mémoire de tous: memory of everyone, everyone's memory]."

Duras: He has a mind like a sieve, yes, full of holes . . . Since he is nothing he offers no resistance to anything, and memory for me is something spread out everywhere, and I see places that way. . . . He's porous, the madman. He is nothing, so things pass through him completely. (*Les Lieux de Marguerite Duras,* 96, my translation)

In that sense, the narrative, like the characters, is a *passoire,* a strainer, full of holes through which the signifier passes. But we pass along with it. To follow the signifier is to be caught in its defiles; here, quite literally, it is to have a pass-key, a master key, a *passe-partout,* which passes to nowhere. Indeed, it is through such textual functions that the text constructs a "memory" of its own, a memory that confuses itself with that of the reader, thereby calling into question the distance between poles— sender-receiver—and their very stability/possibility, which depends on maintaining a split between them.

To accept the utterly noncontractual pact proposed by this narration, to submit to its fascination, is to follow the detours of its circulation, to be captured by the traces of its passage, the destabilization of positions through its textual syntax, the suspension in its narrative discourse, its perpetually displaced figure—the triangle. If we accept Roland Barthes' description of the conditions of narrative, as exposed in "Structural Analysis of Narratives," we may detect certain connections which Duras' texts seem to elaborate.

> The function of narrative is not to "represent," it is to constitute a spectacle still very enigmatic for us but in any case not of a mimetic order. The "reality" of a sequence lies not in the "natural" succession of the actions composing it, but in the logic there exposed, risked and satisfied. Putting it another way, one could say that the origin of a sequence is not the observation of reality, but the need to vary and transform the first *form* given man, namely repetition: a sequence is essentially a whole within which nothing is repeated. Logic has here an emancipatory value—and with it the entire narrative.[7]

The logic "risked" by Duras' texts is never satisfied. In a logic of a different sort of repetition, these texts perform the obverse of narrativity as it is here described.

Within the same textual sequence, as the conclusion of this essay, Barthes establishes a speculative link between narrative and Oedipus.

> "What takes place" in a narrative is from the referential (reality) point of view literally *nothing*. . . . Although we know scarcely more about the origins of narrative than we do about the origins of language, it can reasonably be suggested that narrative is contemporaneous with monologue, a creation seemingly posterior to that of dialogue. At all events, without wanting to strain the phylogenetic hypothesis, it may be significant that it is at the same moment (around the age of three) that the little human "invents" at once sentence, narrative, and the Oedipus. (124)

In this connection, the interrogation of the narrative functions of sequentiality and repetition posed by Duras' three-text cycle must also be connected to the possibility of a different textual economy. Such an economy is precisely a libidinal economy that *performs* a disruption of narrative positionality and productivity in the conventional sense. It is because it is a question of libidinal economy, however, that Duras' texts may be read as a kind of re-vision of the Oedipal scene, with a difference, the acknowledgment of *sexual* difference. If another economy is at work in Duras' texts, we might seek it in the recesses of *The Ravishing of Lol V. Stein,* at the place where the textual discourse begins to account for the inaccessible origin of the narrative itself, as well as for Lol's inability to narrate.

What would have happened? Lol does not probe very deeply into the unknown into which this moment opens. She has no memory, not even an imaginary one, she has not the faintest notion of this unknown. But what she does believe is that she must enter it, that that was what she had to do, that it would always have meant, for her mind as well as her body, both their greatest pain and their greatest joy, so commingled as to be undefinable, a single entity but unnameable for lack of a word. I like to believe—since I love her— that if Lol is silent in her daily life it is because, for a split second, she believed that this word might exist. Since it does not, she remains silent. It would have been an absence word, a hole-word, whose center would have been hollowed out into a hole in which all other words would have been buried. It would have been impossible to utter it, but it would have been made to reverberate. Enormous, endless, an empty gong, it would have held back anyone who had wanted to leave, it would have convinced them of the impossible, made them deaf to any other word save that one, in one fell swoop it would have defined the future and the moment themselves. By its absence, this word ruins all the others, it contaminates them, it is also the dead dog on the beach at high noon, this hole of flesh. . . . Oh! you've no idea how many there are, how many blood-stained failures are strewn along the horizon, piled up there, and, among them, this word, which does not exist, is none the less there: it waits you just around the corner of language, it defies you—never having been used—to raise it, to make it arise from its kingdom, which is pierced on every side and through which flows the sea, the sand, the eternity of the ball in the cinema of Lol V. Stein. (*The Ravishing,* 38–39)

This passage, which is amply commented on by Lacan, Marini, and Montrelay, might be said to contain the totality of the text, in its very *nothingness.* But if so, it simultaneously obliterates itself, the totality, and the commentary; we might see here the interpretation as a discourse caught up in this (w)hole which "would have held back anyone who wanted to leave, would have convinced them of the impossible." However, this absent word, in its lack-to-be, its wanting, its *nothing,* also constitutes a textual node through which circulate the signifiers that wander through this whole textual cycle. The "dead dog on the beach" is *nothing* but the analog of the *mot-trou,* appearing in *L'Amour* as the "literal" translation of that word. Word into Flesh? Word-flesh.

The word "doesn't exist but is still there [pourtant est là]." Est là: à S. Thala. The word ex-sists, and in specific ways, just as it *exits* this text without ever really appearing, only to resonate in *Le Vice-consul* as Battambang: "Battambang will keep her safe. She will never utter any word but that. It is her shelter, her home" (46).

Battambang, a *mot-trou,* constitutes the voiced materialization of the empty space of Lol V. Stein's missing word. This is a word which is now, however, *present,* externalized as the mark of memory's abolition: "She stretches . . . oh, what it is to be young, to run, to walk out at night, singing the songs of Tonle Sap. All of them. Ten years later, in Calcutta, there will only be one song. It will be the last remnant of memory left to her" (49). The word that resonates and disseminates across the text, a word-presence that only installs the absence of both meaning and language, also unites "the present moment and the future," since it is narrated in the future mode. Furthermore, this word, this sung syllable, or false name, marks the mendiante's condition, stands in for her in her capacity as "death in the midst of life" (139). This perpetually displaced syllabic flow plies its way between presence and absence, life and death, "death in the midst of life, death following but never catching up"—the perpetually missed encounter.

We may read *The Vice-Consul* as the set of threads that bind together the three texts of the cycle, and as the one that is based upon the absence of Lol V. Stein—a text founded on her memory, the space of her absence, but apparently without memory of her. This double-centered text, focused on the two empty figures, "the beggar woman" and the Vice-Consul, is also traversed by a word— "Impossible." This word is repeated by the Vice-Consul, a word whose very repetition contaminates the discourse of the other textual figures. For instance, Anne-Marie Stretter, in the ball scene, is transfixed by the word.

> I don't know how to say . . . the word "impossible" occurs in your personal file. Is that the appropriate word in this instance?
> He is silent. She asks again:
> Is that the word? Answer me . . .

I don't know myself. Like you, I am searching for the word. Perhaps there is another way of putting it? [il y a un autre mot?]
It's not important now. (100)

It is possible that the impossible word, the one that "would have convinced them of the impossible," could be "impossible." Here the textual echo merely launches another circuit of repetition, restarts the quest for an absent term.

We might want to speculate, on the basis of nothing, risking *nothing,* that the *mot-trou* of *The Ravishing* is nothing more than the persistence of "rien," "ne . . . plus," "personne," "aucun," the "ne . . . pas" that suspends textual movement as well as narrative affirmation. The insistence of negations in this text almost obliterates each enunciation as soon as it is posed. Almost. At the very least, it installs contradiction at the textual core: in the word *rien*. Michèle Montrelay speculates on precisely the implications of this word in her remarkable essay on *The Ravishing,* which appears in *L'Ombre et le nom: "The Ravishing of Lol V. Stein* secretes a passionate will to lose, to waste all resources, those it proliferates and your own. It puts everything in the service of a certain nothing. Etymology and grammar give the word contrary meanings. 'Nothing' can mean nothingness, void [néant], but a nothing in the sense of a trifle, that can't equal zero, surely that's something. Does the impoverishment of *Le Ravissement* open on zero, or rather on a nothing with consistency?"[8] For Montrelay, this "nothing" recalls none other than the signifier itself; "in its materiality, the signifier is a nothing that is not without reality, but which is a nothing all the same, because it is not signified" (10).

In her "Inquiry into Femininity," Montrelay also characterizes the *rien,* the hole of the text, as a form of feminine parade: the gap shown to mask the absence of a lack. She writes, "Duras wants to make this lack 'speak' as cry, or as music. Here let us simply recall what is said in *The Ravishing of Lol V. Stein: '*What was needed was a word-hole . . . it could not have been spoken; it could only be made to resound' " (230).

In this appropriation of the word-absence, she is not alone. Jacques Lacan's reading of the passage is similar.

This is to be seen in the first scene where Lol is, properly, robbed of her lover [dérobée à quelqu'un: to steal from someone; also dérober: to hide or conceal], that is to say that it can be followed through the

71

theme of the dress [la robe] which here supports the fantasy to which Lol attaches herself in the time afterwards, a fantasy of a beyond for which she hasn't managed to find the word, that word that, closing the doors on all of them, would have joined her to the moment when her lover took off the woman's black dress and unveiled her nudity. Does this go further? Yes, to the unspeakable of that nudity that insinuates itself to replace her own body. There everything stops.[9]

The absent word here is the *maquillage,* the masquerade (robe) that covers the absence of the gap—that supports the fantasy. It is a word-fetish that immobilizes the text.

For Marcelle Marini, such a word-hole installs itself on the feminine impossibility of symbolizing her sex or her desire. It thus marks or seals the border of a feminine imaginary, as yet inarticulable. Of the "word-hole," she says, "if it existed, it would name sex and death" (*Territoires,* 26). She goes on to specify the relationship of the feminine to this lacking word: "Whether it's a question of men or of women, this missing word has something to do with the enigma of the female body. . . . What is necessary (for the woman) is a term which would situate her in relation to her own sex, in a symbolizable lack-to-be-to-herself [manque-à-être-à-soi]" (26–27).

All these readings touch on the essentials of the text's concentration in this passage. However, what if this nothing, along with the negations that it entails, throughout the text, were to be read as a *knothing,* a knotting, and the *ne*/not as *noeud*/knot?[10]

From a word-hole, a word-absence, to a word-thing, *The Ravishing* effects this transformation through the question of posing, posing a question, posing a word.

"You must," she says, then adds, "I love you, you have no idea how much I love you already."

The word travels through space, seeks and alights [pose]. She has placed the word on me [posé le mot sur moi].

She loves, loves the man who must love Tatiana. No one. No one loves Tatiana in me. I belong to a perspective which she is in the process of constructing with impressive obstinacy. (122)

This scene engages the primary question posed by the text: of posing and positions, the triangular, the necessary third who intervenes, and of insignificance, fascination or seduction by the in- or non-significant.

In *De la séduction,* Jean Baudrillard characterizes the process of seduction as related to signs, but beyond signification. To illustrate the
seductiveness of the non-sensical or non-representing sign, Baudrillard
recounts the legend of a soldier who meets Death on the road and,
terrified, begs the king to lend him a horse so that he may flee one night's
ride, to the town farthest from the fateful encounter. When the king later
reproaches Death for frightening the man, Death replies that he was only
expressing surprise to the man, with whom he had a meeting on the
following day, in the town to which the soldier is fleeing. For Baudrillard:
"We are only absorbed by vacant, absurd or elliptical signs, those without reference."[11] As he explains, the man of the legend dies because he
has posed himself as the *destinataire* and interpreter of a gesture *not*
addressed to him. "He took for himself something that wasn't addressed
to him. . . . The seduced man is taken up in spite of himself in the
network of signs getting lost. And it is because the sign is diverted from
its sense [sens: as both meaning and direction], because it is 'seduced'
that this story itself is seductive. It is when signs are seduced that they
become seductive" (104).

Such a reading of the seductive function of signs, as dependent on
one's mistakenly coming into the place of their addressee, on one's
missing their sense along with their destination, seems particularly
applicable to *Le Ravissement:* "She has placed the word on me." The
question of address, destination, and reception is at work throughout
the text, built into its network of circulating signs and looks, and establishing a perpetual cycle of interferences and detours, as in the following passage:

> She has just said that Tatiana is naked beneath her dark hair. That
> sentence is the last to have been uttered. I hear: "naked beneath her
> dark hair, naked, naked, dark hair." The last words especially strike
> with a strange and equal intensity. It's true that Tatiana was as Lol
> has just described her, naked beneath her dark hair . . . The sentence
> explodes, it blows the meaning apart [elle crève le sens]. I hear it
> with a deafening roar and I fail to understand it. I no longer even
> understand that it means nothing. (105–6)

This passage invokes the problem of the referent, of exchange of equiva-
lent terms, in connection with the abolition of distinction between
sender and receiver, subject and object of the exchange, once it is "short-

circuited." In effect, it is precisely this function that is at work in the text's very title: *Le Ravissement de Lol V. Stein.*

It is with this indeterminacy that Jacques Lacan begins his analysis of the text. The word *ravissement* can mean ravishing or rapture, a violent forcing or a state of ecstasy. Such an ambiguity extends to the structure of the phrase itself: le ravissement de Lol V. Stein, the ravishing of Lol V. Stein, because the possessive, *de,* "of"—meaning by her or upon her— allows Lol V. Stein to be imagined as subject and object of the ravishing. One may apply the term "ravishing," as Lacan does, to Lol herself—as ravishing figure, one who fascinates *us* ("Hommage," 131).

Such a description already recalls the structure of fantasy, where the subject is always a participant, but not exclusively as subject. The floating or shifting of positionality in this structure is related to its "grammar," to the syntactic admissibility of a variety of combinations, or the multiplicity of "points of insertion" in the signifying chain. Clearly, the narrative subjectivity, the "je" of Jacques Hold, already constitutes one of the figures susceptible to this fantasmatic structure, in its oscillation between third- and first-person enunciations.

In his article, "Comment elle fait," Benoît Jacquot sees this structure as conditioning Duras' larger narrative enterprise, suggesting that she employs a minimal signifying repertoire which is perpetually recombined. He compares this work to Freud's discovery of the lability of the fantasy, "A Child Is Being Beaten," where the fantasy reduces to a simple phrase out of which several combinations may be generated around an unvarying term—the verb. The invariant for Duras, he contends, is "a blank, a not-said."[12]

If the narrative-grammatical combinatory of *The Ravishing* turns on an invariant blank or *non-dit*/not-said, whose place is held, or designated, by the word-thing "rien," the verbal function that centers the text might well be the word *regarder,* a term that inscribes and reinscribes a set of relations among the figures that remain indeterminate. This function of the verb *regarder,* along with its substantive form, *regard,* constitutes an even greater source of textual pressure in *L'Amour,* which we will examine later. The opening segments of this later text seem entirely based on an alternating rhythm between dialogue and look, looking, as if the narrative itself were propelled by a sort of look-function.

Without a doubt, the look-function in *The Ravishing* is completely imbricated with the "scène du bal"—the absent origin (of the text's

forgetfulness itself). In the early pages of the text, the narrator's speculations on Lol's behavior at the ball run as follows: "Had she looked at
Michael Richardson as she passed? Had this non-look of hers swept over
him as it took in the ballroom? It was impossible to tell . . . her gaze,
from close-up one could see that this defect stemmed from an almost
painful discoloration of the pupil—was diffused over the entire surface
of her eyes and was hard to meet [*capter:* to meet a look, to catch the
eye, to *capture* the gaze]" (6).

The look, here, is already in default, faulty—in the sense that it is
detached from both source and object—a non-look groping across the
surface of the scene. But it is also, within the structure of reversibility
that conditions this passage, just as it does the whole narrative, itself a
surface, a blank, and a vanishing point. A later passage brings back the
ball scene, as Jacques Hold watches Lol watch Tatiana, and recalls the
voyeurism to which his encounters with Tatiana are subject. "As Tatiana
is once again arranging her hair I am thinking back to yesterday—Lol is
watching her—I remember my head buried in her breast, yesterday. I have
no idea that she saw us, and yet the way she is looking at Tatiana is what
prompts me to remember" (71). Here the narrative establishes a circulation of looks, looks looking at looks. Beyond this, however, the look
becomes, increasingly, a detachable, and detached, object: "Lol is still
stroking Tatiana's hair. At first she gazes at her intently, but then she is
staring vacantly into space, she is stroking the way some blind person in
search of her bearings might . . . Her expression [*regard*] is tender,
opaque. Her look, which was meant for Tatiana, falls upon me" (82–83).

The look itself becomes blind here, a point of suspension that inter-
cepts or captures and fascinates another look. But perhaps the most
startling representation of this detachable look occurs at the moment of
Hold's dance with Lol, under "Tatiana's surveillance," a repetition of the
ball scene upon which he has not ceased to speculate.

> Again, like a good girl, Lol is dancing, following me. When Tatiana
> cannot see, I move Lol away from me so that I can see her eyes. I see
> them: a transparency is looking at me. Again I cannot see. I pull her
> back against me, she does not resist; no one, I believe, is paying any
> attention to us. The transparency has gone through me, I can still
> see it, blurred now, it has moved on toward something else, some-
> thing less clear, something endless, it will move on toward something
> else, some endless thing that I will never know. (43–44)

The look that traverses the scene becomes the look of "no one." Tatiana is looking, yet "no one, I believe, is paying any attention to us." A transparency is looking; the look itself is utterly transparent, yet it can cross the scene, define its limits, and rupture them: "it has moved on toward something else, . . . something endless."

Given the concentricity of exteriors here, and their interference, we might see this text as turning around a generative, though empty, center, signaled by the blind look. Our own absorption into the circuit of exchanges and interferences is thereby conditioned by our fascination with this detached look and by the symmetry of our position with that of the "aveugle," since the figure who lacks an exterior is as much the reader of the other figures as we are. This is not surprising in a text which explores the problematic borders of representation through an obsessive attention to a fault in the name, as well as in the look.

This look-function that centers the text is interwoven in a network of functions that provoke the rapture of Jacques Lacan, given the possibility of their determination as a certain textual enactment of his theory. He sees the look's radical separation from the eye, figured in this textual drama, as the function that installs division within the subject ("Hommage," 134). By this he means, I think, that the splitting between the eye and the gaze is replicated in the cutting up of a space by vision, a cutting of space which also installs a separation between the subject, as a hole in the visual field, and the points that mark the distances and limits that determine that field.

We find a similar connection between the look and the cut in Julia Kristeva's work on spatial mapping as support to the subject's accession to language, which she elaborates in *Desire in Language.* As she sees it, the separation or border between inside and outside, necessary to speech, is precipitated from a primary spatial mapping that begins with points of discharge for the excitations of the anaclisis, what she calls "markers of something in the process of becoming stability" (283). These are points that capture and absorb certain libidinal charges: "the breast given and withdrawn, lamplight capturing the gaze; intermittent sounds of voice or music—all these meet with anaclisis . . . , hold it, and thus inhibit and absorb it in such a way that it is discharged and abated through them. . . . At that point, breast, light and sound become a *there:* a place, a spot, a marker" (283).

These points of fixity are engaged in an alternating process of stabilization-destabilization, and participate in the indifferentiation of the semiotic chora, which includes the maternal body and the space surrounding the infant as well. As the first mappings of differentiation, they mark both the cut and the threat of absorption into indifferentiation; for example, the look is indistinguishable from its capture, by absorption, in the bright spot that attracts it.

As a figure of this inseparability of the gaze and its capture, Lol wavers on the border of differentiation-indifferentiation. Lacan characterizes her as the figure of the "non-regard," a dead point in the field of vision, which is, correspondingly, related to the *fascinum,* the suspension, putting to death of the look in fascination. "Because you feel that it is a question of an envelope which has neither outside nor inside, and that in the seam of its center all looks turn back into yours [se retournent dans], that they are yours which saturates them and that forever, Lol, you will lay claim to, call to [réclamerez] all who pass by. So one follows Lol, seizing in its passage from one to the other that talisman which each one hastily gets rid of as a danger: the look. . . ." ("Hommage," 134).

This passage, addressed to Lol herself, constitutes a curious dramatization of the "reading" process this text entails. For Lacan, it is a question of what "vous regarde," in the double sense the French provides: what looks at you, and what concerns you, requires your attention, engages you. In this case, what "nous regarde sans nous regarder" [what concerns us without looking at us] is precisely Lol, whose function Lacan postulates as that of presenting the look object: "There where the look is, Lol makes it emerge in the state of a pure object for Jacques Hold" (135).

For Lacan, this moment of pure look is precisely the switch point at which, through Lol's "voyeurism" (a misnomer, with respect to the foregoing characterization of her look), Hold and Tatiana begin to feel themselves as operators in her fantasy, as figures projected on the screen of her private cinema. We recall that the ball scene is first characterized by its relation to time and to projection: "the eternity of the ball in the cinema of Lol V. Stein" (39).

The repetition of the scene of loss, of irrevocable separation, as generative of the fantasy, is inevitably tied, in this text, to projected images. "In the distance, with fairy-like fingers, the recollection of a certain memory flits past . . . this woman who is gazing up at a small rectangular window, a narrow stage, circumscribed as a stone, on which no actor has yet appeared. And perhaps Lol is afraid, but ever so slightly, of the possibility of an even greater separation from the others" (54). Where fantasy becomes anticipatory and not rememorative, the roles of subject and object are, simultaneously, not reversed, but reversible. For Jacques Hold does not see Lol seeing him, but he imagines her: "Her eyes riveted on the lighted window, a woman hearkens to the void" (54). Later he speculates, "in turn, Tatiana Karl, naked in her black hair, crosses the stage of light, slowly. It is perhaps in Lol's rectangle of vision that she stops. She turns back to the room where the man presumably is" (55). The speaking subject here sees the scene in which he participates through the projected vision of a look located elsewhere, a look that installs an absence, a hypothetical position (where the man probably is) *within* the very space from which he speaks. This, according to Michèle Montrelay, explains why Hold is the figure of the perverse here, in his desire to see the lack-in-being inscribed on the body of the other. With respect to this reading, we must question its implications for our position as readers, desiring to see the lack-in-being inscribed on another body—the body of the text, perhaps.

Hold's own look across the screen-window determines the presence of Lol in the field as follows: "Lol, I can see Lol, she does not stir. . . . Tatiana Karl does not see the dark spot in the rye" (56). In this regard, Lol is positioned as the *projector* of the scene, analogous to the cinematic projector, the blind spot from which images emanate. Moreover, she is the immobilized point of scotomization for the narrator.

> Tatiana Karl traces the origins of that illness back further, further even than the beginning of their friendship. They were latent [elles étaient là] in Lol Stein, but kept from emerging by the deep affection with which she had always been surrounded both at home and, later, at school. She says that in school—and she wasn't the only person to think so—there was already something lacking in Lol, something which kept her from being, in Tatiana's words, "there" [là] . . . Lol was funny, an inveterate wit, and very bright, even though part of her always seemed to be evading you, and the present moment. Going where? . . . Tatiana apparently inclined toward the opinion that it was perhaps, indeed, Lol Stein's heart which wasn't—as she says—there. (2–3)

This description of Lol's condition as always already lacking-to-be-there, which forms part of the narrative's initial inquiry, is later repeated at the moment of Lol's first formal visit to Tatiana—the scene, precisely, of her first effort to recount the history of the past ten years. "Tatiana did not believe that Lol Stein's insanity could be traced back solely to the ball, she traced its origins back further in Lol's life, back to her youth, she saw it as stemming from elsewhere. In school, she says, there was something lacking in Lol [il manquait déjà quelque chose à Lol], she was already strangely incomplete, she had lived her early years as though she were waiting for something she might, but never did, become" (71).

This scene repeats almost exactly the initial speculations, in its insistent displacement of the "original" loss. Loss becomes originary—a loss appealing to or soliciting an inevitably postponed becoming. Moreover, this passage discloses the epistemological drive that conditions the ball scene, as well as the narrative's more general project.

Thus *The Ravishing* constitutes a sort of inverted enigma whose secret lies in not having one: "Now, I alone of all these perverters of the truth know this: that I know nothing. That was my initial discovery about her: to know nothing about Lol was already to know her [ne rien savoir de Lol était la connaître déjà]. One could, it seemed to me, know even less about her, less and less about Lol Stein" (72). While playing on the flexibility French admits for the verb "to know," *savoir* and *connaître*, displacing the question between knowledge and acquaintance, or familiarity, this passage poses the text's contradiction once again: nothing is not absolute. It is impossible to know absolutely nothing of Lol; one must continually know less than nothing, or rather, less and less than nothing.

The lack, loss, or hole becomes the space of *losing, lacking* as a process, rather than a state. In this connection, bearing in mind the centrality of the text's hypothetical drive to name the lack, to find the missing word, we may turn to its naming functions—to the lack in the name, the name's lacking. Here the textual figure presented in the place names, T. Beach, S. Thala, U. Bridge, is not neutral.[13] The use of an initial—one letter for the word— masks under anonymity the topographical junctures of the text, projecting them into an imaginary landscape. The particularly resonant term S. Thala, name of the place of origin, opens larger questions of intertextual connections, in its prominent repetitions throughout this cycle. Here we will confine our examination to a term specific to *Le Ravissement:* U. Bridge. Like the names of the important male characters in the text, this word is English, constituted by an alien linguistic topography. To imagine the shape of the letter itself is significant; the *U* figures an open-ended circuit. We begin at one point and follow a curved trajectory to a parallel, but displaced, terminal point. Imagine this letter as the designation of a bridge—a bridge that metaphorically returns to the same side of the space to be crossed. This is a bridge that fails to bridge anything, but instead reinstalls the unbridgeable gap.

The *U*, as cipher, recalls the name-cipher of Lol V. Stein, described by Lacan as "a cipher that appears in this wisely formed name, in the contour of its writing: Lol V. Stein. Lol V. Stein: Paper wings [ailes]; V.: scissors; Stein: stone; in the *jeu de la mourre*, you lose yourself" ("Hommage," 131). It is impossible to pass this citation without remarking on the sense of Lacan's pun: "au jeu de la mourre"—jeu de l'amour. According to the Robert dictionary, "la mourre" is a game of chance in which players simultaneously show a certain number of fingers while calling out a guess as to the sum represented by the fingers shown by both, the one guessing correctly winning. The connections to be made here are multiple: the love game is a game the winning of which depends on the correct guessing of the sum of one's wager with the other's—a game of intersubjectivity and doubling. Most important, however, the game is a game of numbers—of wager and risk, as well as of counting—just as it is a game of alternation among figures and between subjects; the fingers are hidden, then disclosed. The sum of the fingers of one hand means nothing without the outside additive framework, which always figures in the number hidden in the other's hand. Moreover, "la mourre" derives from the Latin *mora*, delay, which is implicitly central to this game. This sense is linked to the delay which conditions *Le Ravissement*. Indeed, the text might be read as the structure of delays that establishes the possibility of the fantasmatic scene. The ball, the originary scene, always arrives too late, is perpetually delayed, just as Lol is delayed beyond ever arriving.

While Lacan emphasizes the aspects of the text that link it to a "numbers game," a play of ciphers, hidden and disclosed, Marcelle Marini exposes a sexual dimension to this play in her *Territoires du féminin*. Marini sees the name of Lol V. Stein as a cipher for feminine desire, in its lack of access to symbolization of its own lack-in-being: the *o* between two *l*'s (elles/ailes). Referring to *Dix heures et demie du soir en été*, Marini sees in the textual fascination of Duras' narratives with the numbers zero, one, and three the ternary organization of the triangle, an inscription of unsymbolizable femininity. She locates the feminine subject *between* zero and one, posed as zero over and against the unitary identity of the masculine, the One, and yet irrevocably separated from the maternal origin, the zero point. The cipher-name of Lol V. Stein reflects femininity's reduction to a cipher, a nonsubject in the sexual relation that merely repeats, without differences, the identity of the one.

Marini extends this interrogation of the problem of feminine desire and its foreclosure by the symbolic order, in its nonsymbolization, in her examination of the name "S. Thala": "Reste là [stays there], . . . Est-ce ta 'la'? [is that your *la*, feminine article, or your there, *là*]" (38). For her, the sound "la" becomes the unnaming name, "a term which doesn't name," which is, rather, a call, an appeal, a demand posed to the mother. Her reflections on designation and nomination are intimately linked to her examination of *The Ravishing* as an exploration of the means to produce a representation of femininity: "A woman always discovers herself to be 'a woman badly designated' (mis-designated) in the arms of a man, and the child is always mis- or not designated by its father and mother: that's the incest-prison, the child-penis born out of one plus zero, the castrated woman. Or not designated at all: woman-mother-daughter folded over on the unique figure of the virgin-mother, sexuality reduced to the uterus, to wound, to a vagina-hole" (38).

If we look closely at *The Ravishing*, we find a parallel textual impulse, inscribed in the very name of Lol V. Stein, which underlies and, perhaps, also constitutes an interference in relation to the search for the *mot-trou*, a word to name the feminine. The relation I propose here may be precisely an effect of being "out of relation" to one another. There is a connection to be established between the S. Thala—est-ce ta "la"—and Lola Valérie Stein, through the syllable "la," the feminine article (meaningless outside its relation to a noun/name, and yet grammatically charged with the feminine), and the adverbial function "là," "there," indication of place. In fact, it is signicant that it is this "la" that produces, on the literal level, the name of Lol V. Stein as a poor designation, a missed or displaced designation. Moreover, this detached syllable, the terminal "a," floats and disseminates throughout the text, in repeated references to the phrase, "there was already something lacking in Lol, something which kept her from being—there [là]" (3).

The first words of the text establish Lol's abbreviated name as the proper one: "Lol V. Stein was born here in S. Thala, and she lived most of her childhood here" (2). Unlike the missing letters after the initial, V., which are designated by the period, the vacancy, the missing fragment, of "Lol" is in no way indicated: Lol resounds as a full and proper name. Later in the early section of the text, as Lol's mother recounts her version of the ball scene, we read: "She kept repeating the same things: that it wasn't late, it was only the early dawn of summer that made it seem later than it really was. She pronounced her name with rage: Lol V. Stein— that was how she referred to herself" (12). Clearly, the name we have come to attach to this figure is the product of an *autonomase* and is related to the radical "cut" of the ball scene. It is only much later, after delay, or as an effect of retroaction, that we learn the other, the "full" name of this figure: Lola Valérie Stein. "But is it Lol, I'm not mistaken?" (64) inquires Tatiana at her first encounter with Lol. More significantly still, in the scene of the first embrace between Jacques Hold and Lol V. Stein, we witness the following exchange, founded on the process of naming.

> She shakes her head, murmurs my name [Elle fait signe: non, dit mon nom].
> "Jacques Hold."   Lol's virginity uttering that name! Who except her, Lol Stein, the so-called Lol Stein [Lol V. Stein, in the French text], had noticed the inconsistency of the belief in the person so named. . . . For the first time my name, pronounced, names nothing.
> "Lola Valérie Stein."
> "Yes.". . .
> Our emptiness grows. We repeat our names to each other. (103)

Here, the nominal exchange fails to name. The self-saying Lol V. Stein voids the nominative effect of the name, just as her own name, pronounced by the other, acquires the missing, repressed or amputated "a" of its alternation. Paying attention to the transition from "Lol" to "Lola," monosyllabic to disyllabic, we may hear a return of rhythmic pulsation. What returns is the "la," that syllable, word, and object that determines Lol's status as a subject ("there was already something lacking in Lol . . . which kept her from being 'there' [là]"). *The Ravishing* turns on the intermittence of the "la"—thereness—which, once posed, always evaporates or fades.

This structure is precisely *not* a pure opposition: absent-present, far-near. It is structured in and through the varied and indeterminate distance of the "there," and proximity of the "here," throwing these categories themselves into question, since they exist both in relation to each other and to the subject always in the process of its constitution through this mapping. Can we doubt the inscription of death in the intimate and indefinite proximity of the name, when we continue from the exchange of names to the question of memory and its loss in this scene? "Just as my hands touch [se posent sur] Lol, the memory of an unknown man comes back to me: he will serve as the eternal Richardson, the man from Town Beach [T. Beach], we will be mingled with him, willy-nilly, all together, we shall no longer be able to recognize one another, neither before, nor after, nor during, we shall lose sight of one another, forget our names, in this way we shall die for having forgotten—piece by piece, moment by moment, name by name—death" (103).

This passage might well describe the entire textual movement, both across *The Ravishing* and across the three-text cycle. Death resides in the name, in its own self-forgetfulness, lodged in the power of the name to forget, to install absence and division in the subject. Put another way, the naming act becomes a renaming, a repetition effect. This effect is connected to the continually repeated syllable "la" which occasionally returns to attach itself to the "Lol" syllable, and then, as quickly, slips under the name and fades out.

The final voyage of *The Ravishing*, the "return" to an originary scene, itself constitutes a false repetition of Lol's solitary trip there. She tells Hold that she wanted to see T. Beach again with him. When he points out that she has just returned to that site, she responds, "No, I never really went back, not all the way back. The day before yesterday I didn't leave the station. I stayed in the waiting room" (157). The recitation of this scene culminates in Lol's declaration that "the sea was in the waiting room mirror" (162).

Arriving at T. Beach, she has never quite arrived, but instead, has seen the beach, the sea, in a mirror in the station. "The sea [la mer] was in the mirror." Or, *la mère* was in the mirror. In either case, the mirror provides no narcissistic doubling, but reintroduces an exterior space, be it the sea, or the division in the mother's body precisely at the locus of the specular, the reflection. We should note that the mirror is in the waiting room of the train station. Lol never leaves the *waiting* area, the antechamber of the *relay* station; she is always somehow before the fact.

This strange reappearance of the mother, or her homophonic double in French, the sea (whose significance for Duras' texts we will pursue shortly), participates in a certain reversal of the uncanny effect—the mirror reflects the outside and not Lol, and she, rather than doubling or repeating the scene, finds it unrecognizable, utterly different from itself. This peculiar effect is reflected in the place name itself. "T. Beach" suggests the inverted repetition of "S. Thala": *thalassa*, Greek for sea. The tautological name "sea beach" inscribes the borderline within—between the sea and the beach.

In connection with this false doubling, and with names, the penultimate love scene of the text, the first sexual encounter between Lol and Hold, pivots on the axis of names, in their relation to identity and difference.

> She is no longer moving, now doubtless remembers that she is here with Tatiana Karl's lover . . .
>
> But now at last she begins to doubt that identity, the only identity familiar to her, the only one she has used at least as long as I have known her . . .
>
> . . . now there was no longer [il n'y a—present tense] any difference between her and Tatiana Karl except in her eyes, free of remorse, and in the way she referred to herself—Tatiana does not state her own name—and in the two names she gave herself: Tatiana Karl and Lol Stein. (178-79)

The difference between the two figures is established precisely on the point where the one calls herself by the other's name as well as her own, interchangeably, whereas the other doesn't call herself at all.

Elsewhere, Duras has concerned herself directly with the question of naming. Speaking of her film *Aurélia Steiner,* she offers the following meditation.

> Isi Beller says that the sexual act there is a sort of metaphor of what should happen when one calls [appeler: to call or to name] someone: the penetration of Aurélia's body by the black-haired sailor is the name Aurélia Steiner that inscribes itself in the body of Aurélia, and Beller sees Aurélia as the passage of that metaphor. That is, an inscription and an effacement, and again an inscription and an effacement. She can't capture this name, she can't apprehend it except by the penetration of her body, as if the name was written there, in that body.[14]

Such a body-inscription is dispersed and repeated in the three films called *Aurélia Steiner*, each with a different voice-over narrative, all addressed to a never-designated "you," and all covering images that track a natural landscape. Because the filmic narratives all conclude with "My name is Aurélia Steiner, I live in Melbourne/Vancouver/Paris, where my parents are teachers. I am eighteen years old. I write,"[15] all the narratives seem to trace the construction of a name, an "I" opposed to a "you," and a proper name. The proper name always stands in a relation to a place. (Place is necessary to distinguish one Aurélia Steiner from the others, as Aurélia Melbourne, Aurélia Vancouver, and Aurélia Paris. It is significant that these texts, all published under the title *Aurélia Steiner*, must, for their circulation, for filmic distribution, incorporate an "alias" into the title.) The other coordinate to which the proper name stands in relation is a *history*—a social past, a biography, as well as a position in a family discourse.

In at least one case, "Aurélia Vancouver," the "you" figure is the dead father. This narrative is a letter to a father, a lover, and to no one in particular. Taken together, the Aurélias are a set of narratives that repeat a biography, a different one each time, for the "same" name. In a perpetual retelling (of which none of the three can be marked as the original or definitive version), of stories that are not mutually exclusive, but that are in no way coherent, the proper name is cut adrift, as mobile as the displacement from Melbourne to Vancouver to Paris. This noncontinuity is replicated in the relation of image to voice—there is nothing, no diegetic marker, that holds the voice on the image. Instead, the two levels are woven into one another in an explicit *construction*. Just as the narrative constructs the name, the name exists only as an insertion in an intersubjective space, a history and a family discourse of positions: father, mother, daughter.

On another level also, we read the performance of precisely the operations Duras describes, since this passage presents the inscription-effacement of the name of Lol V. Stein, of the sailor from *Le Marin de Gibraltar*, and of the figure of Tatiana Karl, "naked under her black hair."[16] The passage is itself conditioned by, structured on, cryptograms, buried names, fragments of other texts, morsels distributed throughout Duras' "corpus," which produce a series of splits within the text. Thus, the name itself appears explicitly as an introjection, a body-writing, which inscribes the split in being at the emergence of the name, with respect to *Aurélia Steiner*, in a passage whose prose, as body, performs the same incorporative move. This is related to the border of discourse itself, where the sign is grafted onto nourishment in the exchange with the maternal body. The name as "foreign body," so to speak, recalls the strangeness, estrangement, of the love scene in *The Ravishing*, where one woman calls herself by the other's name, the name appearing as absolutely other, and yet somehow utterly defining of identity-as-foreign.

The scene of return to the Casino, however, is itself doubled, falsely repeated, misremembered in the textual circuit formed by the three texts. In *L'Amour*, the casino attendant retains (almost) no memory of the scene, unlike his counterpart in *Le Ravissement*. This false memory or reproduction is, interestingly enough, signaled by the question of a name in *L'Amour*.

> The traveler approaches. He pleads:
> "Recognize her."
> The man waits, asks:
> "Why?"
> The traveler does not answer. The man asks:
> "What is her name?"
> The traveler answers:
> "I don't know anything any more."
> The man says a name.
> " . . ."
> "Is that it?"
> The traveler doesn't answer. He pleads again:
> "Would you repeat that name?"
> "Which?"
> "The one you just said," he pauses, "I'm asking you."
> The man backs off a little, he repeats clearly, completely, the name
> he has just made up. (130–31)

The textual circuit culminates in a falsification of the memory, the invention of a name with which to designate the unknown woman. The text remains on the border between falsification and misrecognition (ultimately, miscognition), haunted by their overlap.

It is impossible to dislodge the impossibility of memory, and of reenactment, repetition of the same, from the problem of narrative impossibility posed by *The Ravishing*. As Lol returns to the stage of the ball scene, reenters that "originary" scene, and lives it as presence, Jacques Hold finds himself losing his memory to hers.

> Behind her, I was trying to accord my look so closely to hers that, with every passing second, I began to remember her memories. I remembered events contiguous to those events she remembered having been present at, sharp profiles of similarities that vanished the moment they were seen into the dark night of the room . . . One trace remains, one. A single, indelible trace, at first we know not where. What? You don't know where? No trace, none, all has been buried, and Lol with it. (170)

When the memory trace is actualized, when memory "returns," so to speak, it is already another's—his memory of her memory. And the trace itself is only a disappearance: the "nothing" of the "word-hole" has become the "all" with which Lol herself disappears.

The impossibility of remembering this scene while returning to it, or of returning if one does remember it, of repeating the scene remembered, or remembering it *as if* one had lived it, is clearly sketched here, in the transference of memory from Lol to Jacques Hold, and in Hold's slippage from the pronominal position "je" to the vague, anonymous "on." The pronominal, figural, and scenic space of repetition thus collapses, and with it the narrativization of the scene itself. The narrative impossibility that poses itself in the text's perpetual repetitions appears in a particularly intense way at the moment of triangulation, when Hold asks Tatiana and Lol to tell him about Michael Richardson.

> They are not surprised, they look at each other, endlessly, endlessly, decide that it is impossible to describe, to give an account of those moments, of that evening whose veritable depth and density they, and they alone, are familiar with, that night whose hours they had seen slip by, one by one, until the last had gone, and, by that last hour, love had changed hands, identity, one error had been exchanged for another. "He never came back, never," Tatiana says. "What a mad night! [quelle nuit!]" (92)

If *The Ravishing* is semantically focused on the impossibility of reproducing, repeating, or re-presenting the "originary" scene, syntactically it is subtended by the unfolding of repetition. Repetition reports, causes a report, an echo, and a doubling, installs a distance, joining absence and presence in a re-calling, a calling one back to or through the other in a constant alternation.

This repetition function may be tied to certain questions of memory, and of narrative memory, at that. If we consider *The Ravishing*'s compulsion to repeat, which abolishes all narrative coherence, all advance, motion, or connection among events, spaces and utterances, we may find that it establishes a radical interrogation of limits, both narrative and signifying, through its progressive emptying of the repetition.

Speaking of Anne-Marie Stretter and of *India Song*, Duras' filmic repetition of the elements of the textual cycle here in question, Viviane Forrester examines the relation of repetition and limits, where because of the impossibility of installing stable limits, separations, "mirrors do nothing but repeat,"[17] rather than reflect a distinct subject, or produce a space. This "story," as an unfurling of the repetitive mechanism, is linked, she adds, to "this ultimate story, where nothing can draw to a close because it is already there" (171). Therefore, the story, "l'histoire," must find a mode of being that sustains itself without the narrative limits of beginning/origin or end/teleology.

Just as the Lol V. Stein story abolishes its own memory in a repetition that never achieves access to the scene it poses or hypothesizes as its origin, the ball at the Casino, it cannot accomplish a closure. Instead, it explicitly disseminates its elements through *Le Vice-consul* and *L'Amour*, as well as through the filmic re-presentations, *India Song, Son nom de Venise dans Calcutta désert*, and *La Femme du Gange* (to name only the obvious references).

Stephen Heath approaches the relationship of repetition and narrativity in his essay "The Question Oshima," which takes as its subject *In the Realm of the Senses*, a film whose repetition of sexual scenes culminates in the death of one partner, but whose obsessive patterns are not altogether divergent from those demonstrated in *The Ravishing*. For Heath, "repetition is the return to the same in order to abolish the difficult time of desire and the resurgence in that very moment of inescapable difference. The edge of repetition—its horizon of abolition, the ultimate collapse of same and different—is then death" (*Questions*, 156). Citing Lacan, Heath states that "desire is interminable, finds itself in a repetition that poses the limit of death as the 'absolutely own possibility' of a historically determined subject" (156). The repetition in which desire is rooted, then, is also a function of death as limit—as absolute past and absolute future toward which the subject tends. Within the bounds of repetition which does not attain the absolute immediacy of desire, of the limit-moment of death, the serial temporality that permits the function of the subject continues.

Departing from this citation, Heath describes the force of *In the Realm of the Senses* as having to do with an approach to that limit of the subject by presenting repetition as a "loss of function, an absolute past to the subject forgotten in the subject-positions" (156). The link with *The Ravishing* is to be made, I think, on the juncture of memory and forgetting, on the welling up of an absolute past which is beyond and resistant to any narrativization or to temporal structuration, and which represents the collapse of differentiation: "The memory itself goes back beyond this memory, back beyond itself. . . . What am I saying?" (*The Ravishing*, 167).

This collapse of past and future poses death as the absolute limit on either "end" of the trajectory when repetition collapses temporal scanning. Indeed, this past is also beyond the limits of the text, for it circulates and insists in successive textual and filmic performances, in a set of transferences that never resolve or dissolve the repetition mechanism. The memory is the memory of a memory, absolutely prior to itself; such a formulation constitutes a rupture in the possibility of even imagining, let alone imaging, a temporal coherence and motion.

We may turn, briefly, to Duras herself, as reader of her own text, for a different approach to this issue. Speaking of *The Ravishing* and *The Vice-Consul*, Duras reports that she has forgotten the book, *The Vice-Consul;* "I have forgotten it because cinema has passed over it . . . Lol V. Stein has remained intact, locked up in the book, cloistered inside" (*Les Yeux verts*, 56). This passage establishes a certain double imperative that characterizes Duras' work, as an elaboration of particular repetitive structures. The filmic repetition, precisely, abolishes memory, while the textual entity, without the superimposition of filmed images, acts as a kind of preserving crypt. In this context, it is not without interest that Duras is quite clear about a distinction between text and film, which she establishes at the junction of what she calls "l'imaginaire" (the imaginary). "Cinema arrests the text, beats its descendance to death: the imaginary. Its very virtue is there: to close. To arrest the imaginary . . . the fixation of representation once and for all."[18]

If the cinematic repetition is a kind of "putting to death" of the written or textual figure, there is reason to question both the function of an "imaginary" in Duras' texts, and the function of textual repetitions and circulations. Do these repetitions put figures in motion, animate an imaginary charge or circuit, or do they establish a sort of crypt, turning the figures themselves into "cryptograms"?

Interestingly enough, in conversation with Michelle Porte Duras addresses this issue in direct connection with Lol V. Stein.

> Duras: Obviously, I can show Lol V. Stein in film, but I can only show her hidden, when she is a dead dog on the beach, covered with sand, you see . . .
>
> Porte: If you make a film of Lol V. Stein, of the ballroom scene, you won't show her?
>
> Duras: Yes, her, her, but destroyed, already filmed, not having left the book, not emerging from the book, but already ruined by commentary, by readings. . . . She belongs to you, Lol V. Stein, she belongs to others, you see, she has no meaning. Lol V. Stein, you see, it's what you make of it, it doesn't exist otherwise. (*Les Lieux de Marguerite Duras*, 100–101)

It is surely no accident that this passage grounds itself on the question of memory, as opposed to forgetting, and on the figure of "un chien mort"—that image that appears once in *The Ravishing* and returns to figure centrally in *L'Amour*, a *revenant* (in French: ghost, from the verb *revenir*, to come back), a haunting figure of return.

The dead dog, an utterly unassimilable figure, a disgusting cadaver that punctures the beach scene, precisely by its *not* belonging there, ruptures the semantic, thematic, and even logical continuity of the text in *Le Ravissement*. An enigmatic figure of death and disgust, it signifies only a pure, stupid resistance to sense, while simultaneously attracting to itself the sense-making, epistemological drive—a function confirmed by the figure's centrality and frequency of appearance in *L'Amour*. In its resistance, its operation as a pure point of resistance to any mastery, this figure also doubles Lol V. Stein.

We find the connection clearly inscribed toward the end of *Le Ravissement*, where Jacques Hold remarks: "There is some commotion, a crowd gathering around something I cannot see, perhaps a dead dog. She gets up, takes me to a little restaurant she knows. She is famished" (173). The introduction of the dead dog is obliquely connected to Lol's hunger, a need whose satisfaction is the site/source of extreme fascination for the narrator.

Lol is eating, gathering sustenance.
  I refuse to admit the end [je nie la fin] which is probably going to come and separate us, how easy it will be, how distressingly simple, for the moment I refuse to accept it, to accept this end, I accept the other, the end which has still to be invented, the end I do not yet know, that no one has invented: the endless end [la fin sans fin], the endless beginning of Lol V. Stein.
  Watching her eat, I forget. (174–75)

She eats; he forgets. In the midst of anxious speculations about the end whose denial forces acceptance of another inconceivable ending without end, unending ending, we hear: "la fin sans fin." We give in to the ear (as we must, in all of Duras' narratives, since they lodge themselves in the ambivalent relation of reading eye/listening ear), a relation established through the intervention of the voice. And the voice is, as Régis Durand puts it, "body of language, the body of the speaker. . . . The voice speaks of the body; of its dualities (interior/exterior, front/back, eye/ear, etc.). It speaks of the unconscious drives or fantasies."[19]
  The phrase shatters into several forms, all of which recall the body as referent: "la fin sans faim," "la faim sans fin," "la faim sans faim" (the end without hunger; the endless hunger; hunger without hunger). Furthermore, the relationship between hunger and the end, ending, or its impossibility—continuation—catches up the problem of memory. To eat, in this scene, is to begin the process of forgetting.
  Perhaps these tenuous connections would not take root so firmly were they not stressed by the repetition function of the text. However, the approach to S. Thala, and to the memory scene, inscribes exactly the inverse relation of terms: to remember is to vomit.

She is completely preoccupied by her effort to recognize things. . . . And yet, every once in a while, she turns her head and smiles at me like someone who has not forgotten, though I must not let myself believe in it.
  . . . at the end she talks almost without interruption. I don't hear it all. I'm still holding her in my arms. When someone is vomiting, you hold him tenderly. I too begin to pay attention to these indestructible places, which at this moment in time are becoming the

sites of my arrival on the scene. Now the hour of my entering Lol's memory is at hand. (164–65)

Lol's memory opens up, surges into words that fail to signify, words vomited, precisely; the indestructible places appear as morsels, fragments preserved intact, that is, undigested. This passage stresses the insistent relation these texts express between the sign and the oral functions. As such, it relates to the imbrication of signifying and vital processes, as, for example, the signifying quality of food. As Laplanche has it, the sign is incorporated by the infant along with the food, or as its substitute.

Undigested memory is the central and repeated obsession of the text: "Nothing about this woman betrayed the slightest hint, even fleetingly, of her strange mourning for Michael Richardson. She had nothing to say to Tatiana, nothing to tell" (68–69). The strange, incomplete mourning work leaves nothing to recount, no story to expose.

Furthermore, the connection the text establishes here between mourning and vomiting resides in their relation to the border inscribed and invested through the primary acts of incorporation. For Laplanche and Pontalis, incorporation is the corporeal prototype of psychic introjection, whereby "in fantasy, the subject transposes objects and their inherent qualities from the 'outside' to the 'inside.' "[20] Incorporation itself, however, is focused on the constitution of the bodily limits and is a mode of relation to an object—either as pleasure in the penetration of the body by the object, as destruction of the object, or as assimilation of the object to preserve it within the subject. This last modality is the prototype of introjection, and is also the one which joins the other two; to incorporate the object without destroying it, in order to preserve it, involves the fantasmatic conservation of an exterior within the body—an "alien internal entity." Such an object cannot be destroyed or decathected by mourning—drained or relinquished— nor can it be fully assimilated. It remains a heterogeneous fragment in the interior. Such an object, which menaces the stability of the interior/exterior border, is implicated in the figure of vomit, which is a part of the inside that has "fallen out." As such, vomit designates the possible collapse of the border of the subject; it is neither here nor there, neither me nor not-me. This is very much a question of limits—of the body, of the subject—and of what must be expelled in order to preserve them.

The incomplete mourning work that conditions Lol V. Stein's "manque à être: là," persists in the two other texts of the cycle. The mourning work continues, now as a textual mourning of the Lol V. Stein figure itself. The space of the mourning, which never quite takes place, is, in fact, figured in this sentence, through the interruption of the colon, introducing a connection across an absolutely indeterminate gap. This gap, we might say, is repeated in the suspended time of the ball scene, where Anne-Marie Stretter and Michael Richardson begin to dance on page 6, and Lol only responds to this cut, this rupture, on page 12: "Lol cried out for the first time . . . She had gone on screaming all sorts of things that made perfect sense: it wasn't late, it was only the early summer dawn that made it seem that it really was" (12). The cry attains voice only after an entire evening, whose time is incalculable. The cry itself arrives too late—just as the syllable "la" somehow arrives to complete the sentence just a little late, after delay.

Furthermore, the cry only becomes possible at the point of yet another intervention in the scene, the arrival of the mother. "When her mother had reached her side and had touched her, Lol had at last let go of her grip on the table. It was only then that she realized, vaguely, that something was drawing to a close, without quite knowing what it might be. The screen which her mother formed between them and her was her first inkling of it" (11–12). The mother as screen, then, constitutes a site of projection, as well as a barrier, an inhibition. For Julia Kristeva, it is this double function that facilitates the consolidating of a concept of the subject.

> The *personal* (ego, body) depends on or is constituted by a counterpoise (the point of projection: lamp, mother, parents) that burdens and dramatizes it, but, without being definitively separated (neither barring nor blocking facilitation), by its permissive distance allows the body to discover itself again. . . . An inhibition is thus built up . . . but as *existing elsewhere:* a set place, always there, but separate from the body, which can, only under these conditions, constitute itself as "personal" and reach jouissance at a distance. At this stage we have the necessary conditions that . . . constitute the semiotic disposition and insure its maintenance within the symbolic. (*Desire in Language,* 285)

The memory beyond memory, then, beyond discursive temporality, must be related to the mother.

The mother, as screen-sign, becomes one of the underlying and motivating figures that link the two later texts, *The Vice-Consul* and *L'Amour*, with *The Ravishing*, in a cycle of repetition and displacement. If the memory of the ball scene also entails a memory of the mother, the textual obsession with the word and voice intersects with the problem of maternity. These two narrative threads are further connected through the repeated figures of incorporation, of signs doubled with nourishment, forming a constellation elaborated throughout this cycle.

NOTES

1. Hélène Cixous and Michel Foucault, "A propos de Marguerite Duras," *Cahiers Renauld-Barrault*, no. 89 (1970): 7.

2. Marguerite Duras, *L'Amante anglaise*, trans. Barbara Bray (London: Hamish Hamilton, 1968), 4; (Paris: Gallimard, 1967), 11.

3. Marguerite Duras, *L'Amour* (Paris: Gallimard, 1972), 8; all translations from this work are mine.

4. Marguerite Duras, *The Ravishing of Lol V. Stein*, trans. Richard Seaver (New York: Grove, 1966), 4. All other references will appear in the text.

5. Marguerite Duras, *The Vice-Consul*, trans. Eileen Ellenbogen (London: Hamish Hamilton, 1968), 124–25. In this case, as with all similar ones, I have inserted the original, in brackets, where the translation misses certain important textual effects produced in French.

6. For a more detailed consideration of the implications of a textual and theoretical structure not based on stable opposition, see Derrida's reading of Freud's *Beyond the Pleasure Principle* in *La Carte postale*, especially 287–304. Here Derrida argues that Freud's inability to arrive at a conclusion, because of the tendency of both the text and the theory to veer off, to take detours, is conditioned by that very tendency in its theoretical object: the pleasure principle. Between pleasure and reality as ideal and fictive limits, the detour, he argues, "forms the very effectivity of the process, of the 'psychic' process as well as a 'living' process. . . . The detour thus 'would be' the common—one might as well say different—root of the two principles, a root torn up from itself, necessarily impure and structurally condemned to compromise, to the speculative transaction" (*Carte postale*, 305, my translation).

7. Roland Barthes, *Image-Music-Text*, trans. Stephen Heath (New York: Hill and Wang, 1977), 123–24.

8. Michèle Montrelay, *L'Ombre et le nom* (Paris: Minuit, 1977), 9–10, my translation.

9. Jacques Lacan, "Hommage fait à Marguerite Duras, du *Ravissement de Lol V. Stein*," in *Marguerite Duras,* ed. Marguerite Duras, Joel Farges, and François Barat (Paris: Albatros, 1979), 133, my translation.

10. Cf. Daniel Sibony, "Hamlet: A Writing-Effect," *Yale French Studies* 55/56 (1977): 53–93.

11. Jean Baudrillard, *De la séduction* (Paris: Galilée, 1979), 104, my translation.

12. Benoît Jacquot, "Comment elle fait," in *Marguerite Duras,* 161.

13. This is one area in which the English translation is not simply inadequate, but entirely inappropriate. To replace the initial in each of the place names by a word (T. Beach becomes Town Beach, U Bridge becomes Uxbridge, S. Thala becomes South Thala) is to make a serious error: to reduce the enigmatic ambiguity and polyvalence of the name to a "logical" conclusion/deduction. Such a gesture seems to demonstrate precisely an anxiety about the unnaming name, like an effort to cover the places where the text's fabric is irrevocably rent. (Something of the same is at work in the translation's consistent rendering of Lol V. Stein as Lol Stein, an elimination of the "gratuitous" and troubling *V* which segments the name, constituting a point of resistance and a gap within it.)

14. Marguerite Duras, *Les Yeux verts,* Les Cahiers du cinéma (Paris: Gallimard, 1980), 56–57, my translation, here and following.

15. Marguerite Duras, *Aurélia Steiner,* in *Le Navire Night* (Paris: Mercure de France, 1979), 135, 165, 199, my translations.

16. The inscription-effacement effect here also touches on *Hiroshima mon amour.* Nuclear holocaust is related to the Nazi holocaust, the central historical event to which all the Aurélia Steiner texts refer, again embedding the event in the subjective love story, this time as love letter.

17. Viviane Forrester, "Territoires du cri," in *Marguerite Duras,* 171, my translation, here and following.

18. Duras, "Le Camion," cited in Verena Andermatt, "Big Mach (on *The Truck*)," *Enclitic* 4, no. 1 (1980): 27.

19. Régis Durand, "The Disposition of the Voice," in *Performance in Post-Modern Culture,* ed. Michel Benamou and Charles Caramello (Milwaukee: Center for Twentieth Century Studies, University of Wisconsin, 1977), 101.

20. Jean Laplanche and J.-B. Pontalis, *The Language of Psychoanalysis,* trans. Donald Nicholson-Smith (New York: Norton, 1974), 209.

4

Le Vice-consul and L'Amour: A Word in Default

The Vice-Consul and *L'Amour* inscribe themselves at the connection between the mother-screen-sign and the cry, in a process which resembles the repetition and delay of mourning, that process by which the subject relinquishes a loved object by draining or displacing the object-cathexis. Freud associates mourning work with incorporation, as a means of relinquishing the cathexis on the lost object by incorporating, internalizing, and idealizing its image. As such, this process is linked to primary narcissism: "The narcissistic identification with the object becomes a substitute for the erotic cathexis. . . . We have elsewhere shown that identification is a preliminary state of object-choice, that it is the first way—and one that is expressed in an ambivalent fashion—in which the ego picks out an object. The ego wants to incorporate this object into itself, and in accordance with the oral or cannibalistic phase of libidinal development in which it is, it wants to do so by devouring it."[1] It is clear from this description that the object of this earliest form of identification, from which later objects are derived metaphorically and metonymically, is the maternal body, or the breast. Hence, the connection Freud establishes between this type of identification and hysterical identification has particular pertinence. Hysterical identification differs from this early prototype, according to Freud, in that the object-cathexis is not abandoned, but "persists and manifests its influence" (250). The hysteric's identification is doubled over by a failure to relinquish; the object is, in effect, both there and not there, both inside and outside. Hysterical identification, then, announces the failure, the delay, of the mourning work.

If the labor of mourning is related to incorporation, it is just as much about decathecting memory traces, in a progressive "forgetting," and about the juncture at which the loss itself is committed to memory. At the same time, the incorporative impulse is always bound up with the negative drive of expulsion/rejection, in the first mappings of the oral stage, where the subject may only accept or refuse/expel nourishment.

The complex connection between the two figures, the mother and the cry, is established in Duras' narratives through a certain oral pulsivity of the text. While the tale of the beggar woman traces a repetitive alternance between mother and daughter and daughter as mother, within the frame of starvation, incorporation, and rejection of food, the feminine figure of *L'Amour* obsessively repeats the statement, "I'm expecting a baby. I feel like vomiting" (23; this and all following translations of this text are mine).

The "real" or fantasmatic pregnancy is here connected with "the nauseating movement of the waves, the seagulls that cry and devour the body of sand, the blood" (23). Mer-mère (sea-mother)—the movement of the sea, and the body of the mother, are inextricably bound to the movement of incorporation/rejection. This movement, however, shatters thematic bounds, since the texts themselves effect a cannibalization of the figures and the discourse that appear in *The Ravishing:* the work of mourning becomes a textual condition, a structuring effect as well as a "content."

While *The Ravishing*'s final passages connect hunger and nourishment to forgetting ("Lol is eating, gathering sustenance. I refuse to admit the end . . . Watching her eat, I forget" [174–75]), where incorporation becomes forgetfulness or oblivion of *la faim/la fin, The Vice-Consul*'s opening episodes are concentrated on the biological rhythms of the starving "mendiante," her urges to eat and to vomit. In this case, hunger itself is the locus of a prolonged absence, as the memory of a lack becomes its anticipation. Marcelle Marini calls attention to the text's structuring on this axis, presence-absence of hunger, in connection with the term "mangue" (mango), the mendiante's primary sustenance in the opening passages. The word mango itself condenses the two terms, nourishment and privation, in its phonetic similarity to *mange* (third person singular, or imperative, of "to eat") and *manque:* lack (see *Territoires*, 203).

Extending her line of thought, we might conclude, provisionally, that

Le Vice-consul is a text about consuming/incorporating the lack. However, the resonance of "mangue," as it relates to "mange," engages the mother's remembered discourse, the *parole de mère* as nourishing source; "Her mother said: Eat. Don't go grieving your mother. Eat, eat" (5). Indeed, nourishment and the mother's injunction to eat form the juncture of desire and death, for food is also the mother's anticipated means of killing the daughter (" 'If you come back,' her mother said, 'I shall poison your rice. I will kill you,' " [1]). This double nature of nourishment extends into the relation of memory to forgetting. The object of the beggar's obsessive fantasies of food is "a bowl of warm rice." Already, the quest for nourishment is linked to death. Such a linkage is found in the primary *clivage* of the pulsional object into "good" and "bad" object, whose fold reflects the duality of the drives—turned toward both life and death. Thus, the "bad" object is food which kills, and which must be expelled.[2]

The obsessive cycle of hunting and finding food is punctuated by the act of expulsion: vomiting the mango. "She vomits, retches, hoping to bring up the child, but all she brings up is sour mango juice" (8). The vomited mango is the failed abortion of the persistent and devouring child. But it is also the *last* object incorporated: "There are flames leaping in the pit of her stomach. She vomits blood. No more sour mangoes for her, only rice-shoots" (9). The last mango and the fish, which becomes the dominant form of nourishment, also put an end to the possibility of satisfying hunger ("the strangest thing of all is that no amount of food can satisfy her hunger [c'est l'absence de nourriture qui se prolonge]" [6]), which, in turn, puts an end to the hunger itself. Not surprisingly, within this context (the chapter which concludes with the line, "The old hunger will never return" [13]), the real stake is forgetting of the mother, and of maternal language. This peculiar gap, then, seems to be the locus of an exploration of a feminine jouissance—in the indifferentiation of mother from child—where the text folds over in the mother-daughter folded into the mendiante figure.

The text slips from a definitive address or appeal to the mother to the word "Battambang," the curious word-object that centers the text. "Who else but you should hear the tale I have to tell? Who else does it concern that I now long more for the food I cannot have than I long for you . . . One day she will go back just to say: I have forgotten you" (10–11). The text poses its own impossibility in the project of returning to the forgotten mother in order to address her: "She tends to forget [elle a tendance à oublier l'origine] that they drove her out because she was a fallen woman [elle était tombée enceinte]" (9). Simultaneous with the oblivion of the origin, the text poses the impossibility of recounting without an origin and without an address, a destination. Such an impossibility is also, more important, the impossibility of recounting the *drive* to eat, the need for food, hunger itself. In this sense, the text operates in suspension of the referent, which is infinitely displaced—the drive cannot be spoken—and yet, inevitably recalled as the limit of the text's own discourse, the body that sustains it.

In place of the *récit*, the story, a history to be unrolled, the text installs the three-syllable proper name, *place* name, "Battambang." "Battambang. She has nothing else to say" (11). The word-object arises at the death of sense in the phrase "I have forgotten you," a phrase already committed to memory, which can never be pronounced without the absolute negation of its own sense. Upon the gap, the space left by memory, appears the word-object Battambang, a punctuation: "All three syllables boom tonelessly [sonnent avec la même intensité, sans accent tonique] as though rapped out on a small over-stretched drum" (11).

We may read these words as the sign of an incomplete mourning work, since it is resurgent, vomited up, repeated endlessly, as both appeal and response. For Derrida, the connection to be made between vomiting and mourning intersects questions of representability, a function particularly crucial here, since the text opens on the failed effort to narrate hunger.

> Vomit is related to enjoyment [*jouissance*], if not pleasure. It even forces us to enjoy—in spite of ourselves. But this representation annuls itself, and that is why vomit remains unrepresentable. By limitlessly violating our enjoyment, without granting it any determinate limit, it abolishes representative distance—beauty too—and prevents mourning. It irresistibly forces one to consume, but without allowing any chance for idealization.
>
> Let it be understood in all senses that what the word *disgusting* de-nominates is what one cannot resign oneself to mourn.[3]

The connection between mourning and vomiting here turns on mourning's function as a displacement of cathexis from the object to its *representation* in the ego; the failure of representation, in this case, signifies the failure of mourning. It is all the more striking, in light of this passage, that the word Battambang serves precisely to de-nominate, to abolish the possibility of nomination within the *récit* of the mendiante, and with it, the *récit* itself. De-nomination is related to problems of representation through a destabilization of limits, of borders determining subject and object. In *Powers of Horror,* Julia Kristeva succeeds in connecting the phobic object with a notion of the abject, which is neither subject nor object; it is not something, but not nothing either. Because the abject is always related to the maternal zone, this notion is particularly pertinent for an analysis of hysterical disgust. Moreover, the hysterical symptom, product of a conversion, is really another route taken by the anxiety that is displayed in the phobic reaction.

The primal form of the abject, that limit-object, the object that indicates a limit, is rejected food. To expel the food offered by the parents is to reject the sign of their desire: " 'I' want none of that element, sign of their desire . . . 'I' expel it. But since the food is not an 'other' for 'me,' who am only in their desire, I expel *myself,* I spit *myself* out, I abject *myself* within the same motion through which 'I' can claim to establish *myself*" (3). As a limit to the subject position, Kristeva connects vomit to a series of "abjects"—feces, the cadaver—which *indicate* death, the loss of limits, but without signifying or representing anything by themselves.

> In the presence of signified death—a flat encephalograph, for instance—I would understand, react or accept. No, as in the true theater, without make-up or masks, refuse and corpses *show me* what I permanently thrust aside in order to live. These bodily fluids, this defilement, this shit are what life withstands, hardly and with difficulty, on the part of death. There, I am at the border of my condition as a living being. My body extricates itself, as being alive, from that border. Such wastes drop so that I may live, until, from loss to loss, nothing remains in me and my entire body falls beyond the limit—cadere, cadaver. (3)

Having fallen from the body, the abject both poses and menaces its limits, which is why it cannot be made to signify or to represent.

Indeed, the problem of de-nomination conditions the whole textual progress of *The Vice-Consul.* The Vice-Consul himself comes into being under the sign of the word "impossible." His conversational dance with Anne-Marie Stretter, in fact, does no more than explore its own impossibility. "I don't know how to say it," she explains, "the word impossible occurs in your dossier. Is that the appropriate word in this instance? [Est-ce le mot cette fois?]" (100). Her demand that he answer this question produces the following exchange:

> "Is that the appropriate word? Answer me."
> "I don't know myself. Like you, I'm searching."
> "Perhaps there's another way of putting it? [Peut-être y a-t-il un autre mot?]"
> "It's not important now." (100)

An exchange jammed by the question of the word's sense abolishes itself in its own impossibility, in the search for a missing word. And this particular word circulates across the text, reappearing in the discourse of Michael Richard (the character whose name recalls, but does not repeat, that of the lost lover of *The Ravishing*, Michael Richardson): "The word 'impossible' keeps cropping up in his personal file, I believe. What was impossible?" (126). The question's source is anonymous, just as the word in the dossier is authorless, more the property of the object it designates, the Vice-Consul.

Earlier in the text, the Vice-Consul asks the Director of the European Circle, his habitual interlocutor, how he appears: " 'What's my face like, tell me, Mr. Secretary?' asks the Vice-Consul. 'Also impossible,' says the secretary. The Vice-Consul, impassive [impassible], continues talking" (59). The "impossible" stamped on the dossier is equally inscribed on the face. Moreover, the "impossible" is as much the "impassable"—the unmovable, utterly unaffected deadness of the look—as well as the textual impasse of discursive exchange. On the following page, the conversational structure of question and reply collapses on the impossibility of response.

> The Vice-Consul does not expect any reply from the Club Secretary.
> The secretary does not turn a hair.
> "Mr. Secretary," pursues the Vice-Consul, "you have not answered my question."
> "It did not call for an answer, sir. You did not expect any. No one could answer it." (60)

This aborted discursive exchange founders once the unanswerable demand is posed: "Répondez-moi." This demand both imposes the specular structure of these dialogues—where the director repeats the discourse of the narrative itself—and repeats the perpetual textual impasse, an incommunicability, a failure of exchange.

For Mieke Bal, this communicative impasse, or stagnation, as she calls it, is a determining textual feature. In Bal's reading of *Le Vice-consul*, presented in *Narratologie*, the impossibility of verbal communication is supplemented by the nonverbal, and reflects the morbidity of the social space of language in the narrative. Characters or *names*, who lack consistent or solid identity, and who are determined largely by their discourses, engage in reciprocal monologues, always failing to answer each other, or even to complete sentences. Messages don't reach their addressees, she argues, but are often replaced by nonverbal forms, bound to objects. As she puts it, where verbal communication does establish itself in the text, there is an intense concentration on the phatic function, the simple making contact, a contact established through an object, for instance Anne-Marie Stretter's bicycle.[4]

To push her analysis in the direction of its own inclination, the word-message itself seems to become an "dead object," without source or destination, as the text steadily undermines the possibility of even posing those poles. In their place, Bal argues, the narrative discourse stresses nonverbal communicative functions: the cry, the look, the gesture, the musical fragment. A glance at this set brings to mind the part object, the detachable object which confronts the subject with its own loss—the loss in the signifier. With considerable acuity, she includes in this set, as its very emblem, the word "Battambang"—the word that stands somewhere between the object and the cry. For Bal, it becomes a sign through the very repetition that reduces it, first, to a meaningless form. As such, this empty repetition becomes the sign of something else: the gaps, that which is missing, the textual obsession. Moreover, "Battambang" stands as the only remaining trace of the beggar woman's origin, her source.

This word object seems to play out a drama of separation of word from body, through the part object. Kristeva describes the cry, as part of the anaclisis, in the following manner: "Neither request nor desire, it is an invocation, an anaclisis. Memories of bodily contact, warmth and nourishment: these underlie the breath of the newborn baby as it appeals to a source of support" (*Desire in Language*, 281).

The cry or invocation is one among a system of part objects that constitute and mark the juncture through which the subject passes to enter the discourse of the Other, within which he or she is already passively inscribed. As object (in the Lacanian sense), the cry operates at the beginnings of representation, still enmeshed in the lost object, which can never be refound because it has condensed with others to form the hallucinated object, separated from the pulsional body.

Bal also connects "Battambang" to music. Citing the word's resemblance to the musical fragment of Indiana's Song—whose words are forgotten, another instance of the oblivion of speech, as well as another connection to the maternal locus, the origin—she emphasizes the function of "Battambang" as the point of interdependence between the two textual *récits*, the story of the Vice-Consul and Peter Morgan's novel. In this sense, it is precisely the voice or cry of the woman permanently out of relation to her maternal origin, and to her mother tongue, that constitutes a juncture and a channel of passage between the two *récits*.

This word-cry also becomes the axis of exchange in the text, at the moment when the mendiante gives her child to another woman. "The girl answers, Battambang . . . Battambang will keep her safe, she will never say another word but that one in which she is enclosed" (22). Indeed, it is the word itself that effects the exchange, functioning as assertion, response, demand and refusal, all at once. This word later centers an "inverted" and terrifying version of this exchange, between Charles Rossett and the *mendiante:*

> She waves toward the bay, and says just one word, the same word, over and over:
> "—Battambang" . . .
> He gets some loose change from his pocket, takes a step or two towards her, and stops . . .
> He does not go any nearer, but stands there, with the money in his hands.
> She repeats the word that sounds like "Battambang." (163)

The exchange, however, remains incomplete, for the woman biting the head off a live fish, posing the Medusa image, causes Charles Rossett to flee. The coin he tosses never reaches her, is never accepted, just as the word "Battambang," tossed toward him, disappears in its utterance. The word, however, acquires the status of the coin tossed without currency, outside any possible exchange of equivalencies. It becomes a "dead" center, a *point mort* for the scene. Such a figure repeats that of the beggar, described by the Vice-Consul: " 'Death in the midst of life [la mort dans la vie en cours],' says the Vice-Consul at last. 'Death following but never catching up. Is that it?' " (139).

To consider the relation between the text's opening sentence: " 'She walks on [Elle marche],' writes Peter Morgan" (1), and one of its final scenes, that of the discussion about Morgan's book among the Europeans at the Prince of Wales, is to disclose the function of the beggar as, simultaneously, narrative and frame, center and periphery, "ground" and "figure." In this respect, the "Elle marche" is also the figure of writing, as it unfolds, doubles, and repeats itself. For Peter Morgan, the desire to write this story is bound up with a kind of death in discourse.

> "In Calcutta, she will be a . . . dot at the end of a long line, the last distinguishable fact of her own life? With nothing left but sleep and hunger, no feeling, no correlation between cause and effect?"
>
> "What he means, I think," says Michael Richard, "is something even more extreme. He wants to deprive her of any existence other than her existence in his mind when he is watching her. She herself is not to feel anything."
>
> "What is left of her in Calcutta?" asks George Crawn.
>
> "Her laugh, drained of all color, the word 'Battambang' that she repeats incessantly, the song. Everything else has evaporated."
>
> "How will you trace her past, piece her madness together, distinguish between her madness and madness in general [sa folie de la folie], her laughter from laughter in general [son rire du rire], the name Battambang and Battambang the place [le mot Battambang du mot Battambang]?"
>
> "Her dead children—because she must have had children—and other dead children?"
>
> "Finally, the exchange, if that's what it was, or, to put it another way, the giving up, was not, in the long run, very different from any other exchange or surrender. And yet it did take place." (146)[5]

Morgan's desire to produce a narrative that arrives at a point that has no point—no destination and no causality—a point of indifferentiation ("How will you distinguish her madness and madness in general"), the merger of definite and indefinite articles, is predicated on the explosion of any causal effects. Moreover, the origin of this *récit* is its indefiniteness, a problem related to the question of memory.

Peter Morgan is forced to resort to fragments stored in his own memory to fill in the blanks of the beggar woman's forgotten past [voudrait maintenant substituer à la mémoire de la mendiante le bric-à-brac de la sienne]. Otherwise, Peter Morgan would be at a loss to explain the madness of the beggar-woman of Calcutta . . . How long since she lost her memory? How to put into words the things she never said? How to say what she will not say? How to describe the things that she does not know she has seen, the experiences she does not know she has had? How to reconstruct the forgotten years [tout ce qui a disparu de toute mémoire]? (54–55)

Morgan's "false" memory, entering into the place of the beggar's absent memory, constantly entertains the possibility of its own abolition in and through narrative time. How to write *nothing?* How to establish temporality in the absence of memory? Furthermore, this passage discloses one of the most startling of the narrative contradictions: the substitution of one memory for another, of one's memory for another's in the juncture of two *histoires* (in both senses of the word). Indeed, this is the determining problem of the whole text: two *récits* are embedded, but the seams along which the embedding is sutured have no clear distinction or separation.

Although the story/*récit* of the Vice-Consul and that of the mendiante are connected metonymically through the movement of the latter figure from one textual level to the next, they are likewise bonded metaphorically by a textual system of mirrors: the mendiante and the Vice-Consul are both dead centers or dead looks which attract the fascinated gazes of all the other figures. Both are voices or cries that disrupt the system of discursive articulations, while nevertheless stimulating an endless and fragmented proliferation of commentary.

To the extent that Peter Morgan's narrative focuses on a being without existence, except in the look of the other, who "would watch her live [celui qui la regarderait vivre]," his narrative is also captured by what "le regarde" (in the French sense, what concerns it), without ever addressing or even recognizing it.

The precise point of slippage of one narrative into another, the reversal of the capture, is radically indeterminate here. Even more problematically, this same function repeats itself in the dialogic "exchanges" of the Vice-Consul and the Secretary. These exchanges culminate in a substitution of memories. An early dialogue effects the exchange of remembered scenes, *histoires,* of school days, during which the Vice-Consul trades his story of education at Montfort for the Secretary's reminiscences about his experience at a reform school, at Pas-de-Calais, near Arras (85). Subsequently, in the final scene of the text, the Vice-Consul repeats, as is his habit, a memory:

> "My mother looks at her watch: I have not opened my mouth, except for one remark." "What remark was that?"
> "That you were glad to be in Arras."
> "Correct, Mr. Secretary. It's February. Night is falling in the Pas-de-Calais. I do not want cakes or chocolates; I only want to be allowed to stay there." (106–7)

In this case, memory is displaced, effecting a radical resituation of interlocutors, the exchange of histories. Certainly, this impossible exchange has the features of a transference, in the context of the scene in which the Vice-Consul endlessly repeats and reworks his past, before the almost neutral figure of the Secretary. In more general terms, this transference disturbs the possible positional boundaries that condition the movement of narration: where the speaker/source recounts a history to an addressee. Similarly, the disruption and detachment of memory signals the abolition of its relation to any lived scene, as well as of any property or properness attaching to the subject's identity.

This scene reflects the generation of Peter Morgan's narrative—based on the substitutability of memory, and, ultimately, on its obliteration. Both textual scenes are related to the issue of fixing an impossible narrative origin or source. It is as if the framing story—Peter Morgan's narrative of the beggar woman, with which the text opens—were continually invading, and becoming enfolded inside, the *framed* story. The relationship of margins to the narrative of the Vice-Consul and, metaphorically, that of frame to image, is unstable, contradictory.

Duras' text calls into question the implicit metaphor of figure and ground that such embedding of *récits* installs. Moreover it disturbs the textual relation between controlling narrative voice and its object: narrative *énonciation* to narrative *énoncé*. If the mendiante is nothing but her *histoire* neither is Peter Morgan anything but the story of writing a story. Neither, likewise, is the Vice-Consul anything but the story of the impossibility of telling his story. Just as the story-less beggar crosses the *grillage,* the insistent textual figure for European anxiety to preserve separation from Calcutta, the textual crossing constitutes the explosion of boundaries between narrative layers, and produces an incessant interference among narrative enunciations.

The metaphor of interference is significant here, since these subtexts not only intersect each other, but also merge. Similarly, the textual mirror-effects inevitably produce an indifferentiation among levels and figures. This narrative anxiety is clearly reflected in Peter Morgan's interrogation of his own project, "Comment séparer sa folie de la folie," but it conditions the entire text as well; where does the narration go when it has nothing to recount, when its own origin is absent?

Such a complete inaccessibility of a presumed originary scene accounts for the textual fascination and the "uncanny" effects attaching to the Vice-Consul. The extended ballroom scene, the textual center, which pivots upon the figure of the Vice-Consul, is governed by the indeterminate discursive locus "on," often marked by the conditional, "on dirait que. . . ." The anonymous voices speculate on the blank screen of the Vice-Consul. Yet the scene is equally conditioned by the Vice-Consul's impossible dialogue with Anne-Marie Stretter on the "subject" of Lahore:

> "Why do you speak to me of leprosy?"
> "Because I have the feeling that if I tried to say what I really want to say to you, everything would crumble into dust"—he is trembling—"for what I want to say . . . to you . . . from me to you . . . there are no words. I should fumble . . . I should say something different from what I intended . . . one thing leads to another." . . .
> "What I want to try and explain, then, is that afterwards, although one knows that it was oneself who was in Lahore, it seems impossible, unreal. It is I who . . . am talking to you now . . . who am that man. I would like you to listen to the Vice-Consul of Lahore. I am he."
> "What has he to say to me?"
> "That there is nothing that he can say about Lahore, nothing. . . . And that you must understand why." . . .
> "I would like to hear you say that you can see the inevitability of Lahore. Please answer me."
> She does not answer. (98–100)

The curious alienation effect of this scene reproduces the disembodiment of the utterance that characterizes its discursive context, its surroundings. Further, however, the utterances escape pronominal anchoring—"One knows that it was oneself who was in Lahore." "I would like you to listen [je voudrais que vous entendiez: hear or understand] to the Vice-Consul of Lahore. I am he [je suis celui-là: that one]" (98). The dispossession of the subject pronoun, the intermittence of the speaking "I," is foregrounded in the contradictory expression, "Je suis celui-là," where an incalculable, not to say impossible, distance emerges in the speech act itself. What is at stake here is the very possibility of any identity-within-speech, of an even momentary appropriation of the subject-I, or of an unequivocal *occupation* of that position.

Consequently, the discursive circuit of emission and reception, sending and receiving, that hinges on these pronominal poles is faulty, if not ruptured: "Answer me. She does not answer" (100). (*Répondre:* repondere—to give in return for, satisfy an agreement, agree, to contract, to return, repay, re-echo). As in most dialogic exchanges in this text, there is no return, no reply; nothing comes back to the speaker/sender. Moreover, just as Lahore itself is both inevitable and unrepeatable—it cannot be spoken about, its story cannot be told—this conversation cannot sustain repetition. The next encounter between Anne-Marie Stretter and the Vice-Consul stresses this feature: "You repeated nothing?" — "Nothing" (115).

If their exchange, like the Vice-Consul's story, bears no repetition and provides no return, the Vice-Consul himself appears in the uncanny aspect of a *revenant* (a ghost), whose presence troubles the entire ballroom scene. Yet this figure is the ghostly return of something that was never there. Similarly, both his look and his voice are repeatedly characterized as dead, or empty; they are sourceless, detached: " 'It's true what you said about his voice . . . but it's also true of the way he looks at one [le regard]. It's as though another man were looking out of his eyes. It hadn't struck me before. Perhaps one could say his face is blank [Peut-être il n'a pas de regard].' 'A complete blank?' 'All but, there is an occasional flicker of expression' " (103–4). Or, earlier, "Once again the ambassador seems on the point of moving away and once again he thinks the better of it. He must stay and talk with this man tonight. This man who is looking at him with death in his eyes [cet homme au regard mort qui le regarde]" (92). The Vice-Consul is the petrifying figure of a dead look looking, and failing to feel the look of another upon it. Furthermore, the man himself is described by Charles Rossett as "Oh a dead man. Dead. The word escapes from pursed lips, moist lips, pale at this late hour" (101). Whose lips, whose speech, pass the word "dead," here? The word produces an inextricable confusion of subject and object of discourse, since it hangs detached from both source and aim.

The dead man returned to life is also the echo chamber through which a peculiar foreign voice filters: "She draws away from him a little, but can not yet bring herself to look at him. Later she will say that she was struck by something in his voice. Later she will say, 'is that what is meant by a toneless voice [une voix blanche]?' You couldn't tell [On ne sait pas] whether he was asking a question or answering it" (87). The ambivalent voice, toneless and strange, fails to establish a distinction between the demand and the offer. Later, "people are thinking [on pense]: the Vice-Consul is laughing, but what a laugh! Like the sound track of a dubbed film, utterly lacking in conviction [faux, faux]" (87).

The image here is striking. The Vice-Consul parades the possibility of absolute disjunction between eye and ear, sound and sight, as in a film whose sound track is minutely out of synch with the motion of the image. (Indeed, it is just such a contradiction that Duras will exploit in *India Song*.) The foreignness of the voice (in the sense of a foreign body inhabiting this figure) is figured similarly by Anne-Marie Stretter:

Anne-Marie Stretter is saying to Charles Rossett:
"His voice is quite different from what one would expect from his appearance. You can't always tell what people's voices will be like just by looking at them. You can't with him."
"It's not a pleasant voice. It's almost as though it had been grafted on to him."
"You mean it's not his voice, but someone else's?"
"Yes, but whose?" (103)

The image of the voice as false, as grafted on, as coming from another, an elsewhere, is striking, since it connects again with the dead look and the part object—the signifier of lack. Along with the parade of the lack, the Vice-Consul signifies the terrifying possibility of a lack of all lack, the death of desire, the utter detachment from an originary scene. Régis Durand discusses the fascination of the voice in Duras' texts and films in his article, "The Disposition of the Voice," in which he explores the voice as situating the subject in the desire of the Other: "The voice is always anchored in desire. . . . There is no such thing as a neutral voice, a voice that does not desire me. If there was, it would be an experience of absolute terror. But even as it is, and even though it may charm, the voice frightens and disturbs. Is it because the voice gives us nothing to *see*, because it has no mirror image? Speaks to us of loss, of absence?" (203).

The fantasmatic image without an image, the voice both within and with*out* desire, is implicated in the textual network of messages and passages, of slides into indifferentiation that Viviane Forrester so poetically ascribes to Duras' project: a domain without limits or frontiers, a domain "where death itself does not establish the slightest difference" ("Territoires du cri," 171). This is a space that seems to figure the intolerability of pure presence, where, according to Forrester, mirrors *repeat*, rather than reflect. This passage recalls the figure of the mendiante, whose hunger obliterates even the division of the subject in language, reducing language to its own oblivion in the cry. That figure, then, becomes the figure of the too proximate body, pure voice, the collapse of the thetic.

Elsewhere, Duras speculates on the status of voice in her work: "If I don't find the text just as it arose on the page, the written voice, I begin again. . . . You see, I don't try at all to deepen the sense of the text when I read it, no, not at all, nothing like that, what I am looking for is the primary state of this text, as one strives to remember a distant event, not lived, but 'heard about' [entendu dire]. The sense will follow, it has no need of a law" (*Les Yeux verts*, 49). Here Duras proposes a notion of the written voice which refers not to any fantasmatic "pure self-presence" of or through the voice, but rather emphasizes that the voice is continually speaking from elsewhere. The "entendu dire" is distinctly related to the fantasmatic primal scene—what is heard and not understood, except by retroaction. We might therefore characterize the sense of the "entendu dire," "hearsay," or what has been heard, as associated with the "originary scene" and with the family discourse, the fragments of narrative drawn from the family romance, the set of positional relations inscribed in the familial structure.

The cry, however, has a multidimensional status in this text. Like the cry in *Le Ravissement*, of whose absent *scène du bal* this text presents a sort of inverted image (as through a lens inversion), the cry becomes a punctuation in the scene. This is itself a curious inversion, for the cry is unarticulated, unpunctuated voice, which then serves precisely to pierce, interrupt, point the scene.

The peculiarity of the Vice-Consul's voice is at least once described as a suppressed cry: "The Vice-Consul, addressing Anne-Marie Stretter for the first time, speaks distinctly, but with a curiously toneless delivery, the voice pitched a fraction too high [un rien trop aigue], as though he were with difficulty restraining himself from shouting" (97). Here, as in much of the text, it is this "rien," a nothing, an insignificance, that makes all the difference. The cry held back, retained or withheld, will emerge later in the ballroom scene, as its central "event."

The dialogue between Anne-Marie Stretter and the Vice-Consul produces a frame for the suspended central scene, the ambassador's ball, which is then ruptured by the following drama.

> "I shall proceed as though it were possible for me to stay on here with you tonight," says the Vice-Consul of Lahore.
> "There's no hope of that."
> "No hope at all?"
> "None. But there's no reason why you shouldn't pretend there is."
> "What will they do?"
> "Drive you out."
> "I shall proceed as though it were possible for you to prevent it."
> "Yes, what is all this leading up to?"
> "It will precipitate things [Pour que quelque chose ait eu lieu]."
> "Between you and me?"
> "Yes, between you and me."
> "When you are outside in the street, shout at the top of your voice."
> "Yes."
> "I shall say that it is not you who are shouting. No, I shall say nothing." (113–14)

The retention of the cry is transposed into a desire to be retained, to resist separation. The larger interest, however, is the production of an event, so that something "will have happened." Temporally, the narrative installs the possibility of a "will have happened" upon the ground of the "already there," within the subjunctive mood: that something may have happened—a hypothetical anterior future. For Forrester, *India Song*, the filmic repetition of *The Vice-Consul*, might also be characterized this way, since she describes its story as "an ultimate story, where nothing can happen since it already was" (171). The text, then, poses an anterior future, where something will have already happened, will be past,

111

as if the past were bypassed, where the event can claim no temporal grounding.

Furthermore, the cry, like all utterances in this text, receives no answer: "Someone says [on dit]: 'He is dead drunk.' 'I shall stay here tonight with you!' he shouts. They behave as though they had not heard [Ils font les morts: literally, they play dead]" (115). They "play dead," like Lol V. Stein, who plays dead during the ball scene, where "l'heure trompait," time failed to pass, until the suspension is broken by a cry.

In this case, as in the ball scene, the cry marks separation, interruption, as it ruptures a suspended moment. From this point forward, the Vice-Consul will exist for Anne-Marie Stretter and her friends only as a discursive function, as *story,* the double of the beggar. The last remark exchanged before their separation is Peter Morgan's: " 'It isn't possible,' says Peter Morgan, 'forgive me, but a man of your sort is only interesting in his absence' " (116). The Vice-Consul, then, must be the figure of absence recalled. But he is also the impossible being, as Morgan declares just prior to his ejection (146). This figure—impossible—just as Lahore is impossible (Lahore: "Là-hors," "there outside," Marini), merges with that originary and empty scene, source and end of the narration.

This scene of separation and the cry it produces echoes and repeats itself throughout the textual cycle. For Pierre Fédida, the scene is connected to questions of sexual difference and the body, just as the primal scene and its fantasmatic versions are related to the question of origins: the origin both as birth, and as the origin of difference between the sexes.[6]

Indeed, *The Vice-Consul* is a text that turns on the posing of sexual difference and its effacement in doublings and repetition, in the oscillation of presence and absence. In its most striking movements, these issues are focused by the repeated image of the mirror, the fantasy of a shattered mirror, as a failure or explosion of the moment that is based on the narcissistic and thetic instances. For example, the fascinating rumors about the Vice-Consul turn not to his random shooting into the garden, but to his firing into the mirrors in his house: "There was something else too. The mirrors of his residence in Lahore were riddled with bullets, you know" (72). This notion is repeated in the Europeans' discussion of the Vice-Consul as a "personnage absent." "In Lahore he shattered the mirrors as well . . . 'I'm almost sure,' says Peter Morgan, 'that he felt obliged to do what he did because he had believed all his life that one day he would have to commit himself through action, and after that . . .' " (127).

It is by no means insignificant, then, that Duras filmed the cinematic version of this narrative with frequent use of a mirror as background. The film literalizes, or concretizes, the textual figure of a mirror that only repeats, and does not reflect, since we as spectators would find ourselves before a mirror that repeats images of the figures onscreen, while denying us any narcissistic pleasure in our own anticipated reflection. This is a film, then, that deprives us of a *point de fuite* (vanishing point), as well as of a position of mastery, by inscribing our own absence precisely there.[7]

Concerning the mirror in her films, Duras says: "Yes, it's like holes in which the image is engulfed and then comes back to the surface: I never know where it is going to come out . . . or else a putting into question . . . of the real presence of the word" (*Les Lieux de Marguerite Duras*, 71–72). In this case, the mirror is related to the imaginary—the mirror stage—as well as to incorporation and resurgence. This intermittence of presence may account for Duras' fascination with cinematic re-vision of textuality. If the mirror is an engulfing space, however, Duras' work is all the more emphatic about this function as the locus of loss, loss of speech, sense, and subjectivity.

Anne-Marie Stretter is the figure most present in the text as image or object of desire, for both the Vice-Consul and the mendiante (" 'It's the woman from Savannakhet,' he says, 'It really does seem that she follows her about' " [159]), or as image remembered for Charles Rossett: "He sees Anne-Marie Stretter again [l'image lui revient d'Anne-Marie Stretter] rigid under the electric fan" (161). At most, she is largely the echoing or responding voice, often repeating discursive fragments uttered by others. However, one of the last chapters of the text presents this figure more descriptively: "She stops short of the beach. She stretches out on the ground, resting her chin on the palm of her hand, as she might if she were reading. She scoops up a handful of gravel and throws it. After a time, she stops flinging gravel and lies there, flat on her stomach, with her head resting on her folded arms" (159).

This last image is, precisely, mimed by the textual movement itself, which gathers and scatters fragments; here it interposes the Vice-Consul's "rose reader rose" fantasy with the woman on the beach. If Anne-Marie Stretter's existence as descriptive figure both opens and closes in the movement from inside the Prince of Wales to the water's edge, the entire textual movement of *L'Amour* is suspended on this point, "au bord de la mer." The text re-poses the fragment, "reste là," of "S. Thala" and Thalassa, from *Le Ravissement,* where Lol perpetually "reste là." Indeed, to that extent, all of *L'Amour* takes place, takes its place through that phrase, read either as constative or imperative, as description or demand.

This image itself, then, is a fragmented mirror, that disseminates incomplete reflections of the triadic narrative. Moreover, if it can lay claim to the category of *mise en abîme,* its function is unstable, oscillating. In this case, the indeterminacy of the *mise en abîme* effect repeats the textual instability of the source-destination, inside-outside polarities. This question is particularly interesting when applied to the problem of textual mirroring, of a textual mirror scene, which is, in this last figure, particularly bound up with the proximity of "la mer/la mère."

Speaking of Anne-Marie Stretter, as both a narrative and a cinematic figure, and one whose death is much more fully indicated in *India Song* than in *The Vice-Consul,* where it is barely suggested, Duras describes its relation to death: "I don't know if it's a suicide. She meets something like a sea. She rejoins the Indian Ocean, like a sort of matrix" (*Les Lieux,* 78). This almost too transparent passage plays on the homophony of *mer-mère:* the *mer* as origin, as mold, as medium and enclosing mass—matrix. More interestingly, perhaps, Duras herself rediscovers and determines the particular resonance of this play in all of her work, beginning with one of her first novels, *Un barrage contre le Pacifique.* "I've always been by the edge of the sea [au bord de la mer] in my books . . . I was involved with the sea from an early age, when my mother bought the flood plain, the land of *Un barrage contre le Pacifique* and the sea swept through it all and we were ruined" (*Les Lieux,* 84).

Here we need only remark the potential pun's effect. "J'ai eu affaire à la mèr[e] très jeune dans ma vie [I was involved with the sea]"; "j'ai toujours été au bord de la mèr[e]." Moreover, the early narrative, *Un barrage contre le Pacifique,* is explicitly concerned with the invading presence of both the sea and the mother. Until recently the only overtly autobiographical text of Duras' corpus, this novel establishes the historical referent of the mother's purchase of land in a tidal plain and the ensuing struggle to protect it from the seasonal flooding, as the simultaneous annihilation of time/history. The sea overwhelms all barricades and stops time, prevents advance through time. Its invading propensity abolishes all construction, causing the family's bankruptcy. Simultaneously, however, the family itself crumbles to ruin under pressure of the mother's suffocating investment in her children and her ponderous inertia, which abolishes any future.

Marcelle Marini takes up the question of the phrase "au bord de la mer" in her extended analysis of *The Vice-Consul, Territoires du féminin avec Marguerite Duras*. As she points out, "au bord de la mer[e]" is precisely the feminine territory, always in vague proximity to the mother. The phrase itself implies both separation and proximity, and hence poses the problem of limits, boundaries. For Marini, *Le Vice-Consul*, like most of Duras' texts, meditates on the question of femininity as that which is, not repressed or censored, but rather foreclosed by the symbolic order. Consequently, she sees these texts as an elaborate search for the signifier of woman's desire, for the Name-of-the-Mother, which would guarantee an access to subjectivity as feminine, and hence, a feminine access to history, as well as to History. Alternately, Marini sees this text as a reinscription of a positive mythology of femininity, where the story of the mendiante may be read as privileging the maternal axis of the family discourse. But, again, she also reads the textual inscription of what she calls "cryptograms of the feminine sex," traced by the mendiante's trajectory, with the result that "the text figures what language does not allow it to say" (188).

For Marini, these issues condition Duras' narrative project in general, thereby accounting for the curious triangulations that subtend it. She sees the intervention of the masculine term, or of death, as the institution of a certain separation between feminine doubles, and as figuring a textual movement from the imaginary dyad to the symbolic order (*The Ravishing, L'Amante anglaise*, etc.). For her, this obsessive figuration and refiguration is linked to the ambivalence of the mother-daughter relation. Concerning what she calls "the myth of the beggar-woman," she contends that it plays out the ambivalence of the mother-daughter dyad. At its core is the combination of hostile, aggressive feelings, desire, identification, and the fantasmatic menace of absorption into the maternal body that conditions the mother-child dyad. What can be seen as specifically feminine here is what is known as the female Oedipus: the extra turn that girls must take through the Oedipal drama, in Freud's estimation. Since the female child is not so intensely the object of an incest prohibition which forbids sexual access to the mother, her separation from this figure and, hence, her attainment of enough distance from the mother to "separate" the fields of desire and identification along gender lines is more complicated, more slowly achieved. At the other end of the trajectory through which gender position is acquired, she will herself become a mother, will occupy the maternal body as a speaking subject. The narrative of the beggar woman seems peculiarly intent on exploring the threats, murderous aggression, and desire that characterize the mirror stage, lived in overwhelming proximity to the mother's body.

Examining the maternal fatality of this text, or perhaps better, its morbid maternity—all the characters are, one way or another, motherless, and the mendiante produces children that are continually abandoned—Marini relates it to the problem of feminine access to the symbolic in general.

> The reading of this text shows sufficiently that [the woman] is caught between the impossibility of symbolizing her relation to the maternal body as imaginary body—as the sustenance from which she separates herself—, and as feminine body where she must represent herself, and, on the other hand, the impossibility of abandoning it except by alienating herself as subject and becoming affiliated with paternal values that are only valid for a male subject. (227, my translation)

To this particular bind, Marini proposes a very specific elaboration and emphasis. She finds that the narrative of sexual difference, with its fictive "historical" temporalization, needs a beginning and an end "proper" to the feminine—one that, in a sense, redeems or restores a lost past. That is, she calls for a feminized narration, which is nonetheless a linear narrative organization. Such a reading, it seems, would contradict Duras' narrative project in its demystification of narrative origins.

Marini's analysis is more complicated, however, at other points. For instance, speaking of the mendiante's journey, which she nonetheless characterizes as a "search for the maternal signifier," she situates its contradictory consequences: as the struggle to separate an archaic fantasmatic image of the mother from an "alienated" image of woman, and from an image of anticipated femininity, a space where a woman might find her "proper" place (*Territoires,* 199). Here the tensions residing in

Marini's own text are evident, for indeed, the utopic feminine territory she proposes is never attained in Duras' text or her own, which remains fixed, anchored in in its own bind, between the two possibilities. Part of the problem, posed more strongly in Marini's text, although hinted at in Duras', is the dream of a "proper" femininity, a place where Woman comes into her own, an ideal and homogenized, though different, identity. This myth can only constitute the "other side" of a mythological "masculinity." Increasingly, in her more recent texts, Duras' narrative strategies seem aimed at disclosing the mobility of gender positions, in their discursive construction.

However, Marini will push at the limits of Duras' text, remythologizing the feminine, in what she characterizes as a radically different form of exchange, the exchange of the infant among women. As she reads it, the moment of exchange is the institution of genealogy and symbolization in and for the feminine. The possibility of exchanging the child, for her, puts an end to the specular fascination of the imaginary, what she calls "la fascination mortelle," while it introduces the subject, the beggar and mother, into intersubjectivity (257).

It seems to me, however, that the "fascination mortelle" is here displaced onto the narrative progress itself, as the text imagines the infant suspended on the point of death. Moreover, this scene of exchange signals the beggar's complete withdrawal from linguistic space into muteness: the word "Battambang" emerges to mark this point of separation. Further, the complex exchange only serves to open the space of its own repetition, since the beggar will repeat the conception, production, and abandonment of children throughout the story.

If anything, in fact, this scene seems to be the institution of the text's perpetual plying between "here" and "away." The proximity of the infant, the "semblable," the image, is rejected, cast off, abandoned, installing a rhythm of presence and absence. Furthermore, Marini's assertion that this scene marks a passage from imaginary to symbolic will apply equally well to the beggar's violent "symbolization" in the last scene of the text. For it is she who has the power to make the cut, biting the head off the fish—the Medusa's head that menaces Charles Rossett.

In focusing on the so-called mythic figure of the beggar, Marini's text makes a utopic detour, occluding the possible significance of the Anne-Marie Stretter figure, the "speaking" double (or perhaps triple, given the specular balance struck with this figure by the Vice-Consul) of the beggar. Such an occlusion may be related to Marini's more general tendency to find in the Vice-Consul a thematic reflection or performance of certain issues of feminist theory. But, indeed, such a move leads her to veer away from the last appearance of Anne-Marie Stretter, who is precisely, in her place, which is no place, a space "au bord de la mer," in default of separation, where distance is indeterminate.

As regards the orality inscribed in the narrative image of the beggar: it figures the movement of separation from the mother, the presence-absence, the offer and withdrawal of the breast, the zone of hallu-cinatory satisfaction giving way to representations, where one eats the object or eats the "nothing," the part object. But it is precisely this "nothing" or not-thing, which is already something—the cut already in-scribed in the imaginary plenitude of the mirror stage—that is important here.

What if Anne-Marie Stretter were the figure of this unassimilable, irrecuperable lost object? Addressing the fascination this figure holds for her, Duras gives the following "description" of Anne-Marie Stretter.

She has exceeded all presumptions concerning intelligence, knowl-edge or theory. It's a despair . . . In embracing what is most general in the world, the generality of the world, she is most herself. In being the most entirely open to everything, Calcutta, misery, hunger, love, prostitution, desire, she is most herself. When I say "prostitution," I mean prostitution passes through her like hunger, like tears, like desire; she's a hollow that receives, things inhabit her. (*Les Lieux,* 74)

This is a figure without properties, without property, without proper-ness. Perhaps, in fact, Anne-Marie Stretter is the mirror that swallows, permitting no reflection, allowing no image to realize itself. Further, this infinitely receptive space has particular resonance for Duras, as she says in *Les Yeux verts:* "I've come to envision a master-key image, indefinitely superimposable upon a series of texts, an image that would have no meaning in itself, that would be neither beautiful nor ugly, that would only take its meaning from the text that passed over it" (49).

This paradoxical image would then be both figure, and the ground upon which individual narratives produce their figures—on the order of a screen—receiving projections, yet superimposed on the textual surface: a *passe-partout,* a pass-key, master-key. Such an image explodes the relationship of priority that traditionally governs the pair, figure and ground, routing it through the triadic organization, image-projector-screen, and establishing an utterly reversible directionality for that process. Furthermore, this characterization of the image renders radically problematic the status of the image as a function of representivity. Again, I might describe Duras' textual production as more closely related to mourning work, or to its incompletion, than to any specific reproduction of the Lacanian mirror stage's fantasmatic structures. Consequently, the textual process at once poses and undermines the notion of repeatability, subsuming it under the repetition itself.[8]

We might return to Duras' figuration of the maternal, in order to elaborate some of the complexities it involves. To Marini's purely feminine realm of exchange, we may juxtapose Jane Gallop's argument about Kristeva's strategy for speaking of the mother, in *The Daughter's Seduction*. Gallop focuses on a statement of Kristeva's in *Polylogue*, concerning the mother and the phallus: "That the very subject poses him/herself in relation to the phallus has been understood. But that the phallus is the mother, it is said, but here we are all *arrêtés* [stopped, arrested, fixed, stuck, paralyzed] by this 'truth.' "[9] Analyzing this formulation, Gallop goes on to suggest that it has particular pertinence when applied to the idea of an exclusively feminine space.

> The idyllic space of women together is supposed to exclude the phallus. The assumption that the "phallus" is male expects the exclusion of males to be sufficient to make a non-phallic space. The threat represented by the mother to this idyll might be understood through the notion that Mother, though female, is nonetheless phallic. So, as an afterthought, not only men, but Mother must be expelled from the innocent, non-phallic paradise. The inability to separate the daughter, the woman, from the mother then becomes the structural impossibility of evading the Phallus. (*The Daughter's Seduction*, 118)

In a precisely tuned argument, Gallop proposes that the Kristevan enterprise consists in exposing the fraud and the ideological status of the phallus, precisely by repeating and stressing the term "Phallic Mother": "The Phallic Mother is undeniably a fraud, yet one to which we are all infantilely susceptible. If the phallus were understood as the veiled attribute of the Mother, then perhaps this logical scandal could expose the joint imposture of both Phallus and Mother" (117). Such a strategy may work, according to Gallop, because, after all, the phallus is that which functions-as-veiled, and therefore, is most "phallic" precisely where it is most veiled: in the mother. For this reason, Kristeva's most subversive move may be in the theatricalization of the phallic mother: "not merely to theorize the phallic mother, but to theatricalize her, give her as spectacle, open the curtain" (118).

We might begin to see Duras' narrative cycle as a similar type of performance, or spectacle. Parading, alternately, the figure of the woman as lack—Lol V. Stein, the beggar—and the woman as phallic mother, the narcissistically full, self-referential body—Anne-Marie Stretter, Tatiana Karl, the beggar's mother—the texts reinscribe and disfigure a certain imposing libidinal economy. It is surely no accident that Anne-Marie Stretter on the beach, one of the three "vanishing points" of *The Vice-Consul*, emerges and disappears on the site where Lol V. Stein's absence must be marked, or remarked. Such a reading finds some confirmation in the reappearance of the unnamed Lol V. Stein of *L'Amour*. No doubt, however, it is particularly significant to note as well that these polarities are peeled away from discursive gender-binding, as demonstrated by the Vice-Consul and the traveler of *L'Amour*.

We must also investigate the maternal within at least one other structure of triangulation, as constituted by the intervention of the symbolic in the imaginary at the mirror stage itself. Colin MacCabe presents a convincing account in "Theory and Film: Principles of Realism and Pleasure": "The infant verifies its reflection by looking to the mother who holds it in front of the mirror. It is the mother's look that confirms the validity of the infant's image and with this look, we find that at the very foundation of the dual imaginary relationship, there is a third term already unsettling it. The mother verifies the relationship for the child, but at the cost of introducing a look, difference where there should be only similitude."[10] This is to say that the process by which the subject identifies the imagined plenitude of the specular image as his or her own image, the totality of his or her body, itself only takes place through the intervention of the Other's look.

Such a version of this scene then locates the force of intervention as already there in the imaginary dyad. Furthermore, because it stresses the imbrication of imaginary and symbolic, it obviates the possibility of theorizing the relation between the two on the model of chronological narrative development, from one phase to another. Additionally, for my purposes, it has the advantage of establishing the constitutive intervention of the third look within the "narcissistic" space.

In a slightly different vein, Marini sees the narrative project of *The Vice-Consul* as a shifting of the form of triangulation, since the origin is doubled in the organization mother–father–daughter, and mother–daughter–daughter of the daughter, or mother of the mother. The second triangle remains unclosed, in constant displacement, pivoting around one point, a movement Marini sees as marked out in the zigzagging pattern of the beggar's itinerary. This narrative disturbs any fixed triangular base and instead puts that structure in constant motion, transfiguration, exchange among poles, as in the opening passage of *L'Amour:* "Because of the man who is walking, constantly, with equal slowness, the triangle is deformed, reformed, without ever breaking" (8).

The "closing" piece of the narrative cycle, *L'Amour,* repeats Lol V. Stein in the veiled figure of Elle. This is a text without memory—"There is no more ball" (127)—a text, rather, of cancelled memory, which folds over on *The Vice-Consul* to become one of the two wings of a frame, as anticipated by the *V* that interrupts Lol V. Stein's name and figures the radical break of the ball itself. *L'Amour* is a text without memory, but one which activates a purely textual memory, a reenactment of the text already read. The uncanny effect produced by the already-read might be figured "metonymically" by the following fragment of dialogue between Il and Elle.

She looks, beyond the hotel and the gardens, at the continuous succession of space, the density of time. She adds: "That trip to S. Thala, you know." . . .
"I have never come back [revenue: come back, not retournée: gone back] there since I was young."
The sentence remains suspended for a moment, then it ends [elle se termine].
"I've forgotten." (107–8)

The logical explosiveness of this passage that evokes both memory and the telling, in order to obliterate them, establishing their impossibility, also performs this impossibility in producing an aporia. "The sentence ends," or "she finishes," one reading allows. But it has no beginning. Grammatically, "I've forgotten" is a complete sentence, as is the preceding one. The hiatus framed by these two sentences is the "suspended sentence," which does not exist until it is spoken, at which moment it is no longer suspended, except by the written text. Moreover, this phrase itself constitutes a contradiction when juxtaposed with the previous *ne:* "je n'y suis jamais revenue": "I have never come back here" (implied: where I am). "I have forgotten"; the assertion of forgetfulness here is precisely the sign of the repetition.

In fact, *L'Amour* is about suspense—the suspended phrase, the word suspended outside syntax, the suspended look which sees nothing and comes from nowhere. The *récit* itself is suspended, hung on the frame of two cries. "For a moment, no one hears, no one listens. And then there is a cry . . . A scream. Some one cried out near the sea wall. The scream has been uttered and it was heard in the whole space, full or empty" (12). On the following page appears the explosive passage: "The story [l'histoire]. It begins. It began before the walking at the seashore, the scream, the gesture, the movement of the sea, the movement of the light. But now it becomes visible. It is on the sand that it already settles, on the sea" (13).

The story gives itself as an autonomous inscription, suspended, in a sentence of its own: "L'histoire." "It begins": the story begins after the text has begun, only to begin by telling us that it has already begun, before. It has begun anticipating the cry already emitted. It has, in effect, just remembered, only to forget again, its own beginning—its own anteriority.

The space produced by the cry, in this context, has the same status as the space created by the step.

> The triangle is breaking up, reabsorbing itself. It just broke up: for, the man is passing, one sees him, one hears him.
> One hears; the steps space themselves out. (9)[11]

The step spaces itself, makes space. The step passes; but this step is not only a "step," it is a "pas," negation, as well. The text takes place, makes its space, under the sign of this "pas," the terminal fragment of the negative formation "ne . . . pas," which itself operates as a frame.[12] This step is the step we never "hear" coming, just as we don't hear the story coming, since we know we are already reading it.

If the story hangs on the two cries, the second of these obliquely fulfills the anticipation of the first: "An isolated cry: the mother. She screams that they must leave" (99). Is this the cry—now articulated, developed, and differentiated—that can put an end to the reverberations of the first one, which emanates from nowhere? Or perhaps it is the sirens on the preceding page which it simply voices. "Fire alarms blast throughout the city" (98). At stake here is the impossibility of framing, since *The Ravishing* also pivots on a cry, and a delayed one at that. Indeed, we might speculate that *L'Amour* gives voice to that unvoiced, unpunctual cry of the anterior text, its "generative" moment.

It is precisely the domain of suspense, however, that stages the "continuous succession of space, the density of time," that paradoxical reversal of attributes—density or volume to time, and sequentiality to space. If we consider this operation in light of the function of suspense in general, we may see how, in this case, it explodes the limits narrativity poses for itself. Barthes addresses the issue of suspense in connection with the logical time that governs the production of narrative sequence.

"Suspense" is clearly only a privileged—or exacerbated—form of distortion: on the one hand, by keeping a sequence open (through emphatic procedures of delay and renewal), it reinforces the contact with the reader (the listener), has a manifestly phatic function; while on the other, it offers the threat of an uncompleted sequence, of an open paradigm (if, as we believe, every sequence has two poles), that is to say, of a logical disturbance, it being this disturbance which is consumed with anxiety and pleasure (all the more so because it is always made right in the end). (*Image-Music-Text*, 119)

L'Amour's operative suspense serves only to produce this curious phatic function, the "wink" at the reader, or better, the glance, which fascinates and hangs us up—suspends us. No resolution can be accomplished. The text explodes the anticipation of the two poles of sequence. This is suspense without the "pay-off."

As a temporal function as well, this suspense is overwhelming. I might read it in terms of Colin MacCabe's very concise characterization of the most elementary parameters of narrative.

Narrative is propelled by both a heterogeneity and a surplus—a heterogeneity which must be both overcome and prolonged. The narrative begins with an incoherence, but already promises the resolution of that incoherence. The story is the passage from ignorance to knowledge, but this passage is denied as process—the knowledge is always already there as the comforting resolution of the broken coherence (every narration is always a suspense story). Narrative must deny the time of its own telling—it must refuse its status as discourse (as articulation), in favor of its self-presentation as simple identity, complete knowledge. (17)

This narration is, by contrast, only a suspension, not a story. Because of its character, it abolishes the possibility of coherent polar juxtaposition: story-discourse; *énoncé-énonciation;* writing-reading. If, indeed, the "story" is only the passage itself, between foreclosed source and destination, then it "presents" only the process of articulation: "les pas," steps, beats, pulsation. Furthermore, this text need not deny the time of its telling; its telling *is* its time. But this is also a story which cannot tell time, which denies the possibility of "telling time."

In this connection, it is no accident that the text figures writing itself, but as a "dead letter," caught and suspended, without a trajectory. "Le voyageur" himself is suspended on the immobilized trajectory implied in his name. The letter he writes is central to the text, constituting yet another repetitive mechanism.

> The man takes a piece of paper, he writes: S. Thala, S. Thala, S. Thala.
> He stops. He might be hesitating between the written words. He begins again. Slowly, with certainty, he writes: S. Thala, September 14.
> He underlines the first word. Then he writes again. "Don't come any more, it's not worth it."
> He pushes the letter away. (22)

In this first instance, the letter begins on a repetition, and on a hesitation between words. Curiously, the passage lacks the "hesitations between the words" that are constituted by punctuation. Only the second beginning of the letter can establish even the most primary references: place and time. Finally, the letter *éloignée* is only distanced, not sent. And, indeed, it *can*not be sent.

The last instance of the letter's appearance establishes it as never sent. Its message is already clear to the wife, to whom it is perhaps addressed. " 'I wrote to you. The letter is still there.' She puts the letter back on the table" (88).

This scene turns on the letter's exchange, its repositioning, its return to the table: posed and reposed. But it remains, textually, unread, still a "dead letter"—voided of meaning in the scene of the encounter. And the subject/message of the letter is simply death: the death of the love relation, the intersubjective relation, as well as the possibility of its writer's suicide. In this regard, the figurative quality of the letter is most articulated in its second appearance, the one that is framed by the other two in the repetitive structure; or, read in another way, the point of the triangle framed by its occurrences. This scene is the simultaneous writing and reading of the letter's message:

The traveler pushes the letter away, remains there. . . .
He resumes the letter. He writes.
S. Thala, September 14.
"Don't come any more, don't come, tell the children anything at all."
The hand stops, resumes:
"If you can't manage to explain to them, let them invent." He lays down the pen, picks it up, again.
"Don't regret anything, nothing, silence all your sorrow, don't understand anything, tell yourself that you will be all the closer to"—the hand lifts, resumes, writes "comprehension."
The traveler pushes the letter away. (42–43)

This scene, the scene of inscription of the word "S. Thala," also inscribes, or marks out the space of, S. Thala. In the coming and going, the posing and reposing—"lays down the pen, picks it up again"—the scene articulates a pulsating repetition: "pushes the letter away, resumes it." The repetition here is automatic, since a puppet hand, detached from the writing subject, is the agent of writing. Furthermore, this rewriting of the first instance of the letter adds nothing, produces nothing, it merely reinscribes the first message: the admonition not to come, not to return, not to seek. The promise of sense that binds us in the narrative pact is abolished in the destruction of the letter's circuit, *destinateur-destinataire*. In its ultimate failure to make these poles cohere, such a letter inscribes only death—the abolition of desire in repetition—the collapse of temporal and spatial boundaries.

The full impact of the scene of the letter's writing-reading is situated on the level of the narrative pact or promise, that is, where it concerns the reader. For the ultimate destabilization and displacement wrought by this text concerns the reader's position, implicating his or her desire in its movement. In a sense, the text's repetitions serve to abolish the space and time of a desire: the desire of reading.

In this respect, the moment of discovery, recognition, or recall of the "generative" figure, Lol V. Stein, is remarkable.

> She holds the mirror out to him, shows it to him.
> "He gave me this before leaving."
> She opens her bag: again. She puts the mirror back in it.
> He looks: the bag is empty, it contains only the mirror.
> "A ball." . . .
> She turns around, smiles at him.
> "Yes, after." She returns to pure time, to contemplating the ground—"after, I was married to a musician, I had two children."
> (113)

The recounted facts are indeed those of Lol V. Stein's story. And this is the first time we may establish the connection, which serves to identify Elle through the continuity expressed by this repetition, the recall. The ball, the empty center, source of her story, is also the source of this story; like the ground contemplated, it, too, returns us to "pure time." "Pure time" is the time of narration. Without direction and without the *articulation* necessary for measure, this can only be dead time, a time of death.

It is the conspicuous presence of the mirror that renders the scene even more strange. The mirror itself is almost uncanny; "the bag contains only the mirror." A mirror is enfolded in an empty handbag, and serves as an object of exchange, a gift, spectacle, memento ("he gave it to me before leaving"), and as threshold between a before and an after. Furthermore, this very scene is enfolded in a text which, like the bag, is empty, except for its repetition of images. The mirror, however, becomes a sort of lost object, suspended as it is, like the look that characterizes all these scenes, or the sourceless reverberating cry. This mirror reflects nothing; it only recalls another look. Here, we are reminded of the mirror-as-ground of *India Song*, the mirror that reflects only our absent place as spectators.

It seems that *L'Amour*, in its *mise à mort* (the putting to death) of narrativity, simultaneously inscribes our absence or impossibility as readers. This is the function of the omnipresent and floating pronoun "on," the "on" who "hears the steps space out" (10), and the "on" that governs the last passage of the text.

One hears:
  For a moment she will be blinded.
  Then she will begin to see me again. To distinguish the sand from
the sea, then, the sea from the light, then her body from mine.
Afterwards she will separate the cold from the night and she'll give
it to me. Only afterwards will she hear the noise, you know . . . of
God, . . . of this thing? They are quiet. They survey, keep watch on
the exterior dawn. (143)

It is not insignificant that the last word of the text should be "extérieure," emphasizing an obscure exteriority. The poetic or metaphoric
deviation implied by the connection of "extérieure" to "dawn" is dis-
turbed by the possibility of the literal effect. Exterior to whom or what?
To these anonymous third-person pronouns, "ils," to the scene, to the
text, or to its reading?

Such an effect is linked to the problem posed by the anchoring of
narrative voice in "on." "On entend" controls the last passage, which
then slides into the final sentences, which, presumably, "on" does not
hear, and which exist on another narrative plane. The instability of this
"on" is further augmented by its recalling the "on" of *The Vice-Consul;*
this "on" is sometimes an anchor of the narrative level of discourse, in
opposition to the *récit,* and sometimes textually localized as an indivi-
duation of the collective voice and eye of the European community which
seems to observe the other textual figures.

The "on" of *The Ravishing* and *The Vice-Consul* is always both an
anchor and a relay, since it acts as a switch point between narrative levels:
from the diegetic "on entend" to the more abstract "on dirait": "as if" or
"one *would* say." In such a construction, what "one would say" is already
problematized. What one would say, one probably doesn't say. The "said"
itself becomes discursive subject, either as the ground of hypothesis, the
disturbance of the possibility of speech, or as the "already said," and,
hence, the "already heard," the "heard tell," of rumor or cliché—collective, unspecified discourse.

Moreover, this last signal passage is anticipatory—"she will be blinded
and then she will begin again." The "on" hears a projected discourse
whose own source is unsituated, a passage overheard and not located.
The "on" is further problematized, since its "overhearing" doubles ours.
As readers, we maintain precisely the position of one who overhears.
Moreover, "on" as a narrative anchor point is already shattered and

fragmented as a pronominal function: "we," inclusive, implying complicity; "one," anonymous, possibly veiling the inclusive gesture, a more generalized collective; the loosely floating "they," noninclusive. The shattered image, the dispersion, projected by "on" then produces a set or series of relays through which our position as readers establishes itself, but as always destabilized, displaced. Duras' later texts will bring into play the "you"; *Savannah Bay* carries an initial envoi: "Savannah Bay, c'est toi [it's you]." Similarly, much of *L'Homme atlantique* is written in the second person—to a male other. Such reader-positions repel our investment even as they seem to solicit us all the more directly.

Régis Durand explores the cinematic version of this textual function, embodied (or disembodied) in the "off" voices. For him, the disruption of connection between voice off and figure on screen throws into question the convention of voice as "expressive," as exteriorizing an interiority.

> Because of this different logic and circulation of desire, *India Song* is perhaps the first cinematographic and textual disposition of another scene, in which reader/spectator, writer/director, text/film, characters/actors are equally implicated, equally affected; where no central, omnipotent subject pulls the strings, orders and reorders . . . desire runs from one object, one "person" to another, carrying danger and death to all (including the viewer). ("The Disposition of the Voice," 109)

Durand goes on to emphasize the problematical status of the relation between language and the voice, through which Duras, as he puts it, works to "cancel, displace, the subject as referent. The question she asks is: What happens when voices are freed from the conventions of what E. Benveniste calls written/spoken discourse, in order to become something that does not concern you, even though it affects you deeply? Marguerite Duras approaches the exploration of pure desire, pure intensity and horror" (110).

Such a displacement occurs through the dislodging of subject from "grammatical person," and of pronominal shifters from their function as discursive anchors. Paradoxically, however, the textual displacement also admits the possibility of cancellation of our subjectivity as readers, transforming that conventionally controlling position to the status of grammatical person, implicated within the play of textual relays. In a Lacanian sense, moreover, the speech/voice that "does not concern you, even though it affects you deeply," is precisely the function of "ça regarde," in the sense of "ça vous regarde," the look that looks at you.

Here we may connect Durand's version of Duras' project with her own meditation on the status of textual discourse, a meditation which refuses or fails the boundaries between written and spoken, as well as written and *read* language. In *Les Yeux verts,* a special edition of *Cahiers du cinéma* devoted exclusively to her work, Duras writes consistently of the relationship between her narratives and her films. The following passage is exemplary for its dissolution or occlusion of a distinct boundary between forms.

> Reading aloud suggests itself in the same way that it suggested itself to you alone, the first time, without voice. That slowness, that undisciplined punctuation is as if I were stripping the words, one after another and I discover what was underneath, the isolated word, devoid of all relationships, of all identity, abandoned. Sometimes nothing, barely a space, a form, but open, for the taking. But everything must be read, the empty space too, I mean to say: everything must be found. (49)

The ins and outs of this passage, its gaps and its breakdowns, serve to dislocate the relationship of writing to voice, reading to writing, as well as the relationship of before and after. Sense becomes a sort of *après-coup*. But it is also the *après-coup*, retroaction, or repetition of an impossibility, "the primary state of this text," which is already written, spoken, articulated, even in "that undisciplined punctuation." The "isolated word . . . devoid of all relationships, of all identity," in this context, must be that impossible disengagement of sound from sense, voice from body, reading from writing. What is at stake, then, is a perpetual work of binding and unbinding. Indeed, Durand's "pure desire, pure intensity and horror" suggests that the disruptive quality of these texts is related to a different economy of narrative binding or suturing—a circulation of intensities.

Because it occurs across repetition effects, which produce an internal network of attachments, the text called *L'Amour,* along with the cycle of which it is one circuit, escapes immobilization and legibility. This text establishes a desiring textual body in the unintelligibility of the word at its head, just as it forecloses the pleasurable immobilization purchased by suspense, in favor of another pleasure.

Just what that other pleasure is can only be determined approximately as the suspension of suspense in repetition, a failure to satisfy or consolidate our investment. Durand describes the uncanny quality of voice-over, the transposition of the voice in Duras' films, as related to a failure to satisfy our urge for investment: "Those voices . . . are radically cut off from our demand, our need to fasten on to them and invest them with our desire" (108). A similar failure to consolidate sites of investment is effectuated in Duras' novels, through unceasing translation and repetition, of trauma and of the circulation through subject positions by which the narrating instance continually signals its own dispossession. The voice that speaks through these texts is never localized, but rather wandering, translating itself from text to text.

In the narrative domain, which maintains a relation of reciprocal translation with the filmic in Duras' production, we may read this function in the incessant translation which never succeeds in bringing back the "same," but which nevertheless provides no stable difference, but only a heterogeneity achieved through alterations. In this regard, we might speculate that these texts elaborate a different narrative syntax, where repetition produces more disjunction than coherence.

The voice itself comes increasingly to the fore in all of Duras' work. In her films it floats, unanchored to the narrative movement, continually failing to sustain or assure the fullness of the image through a consistency of shared reference. Just as the work of the voice undermines the frame—the fixation of the image as centered and coherent in the midst of filmic sequentiality, process, loss of image—it also signals a lack in the representation. It calls to us from another, absent space, the space outside the frame. Simultaneously as it disturbs the placement and consistency of the image, however, this voice "off" also destabilizes the form of address. We are not consistently hailed by the film; it speaks to an indeterminate set of addresses from a mobile position. In so doing, it frustrates any simple, comfortable recuperation through identification with the *narrated* subjects—the figures in the film—or with a spectator position that accedes to knowledge, assurance, or stability through a narrative resolution. Instead, dividing the filmic space explicitly into "on" and "off" screen, the voice stresses the absence in representation, and *our* absence to the film.

We find a similar strategy at work in Duras' text *Le Navire Night,* the narrative of an entirely telephonic relationship between a woman who claims to be dying and a young male telephone operator. This is narrative reduced to a dialogic *scene,* but on a one-way circuit, since only one speaker—the woman—calls, and the other—the young man who does not have her telephone number—is called. This is a text of voices, where the two interlocutors are framed by other speakers who pose questions: " 'No image on the text of desire?' 'What image? I don't see what image.' 'Then there is nothing to see. Nothing, no image.' "[13] All that is constructed is a set of repeated appeals, lures, demands, punctuated by interruptions—the nights without calls. It is as if each call merely served to bridge or breach, momentarily, the telephonic gap. Here we have the narrative reduced to a figuration of the *fort-da* spool, where the voice vibrating through the telephone line is the object reeled in and tossed out. But around and through this established and ruptured connection (telecommunications—contact without touch), is absence—absence of the space and the body from which the voice emanates, absence across which it carries, the absence of any possible image to accompany it.

What then is the reader's position? On what level does the text appeal to us? We need to frame our examination of the text with a consideration of the instance of reading. That is to say, how does the experience of dissatisfaction that Durand describes relate to the disjunction within repetition that is produced by the collision of trauma and pleasure, as they work on the woman reader's position? How do we, as readers, operate in response to the continual trauma of loss and refinding that is elaborated in the textual structure and that is also mapped in the varying degrees of legibility the text offers—its oscillation between overdetermination and blankness or muteness? My point is that these texts map a different set of positions for the reader to invest, as well as to occupy, thereby performing the sort of displacement Barthes calls for in "Plaisir/ Ecriture/Lecture": "Bourgeois culture is in us; in our syntax, in the way we speak, perhaps even in a part of our own pleasure. We can not pass into the non-discursive because the non-discursive doesn't exist . . . the only battle . . . is not always a triumph, but we must try to displace languages. One tries to create . . . a new space where the subject of writing and the subject of reading don't occupy exactly the same place."[14]

In this regard, we may feel ourselves participating in and performing a displacement of reading and writing positions, precisely through the loss of subject-effect in the narration. Among the most striking instances of this loss/dispossession of narrating instance appear when Duras' discourse occupies the textual zone coded for suspense: the murder mystery, the narrative of crime and its investigation, involving narrative movements from breach or disturbance of order, through crisis, to resolution by certain transformations. If we see resolution as mastery which involves the solution of the mystery and the restoration of order, then suspense, delay of pleasure, allows for the meticulous production of coherence among dispersed details, with the result that the pleasure in narrative closure is doubled: as both pleasure in knowledge-mastery and in the construction of a consistent subject *for* knowledge.

If suspense is suspended, the reader's position shifts abruptly, if not violently; such a shift forces the reader's consideration of his or her stance. This disruption is the subject of the following investigation, which follows the trail of Duras' continually returning figures, as the oral thematics of the Lol V. Stein "cycle"—*The Ravishing, The Vice-Consul,* and *L'Amour*—is translated into a "detective story" frame.

N O T E S

1. Sigmund Freud, "Mourning and Melancholia," *S.E.,* 14:249–50.

2. Cf., for example, the exposition of Melanie Klein's theory of "good" and "bad" objects in Jean Laplanche and J.-B. Pontalis, *The Language of Psychoanalysis,* trans. Donald Nicholson-Smith (New York: Norton, 1974), 187–89.

3. Jacques Derrida, "Economimesis," *Diacritics* 11, no. 1 (1981): 22–23.

4. See Mieke Bal, *Narratologie* (Paris: Klincksieck, 1977), 79.

5. As for the final parenthetical phrase, the French has "the *word* Battambang for the *word* Battambang." The distinction to be made is between word and word, not name and place. The translation has, "her madness from madness in general," but the words "in general" are too *specific* here; the problem is not only to separate the specific from the general, but also the part from the whole, while each of these terms remains undetermined.

6. Pierre Fédida, "Entre les voix et l'image," in *Marguerite Duras,* 158–59.

7. Cf. Copjec, 46–47, where she connects the filmic function of the mirror with the central reception scene of *India Song,* where the mirror suspends both Anne-Marie Stretter's image and her gaze, figuring her death.

8. See Copjec for a meticulous explication of the repetition mechanism in Duras' films.

9. Kristeva, *Polylogue* (Paris: Seuil, 1977), 204. Also cited in Jane Gallop, *The Daughter's Seduction* (Ithaca, N.Y.: Cornell Univ. Press, 1982), 117.

10. Colin MacCabe, "Theory and Film: Principles of Realism and Pleasure," *Screen* 17, no. 3 (1976): 15.

11. Note the construction "on": "on l'entend, on le voit," which may be read "he is heard, seen," "one hears, sees him," "we" or "they hear, see him." As such, it introduces a pronominal displacement and a mobility of subject and object within the very grammar of the sentence which cannot be reproduced in translation, but which are the mapping, in germ, of this text's movement. Such a syntax itself reproduces the moving triangle that rotates around its three points.

12. On the question of "pas," see Jacques Derrida, *La Carte postale,* 317, for example. This passage is a prolonged speculation on the pun that discloses a connection between repetition and negation, in the repeated "ne . . . pas" in Freud's text, with respect to its inability to advance.

13. Marguerite Duras, *Le Navire Night* (Paris: Mercure de France, 1979), 30, my translation.

14. Roland Barthes, "Plaisir/Ecriture/Lecture," in *Le Grain de la voix* (Paris: Seuil, 1981), 153–54.

CHAPTER
5

Writing on the Body

Again and again, Duras' texts pose an anxious question—Who is this woman?—thus repeating a classic story in displaying the woman as enigma. For instance, *Le Navire Night,* whose unending play of differing voices precludes any resolution of the narrative into a single discourse, is *about* a mystery—the dying woman who "calls," who telephones intermittently. The text questions her identity and her truthfulness all at once (Is she really dying, or just "making up" a story?), and resolves neither.

The missing and the duplicitous woman are both images of the "riddle" of femininity/of the woman, upon which so many traditional filmic and narrative investigations are based. Over against this unstable, disruptive mystery assigned to woman, a coherent subject—a spectator or reader position—is constructed and addressed to a "masculine" spectator. (Here masculine is placed in quotation marks as a way of bracketing it, since we are considering *constructions,* an image's or text's forms of address, the positions it makes available and the way those positions are coded for gender, and not biological sex.)

The narrative production of a set of positions which the reader is invited to take up is particularly evident in such a highly coded genre as the detective story or the thriller. Moreover, such texts exhibit a preoccupation with sexual difference at their core—a preoccupation which acts as a driving force. In this respect, this form of narrative reveals the interdependence of the Oedipal drama—the passage from desire to gender identification through submission to the law and entry into discourse—and narrativity itself: the passage from ignorance, through crisis, to knowledge.

In reworking the ground of the detective story, Duras' texts *L'Amante anglaise* and *Moderato cantabile* disturb the possible resolution of the mystery as well as the coherence of the reader's position *for* knowledge and consumption of the text. In exploring questions of sexual difference within a highly coded genre, effecting radical displacement of narrative and reading positions, these texts share certain strategies with recent feminist work in film theory and practice, although in an overdetermined way. Because these texts display a high degree of ambivalence, such that a feminist reader might even find them estranging, they are useful terrain upon which to demonstrate affinities between practices characterized as feminist with those characterized as non- or even anti-feminist. Moreover, the violent ambivalence of these texts is connected, I hope to show, to the work of sexual difference within narrative in general, and within reading as well as writing.

When Roland Barthes distinguishes between work and text (in "From Work to Text"), he describes the "work" as an object, closed and disposable, which is set in a line of filiation—the canon. "Text," on the other hand, refuses consumption, fails to give itself over completely to the single reading, and resists unequivocal location in literary tradition alone, as cut off from the world. "The Text," he writes, "(if only by its frequent 'unreadability') decants the work (the work permitting) from its consumption and gathers it up as play, activity, production, practice. This means that the Text requires that one try to abolish (or at the very least diminish) the distance between writing and reading, in no way by intensifying the projection of the reader into the work, but by joining them in a single signifying practice" (*Image-Music-Text*, 162). The text abolishes the distance and the polarity of reading and writing, precisely by displaying their interaction in the *production* of the narrative, which must be conceived as ongoing.

If the categorical separation of reading and writing will not hold in the Text, it is because each text, each narrative, is itself readings and rewritings of the field of discourses in which it is grounded. In that sense, the text *stages* representation, operates on the discourses that come to it ready-made, already read, and confronts their contradictions. Reworking structures of representation, texts constitute a passage composed of joining and disjoining, at the "end" of which is the subject, him/herself constituted as reader-*for*-the-text.

Both the text and the subject are social productions, as well as producers. But if the narrative stages the system of representation in which it is bound up, it also stages the process of the subject in language, what Stephen Heath calls "the permanent performance of the subject in language" (*Questions,* 118), which is a perpetual passage in and into language that is constitutive of subjectivity. For Heath, this permanent passage is the place of a variety of forms of regulation, the focus of institutions and practices that aim to "play out the drama of meaning," producing cohesion, identity, and sense. Narrative may be seen as one among many agencies that operate on and around investment, that produce coherence, and even fixation, out of process, loss, lack, absence, and contradiction.

The movement of narrative representation, in its circulation of positions, binding and unbinding investments, both places and displaces the reading subject—fixes it in place and sets it in motion. These processes of segmentation and sequence, alternation and repetition, are peculiarly evident in Duras' narratives, around the site of textual enunciation and around figures of sexual difference. We might take up these issues under the name of narrative syntax, a term chosen to lay stress on the process of selection, ordering, segmentation—in short, articulation.

At the conclusion of her "Women's Stake: Filming the Female Body," Mary Ann Doane turns her attention to the question of syntax in representation, and to two recent feminist films which play with the codes of suspense. She explains her concern with syntax in relation to the body by reminding us that the body and its discourse never exist in isolation from context, nor from encoding; there is no image or representation of the feminine in isolation: "The attempt to 'lean' on the body in order to formulate women's different relation to speech, to language, clarifies the fact that what is at stake is, rather, the syntax which constitutes the female body as term."[1] That is, the filmic or textual process must be understood as producing constructions of gender, or of the body, just as they produce a subject *for* that representation.

A focus on syntactic organization, ordering, permits Doane to approach the problem of the insertion of the feminine into already coded spaces—both discursive and nondiscursive—and thereby to consider representations in/of the feminine as contextual, rather than autonomous.

136

In so doing, she chooses to explore feminist films that confront the suspense genre, as one of the most elaborately coded of narrative formations. For the same reason, I turn to Duras' narratives of suspense, because they seem to present the most explicit confrontation with the laws of generic coding, within a genre whose preoccupation with the law and its transgression is undeniable. At the same time, however, because of their fundamental relationship to suspense, narratives of crime and detection offer themselves as texts for smooth consumption, whose suspense rewards our curiosity and appetite with the solution-discharge of the mystery.

Such texts facilitate smooth consumption, provide little resistance, precisely because the narrating instance and the reader's position are both highly coded as stable points where progressive acquisitions of knowledge accumulate. What they rehearse and guarantee, through the trajectory of investigation, suspense, and delivery of the "solution," is a full disclosure, an access to mastery of the signifying process.

It is not surprising, then, that this genre is the frame that "gets framed," or reframed, in Duras' textual practice, for it is here that a thematization of death may be made to give way to an inscription of death as the border of discursive practices. It is also here that discursive mastery of the crime, the mystery, can be called into question, that its limit may be disclosed, forcing a missed encounter between discourse and the nondiscursive— that zone which exists in function of its constituting the limits of discourse itself.

In positing death as the source of their narrative projects, in their search for the "body" and in their figuration of the mute textual scream, *L'Amante anglaise* and *Moderato cantabile* dramatize the confrontation of discourse and the nondiscursive. These are texts that seek to approach the limits of narrative discourse while elaborating, specifically, the displacement of limits, of framings, that any such approach to them entails. That they do so within a feminine thematics of oral pulsions, maternity, and hysteria is particularly significant, for the interplay between thematics and textual structuration is at times mutually absorbing to the extent that no absolute separation between categories is possible. Discourse is propped on desire, as sexuality is propped on both the body and language. Moreover, these texts thematize consumption as well, implicating the reader's position in this configuration.

Because they exploit the codes of the detective genre, these texts also figure a discursive encounter, since all detective novels take up, however peripherally, the question of law, in the sense that the crime at their center implies its transgression. This question is all the more pertinent, given the conventional association of detection with the primal scene and with investigative impulses directed toward the hidden recesses of the maternal body.[2] If these texts flagrantly toy with the detective model and then fail to produce, to disclose the corpse, the killer, or the scene of the crime, they then present a radical interrogation of the limits and underpinnings of the investigative economy. What they give us instead is a circulation of positions so unstable as to subvert the narrative frame, the movement from ignorance to disclosure.

Here we might recall that, even on the thematic level, both of these texts involve the performance or reproduction of a murder. In *L'Amante* a woman murders her female cousin; in *Moderato* a man and a woman fantasmatically restage a woman's murder by her lover. In each case, the text takes up the model of a sadistic, aggressive fantasy. In his famous analysis of sadistic fantasy, "A Child Is Being Beaten," Freud discloses not only the interpenetration and reversible interactions of sadism and masochism, but, more profoundly, the split that underpins and is articulated through this fantasy. There is a slippage of positions revealed in the fantasy's movement, as articulated in the syntactic transformations of a sentence, "A child is being beaten." This phrase is progressively transformed, moving from, "The father is beating the child (a boy)," to, finally, "I (a girl) am being beaten by my father." These fantasies, discovered in female patients, reveal a turning round, a reversion, that pivots on the verb of the sentence, and transforms subject into object, active into passive.

As Jacqueline Rose puts it: "The essay demonstrates that male and female cannot be assimilated to active and passive and that there is a potential split always between the sexual object and the sexual aim, between subject and object of desire. What it could be said to reveal is the splitting of subjectivity in the process of being held to a sexual representation (male *or* female), a representation without which it has no place."[3]

Such a split identification, as fundamental in our relationship to sexual representation, is crucial in Duras' earlier texts and in a later work, "The Seated Man in the Passage," where the introduction of a woman as the voyeur of a violent sexual scene—a woman being beaten—complicates the issue.[4] Such a staging of fantasy structures in representation calls attention to the split that inheres within the positions it allows us to take up, and thus radically questions its formal oppositions, active/passive, subject/object, voyeur/object of gaze, along with the classical alignments of those positions around sexual difference: masculine/feminine.

At the same time, however, a feminine voyeur, or a female murderer who dismembers a woman's body (assuming an aggressive pose that might be read as, variously: exploration of the maternal interior, murderous hostility toward the castrated other, a warding off of that anxiety by producing a Medusa effect through dismembering the body into fragments inscribing lack and loss), also destabilizes the gender association of the reader's position as attached to mastery-voyeurism, through the relay of the narrating instance. The detective or the law, the narrating instance of *L'Amante*, is transformed into the voyeur narrating "The Seated Man."

Through repetition and revision which are internal to given narratives, and which also persist from text to text, Duras' enterprise raises the question of the frame, the scene of reading. Just as the primal fantasy structure (as Laplanche and Pontalis describe it) admits the subject into the scene, capturing it in the mobility of positions and setting it in circulation, it also "absorbs" the frame of the scene, resisting any separation between the subject/voyeur and the objects of the gaze. For Catherine Clément, in her remarkable article on this fantasy and misrecognition, "De la méconnaissance: fantasme, scène, texte," the voyeuristic fantasy of seeing a sexual scene, the primal scene, always stages a look *and* a frame, as well as a scene.[5]

The frame here is not only the frame of the scene, its immobilization by the look, but also the frame of the look itself, the passage through which the gaze passes in its constitution *as* gaze. The gaze and the frame are confounded here (in the join of the imaginary—unstable reflection—and in the cut, separation or enframing, of the symbolic). So the fantasy is a fantasy of the look itself as framing and framed. Duras' narratives seem to work aggressively upon the frame—textual or generic—upon the limits of narrative, its arrival at solution, and upon the scene of reading, denying a separation of reading subject from textual processes.

In texts thematically concerned with crime, it seems that an obsession with the law and its transgression must be related to an inscription of desire in narrative. To a greater or lesser degree, narrative poses a lack

139

or a loss that it then satisfies. (In so doing, however, it exposes what Stephen Heath calls the "insistence of the symbolic against an imaginary center" [*Questions,* 86]). In their very process of making meaning, narratives also construct a subject for that meaning. In its flow, its loss and wandering, narrative seeks, on some level, the establishment of a coherence and identity, providing fictions or images that a subject may invest, at the same time that it constructs the subject-position. Any narrative works both within, and to some extent against, the preformed, preexistent discourses from which it is produced. To some degree any text reveals its foundations in other discourses and establishes divergent and critical, or coherent and uncritical, relations with them.

The law, particularly where the detective genre is concerned, and in conventional narrative tradition, tends to locate the woman on "the other side of the Law," in the imaginary, pre-Oedipal mobility where sexual difference and sexual identity are unstable.[6] We must also raise the question more generally, in terms of the female body as the place of the law's inscription. Any interrogation of the law of the father, as of the law in general, will then open questions of gender under the law, of maternity, of the body of the law, and of the body in its relation to discourse and truth. In this reading, woman embodies the law; the maternal body is the site of the law's inscription. Woman is therefore the embodiment of the law, as well as its subject. It is this *clivage* that marks the law's installation.

It is on this site, with this at stake, that Duras' narratives of detection open the gender question and the generic question—the question of textual generation, the crime at the origin—within a relation to the maternal body, to maternity, and to sexual difference. These texts inscribe a certain relation to the law of speech, to textual and discursive laws, and to the maternal body, both in their figurations of maternity and murder, of desire as desire of death, and in their continual drift, circulation, and scattering of fragments, the production of a discourse not of communication, but of affectivity, perpetual displacement beyond exchange. In that sense, they figure the oral zone of "exchanges," where the sexual itself is produced in the space between satisfaction and the call of demand, where discourse arises as propped upon the maternal body.

As a genre the detective story, in its variety of structural versions, elaborates a relationship of knowledge and power in discourse, while stressing certain effects of pleasure, thereby constituting a privileged site for interrogation of these impulses. For Roland Barthes, "Suspense, therefore, is a game with structure, designed to endanger and glorify it, constituting a veritable 'thrilling' of intelligibility: by representing order (and no longer series) in its fragility, 'suspense' accomplishes the very idea of language: what seems the most pathetic is also the most intellectual— suspense grips you in the 'mind,' not in the 'guts' " (*Image-Music-Text*, 119). This reading of suspense resembles the structure of the fetish, the suspension of the look, the reading, and the telling on the point of the threatening disclosure. In this case, it may be the "idea of language" that the suspenseful text reinstates and preserves.

It is a certain fetishizing economy of pleasure that underlies the classical mode of suspense, according to Mary Ann Doane, who sees the "different syntax" of some recent feminist films as an effort to disarticulate suspense in favor of a radical reinscription of the feminine, within a different economy of pleasure. This she calls "suspense without expectation," meaning that the suspenseful pause does not bear within it the clear indication of its aim, the signs indicating its ultimate resolution. We may see clearly in both *L'Amante* and *Moderato* a suspense that leads nowhere, constituting a shift in the economy of pleasure—in favor of process, over pause.

A reinscription of the suspenseful narrative in Duras' later texts operates upon the conflict between narrative movement and its immobilization in scenes. Texts like "The Seated Man in the Passage," *L'Homme atlantique,* and *La Maladie de la mort* are weighted toward the side of spectacle—a scene frozen in "frame." This gesture tends to overturn, destabilize the reader's position in different ways, figuring a voyeuristic fascination, a capture, which constitutes a resistance to the movement toward closure, and catches the reader up in a play between positions. None of the roles in which the reader is cast can be consolidated, because of the pronominal shifts and the oscillation between narrative progress and immobilization, where the reader is lured, and temporarily positioned, in a textual fantasy structure that marks his/her place in its syntax. A similar approach might apply to the problem of the enigma. The *roman à énigme* solicits our curiosity to know the answer, to find the cause or explanation of the effect. But the discovery of a solution implies a certain libidinal pleasure as well—a pleasure in exploration, and in resolution.

This pleasure in resolution involves an unbinding. However, as its etymology implies, dissolution coexists with payment, return, repaying. The analysis of the enigma unbinds it, in order to rebind its elements in an interpretive discourse. Enigmatic discourse is dissolved and rebound in the gesture that masters it through interpretation, or "full" disclosure, which permits the analyst to *see* it all. Jane Gallop presents a suggestive analysis of the problem of the enigma, relating it to psychoanalysis and the feminine enigma as well. "We think of Oedipus and the way solving riddles leads to blindness. A 'solved' riddle is the reduction of heterogeneous material to logic, to the homogeneity of logical thought, which produces a blind spot, the inability to see the otherness that gets lost in the reduction. Only the unsolved riddle, the process of the riddle-work before its final completion, is a confrontation with otherness" (*The Daughter's Seduction*, 61).

Indeed, Duras' detective narratives would seem to play upon the "riddle-work," on the heterogeneity of details irreducible to a logical structure. In this connection, they work with the structural impulse of identification that subtends the detective genre, where the detective's pursuit of the criminal, his reading and interpretation of the clues, increasingly produces a certain identification between the two figures. Or, as Erica Eisinger puts it, Duras' texts play on the function whereby "investigation becomes identification."[7]

In this connection, however, it is worth distinguishing between the enigma and the riddle. While the riddle is that which mystifies or puzzles, disguising its answer by paradoxical or contradictory statements, and which is thereby structured in function of an answer, the enigma presupposes no answer. It is irreducible to "solution," or else its solution is achieved by following strategies of allusion, indirect reference, proceeding to somewhere else. That is, the enigma's reference or answer is always *elsewhere*. If the laws framing the detective story are structured on the model of the riddle, Duras' narratives privilege the enigma, in order to reveal the particular investments that condition its status as enigma/ secret, and how that status is related to a discursive field which locates "woman" in the same space.[8]

This may lead us to interrogate the rhetorical status and power of the enigmatic detail in Duras' *L'Amante anglaise,* where the detail is "capital," although neither the detective nor the textual investigation gets to "capitalize" on it. The location of the missing puzzle piece, the head, becomes the obsessional focus of the interrogation.

—*Now, you must tell me where the head is.*
—Was it to get to that question that you asked me all the others?
—*No. . . .*
—*Just a vague indication would be enough. Just a word. Forest. Bank.*
—But why?
—*Curiosity.*
—You mean to say that only one word counts among all the others? And you think I'm going to let you get it out of me? So that all the others can be buried alive, and me with them, in the asylum? (120–21)

The culminating detail, the one which could make all the others cohere, is withheld, along with any word which might be a clue to the concealment. In the face of the law and its interrogation, Claire Lannes refuses to order the details, or to permit an end to discursive delay and displacement by supplying the fascinating missing detail. In a second "castration" of the "truth," the decapitated head is hidden/secreted, and the name of its location withheld from the discursive reconstruction of the body.

Both Duras' detective stories center on a dramatization of an analytic dialogue. *Moderato cantabile* orients itself on a dialogic interpretation of the crime, in repeated encounters structured by question and response passing back and forth between the two "investigators" (or "interested" parties) and suggesting an uneasy movement from the constative to the performative, modes the confession articulates upon one another.[9] *L'Amante anglaise,* on the other hand, dramatizes the effort to obtain a full confession from the female subject as criminal, a process that poses itself as a sort of "climactic" conclusion to an orchestration of various *versions* of the criminal act and its motive. Both narratives focus obsessively on the question of "truth," a veracity, and an accumulation of detail. Their double articulation—establishing a web of connecting details and reconstructing the scenario of the crime—elaborates a set of relations between the narrative account and the law/power, while dramatizing, at the same time, the doubleness of that law.

L'Amante anglaise, curiously enough, seems structured around this kind of displacement, since its refusal to supply the missing solution, the location of the head, repeats Claire's ultimate refusal to reveal that fragment, thereby subverting the investigation. The corresponding gesture of

143

Moderato cantabile is to supply a proliferation of detail unrelated to the crime, and, simultaneously, to reconstruct it in a mode which exceeds the code of detection—by suspending the narrative on the point of a reenactment of the still entirely enigmatic scene.

These texts open the question of interpretation at precisely the point where mastery intersects the law—interpretive and narrative mastery, to be specific. For, as Derrida puts it in "The Law of Genre," "the Law demands a narrative account."[10] In both cases, the narrative problematizes the question of the *récit,* the recitation or account, a word whose very ambiguity is played out textually. Derrida's argument engages the peculiar etymological charge of the word *récit,* which recalls recollection, repetition, and formal nomination, the summons, naming, and accounting as a legal procedure. The narrative account, then, is always haunted by the instability of citation, which brings along with it metonymical and metaphorical connections with a text or texts, a discourse, a genre. In short, how to stop or enclose the citational movement, prevent it from destabilizing the text that incorporates it?

Duras' texts disclose the operation of such instability through their repetition, "self-citation," which explodes the very genre they cite in the interests of a different syntax and economy. This question of the *récit* and the law touches on the problem of the border, the edge, or, in Shoshana Felman's term, "the boundary." "The principle of totality is the very principle of a boundary and of the repression inherent in it."[11] In their very elaboration of investigative accounts which dramatize the production of the *récit,* both Duras' narratives constitute an interrogation of and a possible disruption of the boundaries of their genre. Specifically, these texts question narrativity in general, through their explorations of the space of reading and interpretation, and of representation of the feminine as enigma, or as death. In any event, these texts stage the figure of woman before the law, in connection with the uncanny effect recalled in the missing dead woman—the dead body which constitutes the fictional origin of the account.

A privileged site of interrogation, which is both central and framing, and which translates uncannily from *Moderato cantabile* to *L'Amante anglaise,* is the oral zone. Both texts thematize orality, in the dialogic discourse that governs the construction of the *récit* and in the thematic obsessions of the female characters, Anne Desbaresdes and Claire

Lannes; at the same time, the texts' metaphoric relays maintain the axes of incorporation and expulsion, as well as the structuration and dissolution of specular identifications. Moreover, the privileged status of the voice as narrative figure and frame in *Moderato* is rearticulated in *L'Amante* on the level of its signifiers, since the title itself constitutes a pun (on *la menthe anglaise*) whose dependence on the simultaneous articulation of the written and the oral opens one of the text's central issues: what is the status of the word? Beyond that, a hidden question that haunts the text is: what is the status of *a* word, someone's word, the voice?

Another way of putting the question is, quite simply, what is the relation of the word to the body?—the body, in this case, in both senses, as the cadaver that marks the crime, and as the flesh, the living, desiring body. This question is central to both of Duras' earlier texts, the later one in a sense rewriting the earlier, unwriting it, transforming and translating it. The relation between discourse and the body is elaborated in each text along two interwoven trajectories: that of discursive repetition/reenactment, and that of consumption, circuits whose interdependence the text exposes. This suspense, suspended and repeated, calls into question narrative unfolding and chronological development, which inflects the whole corpus.

A central figure in *L'Amante anglaise* is the writing on the body fragments. Each piece of the dismembered body has been inscribed with the words "Alfonso" and "Cahors." Such nominal inscriptions, that of a proper name and a place name, already establish as problematic the status of words and referents. This operation is all the more significant because it recalls and elaborates another form of coincidence between proper name and place, that of the last scene of *Hiroshima mon amour*. Their appearance on body parts constitutes a mutilation, both part of the crime itself, and a clue, which implicates the referents of these names in the crime. Through their hideous impropriety, these words explode the conventional possibilities encoded in the inscription of a name on an object—to suggest belonging, as in private property, or place or origin or destination; to indicate person and place of delivery, on a letter or package; to mark production by an individual, or the place of production of goods. Given their multiple occurrence, these names serve instead as a means of reuniting the fragments which no longer form a whole. Furthermore, they embed the problem of dislocation and contextuality in the very concept of the name, by exposing a radical disjunction between name and reference.

The fragmented body whose parts bear these inscriptions becomes the textual emblem of Claire's discourse.

—Ten different things at once. Floods of words. And then suddenly silence.
—*Without head or tail to it?*
— . . . I did try, but I never once stuck it out till she'd finished.
—*What she said did have a beginning and an end then?*
—Yes, I expect so, but you couldn't make them out. Before you knew where you were she was off in all directions, everything would connect with everything else [c'était des relations entre tout et tout]. (32–33)

Patricia Fedkiw characterizes this discourse as constituting a hysterical economy: "To misspell is to dispel phallic authority and to propel unbound energy anew into circulation. As brought out in the dialogue between the interviewer and Robert, that which is apparently without head or tail recovers another logic. When Claire's words fall on deaf ears, they congeal *en glaise,* but when paid heed to, 'this other logic, the hysterical discourse conversely goes off in ten directions at once.' "[12] It is precisely this scattering of discourse that the investigative project wishes to master, to bring back into logical order, of course, but I want to consider this "hysterical logic" as also conditioning of the textual logic itself. For, indeed, the interviewer's project itself is fragmented into several directions—each interview providing another version, another turning of the story, another "truth," *sens,* as direction *and* meaning.

The insistence of this discourse on moving "in all directions," all senses, relating everything to everything else, results in the impossibility of establishing the parts in relation to a whole, of hierarchizing the elements in a logical or linear progression. Beginning with the figure of the body parts disseminated across the railway system, the textual enterprise transforms this system into a set of channelings whose orientation we cannot fix.

Similarly, this textual emblem problematizes the relation of part to whole, along with the question of property and belonging. Since the detail refers only to another detail, without leading back to a whole from which it has been detached, the concepts of totality and totalization undergo a radical shift.[13] In the literally "disarticulated" body, *L'Amante* figures a fragmented femininity, along with a disorganization of *communicative* structure.

But the railway system with which *L'Amante anglaise* opens is not the only textual figure of communication at stake here, since the inscribed body fragments might figure the movements of the postal system as well. Claire's relationship to the letter is itself complicated. We recall that she is known to write to newspapers, and that her relationship to discourse in general establishes what are apparently complete separations between reading, writing, and speech. Moreover, although her husband claims she has forgotten how to read, "and sometimes she used to talk very strangely, rather as if she were reciting something out of one of those modern books, whereas of course . . ." (53). As if she were reading aloud, or reciting memorized phrases?—such that, for Claire an act of reading would be an act of memorization? Such a configuration emphasizes the problematic nature of citationality, and, correspondingly, of recitation, of the *récit* that haunts this text's investigative project. Claire re-cites phrases whose original anchor is displaced, missing, and whose very existence is questionable. At the same time, the idea of a *récit*ation or reading aloud implicates the status of the reader in this disrupted communicational circuit.

Claire's motives for writing pose a similar problem, since writing for her relates to desire, in the cry or scream.

> — . . . When you [on] think of what it was like with the policeman in Cahors, you could say nothing exists beside that. But that's not true. I've never been separated from the happiness I had in Cahors, it overflowed on to all my life. . . . I've always felt I'd like to tell someone about it, but who was there I could talk to about him? And now it's too late. Too far, too late.
> I could have written letters about him, but who to?
> —*To him?*
> —No, he wouldn't have understood.
> No, they ought to have been written to just anybody. But just anybody isn't easy to find. Still, that's what I ought to have done: sent them to someone who didn't know either of us, so that it could all be completely understood.

—*To the papers perhaps?*
—No. I did write to the papers two or three times . . . but never about anything so important. (99–100)

The writing Claire might produce, the recounting of the story of the policeman of Cahors, would be understandable only outside any reference to that scene or its participants. Only the letter without a proper *destinataire*, to "just anybody," is possible. Thus, Claire's wish becomes a desire for writing without address, a writing, precisely, that escapes the limits of a communicational circuit. As such, this writing destabilizes the positionality on which the missive/message depends, and along with it orientation, directionality.

When Claire is asked to account for her inscription of Alfonso's name on the cellar wall, she offers the following hypothesis: "Perhaps I wanted to call him to come and help me? And because I couldn't shout, for fear of waking my husband, I wrote it? . . . I've written before to call for help when I knew all the time that it wasn't any good [pour appeler tout: in French, simply to *call*, not call for help]" (111–12). Writing becomes a substitute for the cry, the call for help, the appeal. To write, "to call when I knew all the time it wasn't any good," is itself a pun: appeler: to call or to name. This writing effect installs itself between the name and the call, between the appeal and its *destinataire* or referent. As such, it constitutes a different syntax, approaching and "incorporating" the border, the limit-case of writing, the scream, the unarticulated voice.

The problem of the call or appeal engages the entire system of Claire's discourse and its dependence on a peculiar separation of reading and writing. "She was writing for advice about the garden, yes, it was about the English mint. . . . Mint [la menthe], she wrote like lover [l'amante], and English [anglaise], 'en anglaise,' like 'in earth, in sand' " (76). This suspicious wordplay that proliferates on the title phrase, one might say, the *capital* phrase of the text, covers a variety of nominal possibilities. These operate on the feminine: lover, mantis, nun's mantle, on the ambiguity of the sounded word (amant[e] followed by "en"), and on the possibility of hearing "anglaise" as "en glaise." Sanford Ames adds to this series a set of associations on the phrase itself: " 'filer à l'anglaise': to slip away, drift off; the culinary suggestions that attend it are: 'en glaise,' like 'boeuf en daube,' as if it referred to a woman 'smothered and served up in clay.' "[14] However, even more interestingly for a consideration of this text's structure, Ames stresses the particular quality of this phrase's polysemy, since it results from a "non-homographic homonym." That is, only writing can *right* the meaning.

Claire's writing translates the madness of her voice, voicing the silent and simultaneous possibilities—going in ten directions at once: calling, appealing to its referent, only to bypass or disengage it. But this madness of speech and writing traverses the entire textual enterprise. It appears in the opening passages: "I said: 'And do the lady and gentlemen come from Seine et Oise?' The girl said she was from Paris—she'd come to have a look at the scene of the crime and . . . He smiled and made a pun that didn't make anyone laugh. He said: 'No, I'm from the Seine'" (10). Here one pun would be Seine-scène, homonyms in French, while the other would be nom-non, as in "non, de la Seine," or "non, de la scène," or "nom de la scène," or "nom de la Seine." All this in a text whose point is to identify the scene of the crime, a text which effects the simultaneous invention of that crime: "We were inventing a crime. That crime is the very one that has just been committed in Viorne" (12).

From its very inception, its fictive auto-generation, this text poses the problem of voice and language. To pose the problem of orality is to call into question our positions as *consumers* of the text, and the status of reading as consumption, as well as the relation among hunger, desire, and language. Opening as it does on the problem of mechanical reproduction of speech, a literally disembodied voice, *L'Amante anglaise* questions the occasion and the continuation of speech, figuring it as doubled in this writing.

> —*I have here a copy of the recording [le double de la bande] that was made there that evening without your knowledge . . . but it just repeats the words blindly, opaquely. So it's up to you to set the book in motion. And when what you've said has given that evening back its real depth and dimensions we can let the tape recite what it remembers and the reader can take your place.*
> —How about the difference between what I know and what I say [ce que je dirai]—what will you do about that?
> —*That's the part of the book the reader has to supply for himself. It exists in any book [elle existe toujours]. (3)*

This passage, stressing the incapacities of the tape, which will, literally, *recite* its memory, not *from* memory or *as* memory, but rather, as false presence, figures the image of an unseeing eye and unhearing ear. Mean-

149

while it calls the reader to account for the difference, the lacks that inhere in this method of constructing a *récit*. In her analysis of this passage, Erica Eisinger cites the following issues: "But the novel illustrates the insufficiency of the device . . . for the present keeps on happening while the band of the past unwinds. The tape recorder fails, moreover, because it can only record what is said, not what is unsaid" (513).

It is precisely within this contradiction, this displacement, that the text works. Moreover, encapsulated in this passage, in Robert's question, is the figure of Claire's own discursive strategy: to maintain the space between "what I know and what I say."[15] This is the indefinable distance that the fictional narrative project *L'Amante anglaise* elaborates seeks to measure and to close.

The narrator of *L'Amante* introduces the question of the *récit* directly into account. In fact, this moment is already a doubled recitation of the events of the evening in the café, since it provides both the recitation-citation from the tape and its supplement, the interviewer's own recitation. After the preliminary dialogue, the interviewer then signals the introduction of a second tape recorder: "We'll have the two tape recorders running at the same time. The first will play back the conversation that evening. I'll stop it when you want to add something. I'll leave the second machine running all the time so it'll record both the conversation and the comments" (11).

While admitting the failure of the first machine to reproduce the *reality* it recorded, because of the temporal limits of the tape, the narrator's discourse here introduces the retotalizing gesture of this scene; the perpetually recording machine will register everything, previously recorded dialogue and commentary, text and interpretation. The problem of a totalizing interpretation, or account of the crime, is central to *L'Amante anglaise*, source and end of the text, which calls attention to itself as such.

This opening dialogue constitutes a particular form of appeal to the reader. The splitting that inheres in a textual invitation to voice the written words ("that's the part of the book the reader has to supply"), to hear our own voice reading it, or to speak it in our own voice, then continues and "literalizes" the figure of the tape-recorded voice, a voice that speaks *elsewhere* than from the body of its origin.

This insistence, a literal interpellation of the reader, is marked by the indicators of a certain dispossession, in and through an *address*. By "interpellation" here, I mean the hailing gesture, "You there," which is most often not literally inscribed in a text, but rather is an effect of its operations of meaning production which guarantee both intelligibility and a subject position or positions for that intelligibility. Since a sign always represents something for someone, the movement of textual process sets a subject in place along with representations. Necessarily, then, the text is within the social field where the subject perpetually constitutes itself in language, but only through an insertion in discourse that binds it to certain available positions. Kaja Silverman describes interpellation as "the conjunction of imaginary and symbolic transactions which result in the subject's insertion in an already existing discourse. The individual who is culturally 'hailed' or 'called' simultaneously identifies with the subject of speech and takes his or her place in the syntax which defines that subject position."[16]

In this schema, identification refers to the imaginary, the static reflection, an illusion of wholeness in a pause, which is constantly overlaid by the symbolic operations of syntax, process, movement, articulation, and cutting. The reader of Duras' text is then subjected to the disturbing split of its position at the point of an interpellation that calls attention to itself as such. "You" stands for the spoken subject—spoken by the narrative, and simultaneously for the silent place of another speaking subject, who speaks *to* the narrating instance. "You" is/are the space the narrative calls for and holds off in the same gesture—the always absent, the lost, the possible but never-achieved completion.

This particular stress—pressure and emphasis—on the position of "you," an unanchored address which the reader by virtue of his/her reading necessarily takes up, becomes crucial to the framing of Duras' most recent texts, *La Maladie de la mort*,[17] *Savannah Bay*,[18] and *L'Homme atlantique*,[19] all of which begin with a direct address. *Savannah Bay*'s brief prefatory note concludes by asserting, "Savannah Bay is you" (familiar); both *La Maladie* and *L'Homme atlantique* are perpetually addressed to a "you" figure—in the second case a figure juxtaposed to a speaking "I," and in the first the hearer of its own story, told by an unnamed narrator.

La Maladie de la mort performs a curious ventriloquism: a narrating voice that never refers to itself tells "you" the story of "your" affair with "her." While the reader's position is thus split and the pronominal frame dislocated by the lack of an "I" position in a discourse circulating

151

through second and third persons, where the second person is split between speaking and spoken instance (as a *narrated* term), the textual frame is also shattered since *we*, the readers, as *you*, are both within and without the textual movement. Perhaps most extraordinarily, the split of sexual difference is articulated into this position, since the *you* is marked as masculine within the first line of the text. "You should not know her, having found her everywhere at once . . . in a hotel, a street, a train, a bar, a book, a film, in yourself, in you [tu: familiar], at the accident of your erect sex in the night seeking a place to put itself, to unburden itself of the tears that fill it" (7, my translation). This imposed masculinity within the ungendered "you" is precisely what calls forth in a woman reader a sense of split identification, since she is addressed as "masculine" by the text.

Identification here must be seen as a complex process that involves constructing a relation that somehow places both terms, the subject and the other with whom he or she identifies. Identification, as the basis of ego formation, is a transformative and intersubjective process that produces both a subject and a relation. As Teresa de Lauretis puts it, to identify "is to be actively involved in a process that, it must be stressed, is materially supported by specific practices—textual, discursive, behavioral—in which each relation is inscribed."[20] The feminine figure in narrative or cinema is most often constituted as the object of the look and desire, and as boundary to be crossed, disturbance that must be mastered, passive resistance that the active hero figure overcomes. Thus, argues de Lauretis, woman is eventually constituted by narrative as the figure of its own closure, as its object. Duras' text here genders the narrative object as male; this is a reversal in one register, since narrative frequently sets the "masculine" against a feminine object on which it operates, in an active-passive configuration. But, since this "masculine" figure is also addressed as "you" by the narrating voice, the text shatters conventional narrative polarities.

Concerning cinema and cinematic narrative, de Lauretis describes the splitting that underlies feminine spectatorship, within an apparatus that tends to code the camera's look as "masculine." The split of identification, she argues, is articulated as "identification with the look of the camera, apprehended as temporal, active or in movement, and identification with the image on the screen, perceived as spatially static, fixed, in frame" (123).

The contradictions of *La Maladie* are precisely here: the *you* framed by the text is masculine, but barely held in frame; in fact, Duras' recommendation, which is part of the text, is that if the piece is performed on stage, this "you" should remain absent, and the text be read by a male actor, differentiated from the character. The female actor would appear on stage, and would recite her part from memory. Thus she would represent a certain conventional cohesion of the actor, representing a character, while the male would be a narrator both addressing a "you," and reporting his own speech—as a literal stand-in, a delegate. Meanwhile, simultaneously and implicitly, he would play the part of the reader or the reading, itself staged. The "you" to whom he speaks then would be spread across at least three sites: the absent man, the young woman, and the spectator, thus fracturing the separation of registers proposed by the text, as text or theater. Any reader/spectator would find her/himself oscillating, circulating among these positions and registers; but, indeed, because of the determination of "you" as masculine, and its subsequent subversion, this text calls attention to the binding of gender position into and through representation.

In *L'Amante anglaise* a similar drifting effect is produced by the insistent textual emphasis on voice—both figural and structural—which intensifies the sense of dispossession of the word through the voice. The movement of the first dialogue/interview effects the spatial merger of the earlier taped version of the scene in the Café Balto with the moment of the interview. In the absence of citational marks, the two speech events begin to collapse temporal distance and to confuse the referentiality of the utterances. Robert's comments, which punctuate the tape's account, providing descriptive and contextual indices for it, become "invaginations," rather than a frame for this anterior *récit*. The effect of this slippage is to render problematic the status of the *récit*, the recording and the referentiality of both scenes, to call into question the possibility of *framing*.

The effect of this fiction is to produce, on the discursive plane, the echo of Duras' cinematic practice, to play out in the "taped" replay a rupture in the scene itself, now dispossessed of its visual aspect, which is to be supplied by another voice. The tape's autonomous and automatic discourse, unconscious of Robert's voice, then acts analogously to the images of *India Song*, for instance, in their dislocation with respect to the voices. Robert's discourse, which supplies the punctuation, the articulation, a new syntax and frame to the taped "event," is caught in a peculiar relationship to its own enunciative moment.

Indeed, this moment inscribes an effect similar to that described by Marie-Claire Ropars-Wuilleumier as structuring *India Song*, in its radical tension between voice and image. She writes, "Now it is the referential capacity of vision that is found, because of the asynchronic montage, to be both exasperated and thwarted: the picture leads to referentiality by its analogical status, and escapes from it by the autonomy of its statements. What is said cannot coincide with what is shown" ("The Disembodied Voice," 266). Much the same is suggested by the image of the tape-recorded voice, which installs referential fiction in its analogical relation to the voice it has registered.

Such an image is the figure that Cocteau uses to describe the filmic, "death at work" (cited in Heath, *Questions,* 114), the constant striving of the frame against the loss that works on it. The loss, absence, and fading at work in the film's intermittence, its flickering effect, are the "outside" that haunts the filmic consolidation of an image—what is missing in the image. Repeatedly, obsessively, Duras' texts and films activate our sense of this gap. *L'Homme atlantique* narrates the process of a film to be made, opening with the line, "You will not look at the camera, except when we require it of you . . . You will forget that it is the camera. But especially you will forget that it is you" (7, my translation). Here, a whole narrative movement operates to produce this forgetting: of subject and object of the gaze, of the distance between them, and especially, of the frame. Within a few pages, the text announces: "You have left the camera's field. You are absent. With your departure, your absence has emerged, it has been photographed just as before your presence was" (15, my translation).

This passage figures the fading that the cinematic frame both depends on and strives to conceal, to hold off. Meanwhile, this absence from the frame installs a new textual frame, as it demarcates a new narrative space, where the "I" narrates her reaction to this absence. Finally, "you" returns to the image, to the frame, producing a third segment of the text, a *frame* folding over upon the middle section of the text. Disturbance of the frame and of the image coincides with the "frame of reference" of these pronouns. Consequently, we become aware of the interdependence of our subject-position—as distanced from the image, mastering it through the reading/spectating gaze—and the frame itself, which immobilizes movement against loss, fixes the image against its own prior and virtual absence. In fact, our own potential absence is inmixed with our guaranteed absence from the frame: "You have left the camera's field. You are absent."

The blockages that inhere in the discursive movement of the first dialogue and in Claire's hysterical speech accomplish a similar disturbance of reference and meaning in *L'Amante anglaise*. Claire's discourse concludes with the refusal to speak the missing word—to designate the location of the head, which would permit the total identification of the body, the reestablishment of wholeness, and fulfill the demand for a complete confession: "And you think I'm going to let you get that word out of me so that all the others can be buried, and me with them, in the asylum?" Putting suspense in the place of climax, this discourse ends with a conventional conversational opening, the purely phatic: "If I were you, I'd listen. Listen to me" (122). These are the last words of the text. Built on the structure of shifters, the imperative direct address, they install an unfulfilled pact, a promise of speech and an impossible demand, in which the reader's implication is inescapable. That referential inescapability, founded as it is upon a deferral, the death of discourse, retrospectively conditions the entire textual project as undermining, but not escaping, the foundations of speech as act, communication, or referentiality.

A parallel textual move marks the curious conclusion of *Moderato cantabile*'s repetitive dialogic "reconstruction" of a woman's murder by her lover. " 'I wish you were dead,' Chauvin said. 'I am,' [c'est fait: done] Anne Desbaresdes said."[21] These last lines of dialogue effect a dramatic shift from the constative to the performative that resumes and rewrites the textual movement. Indeed, the textual strategy indicates that the dialogic reconstruction of the crime has become the event's reenactment, the event itself, whose performance we have somehow missed—again. The wish or order has a strange perlocutionary force—but its accomplishment escapes all discursive boundaries. "C'est fait," spoken either as the acceptance of a wager, the formalization of a contract, or the declaration of a fact, remains undecided. The point marked by this unstable "done" is the point of textual undoing, a non-saturation of context and enunciation. We can verify neither meaning nor reference here; nor is it possible to assure that any act at all has taken place.

This scene reflects on the entire problem of this text: what is the event?

And what is its relation to the account? The textual recounting of the event becomes an event in itself, an event which takes place in the mode of recitation/repetition, and which then casts the "original" event in the same frame, as itself a repetition. Framed as it is by the music lessons, the practicing of scales [répétition des gammes], the text continues to interrogate the status and modes of repetition. The problem of the mode itself reverberates from the title to the curious shifts in verb tenses—the mode of telling, and of narrative frames, punctuations, or measure. The question of musical measure and discursive grammatical modes, then, inaugurates the account.

Moreover, the musical repetitions are the scene of the regulation and channeling of the child's energy into the correct measure, the repeated performance, the perfecting of musical scheme, as well as the scene of memorization, in the sense that one repeats or rehearses the piece in preparation for its "recital" from memory. This scene, textually marked by the *passé simple* as anterior, but also marked as habitual through the teacher's remarks, is punctuated by the event of a cry. To the question, "Are you sure you don't know what *moderato cantabile* means?" the child fails to answer, and the scene is immobilized, awaiting the response he withholds. Shortly thereafter, the non-punctual punctuating cry arrives. "In the street downstairs a woman screamed [un cri de femme retentit], a long, drawn-out scream, so shrill it overwhelmed the sound of the sea. Then it stopped, abruptly" (65). But even this pointed end is rendered less than punctual, blunt, as the cry becomes an event: "Scattered shouts followed [rélayèrent] the first, confirming an already established fact [une actualité déjà dépassée], henceforth reassuring" (65).

It is the subsequent relay of cries, scattering and echoing the first, that paradoxically appoints it an event, relates it to the moment of death. But this inaugural rupture, the cry as marking the moment of death, while becoming increasingly indeterminate through its reverberation, repetition, in the crowd, is echoed textually by the repeated interrogation of the meaning of the cry in Anne's dialogue with Chauvin. Its textual relay transforms it from the marker of the moment of death to the trace of separation.

"It was a long, high-pitched scream, that stopped when it was at its loudest," she said.

"She was dying," the man said. "The scream must have stopped when she could no longer see him." . . .

"I think I must have screamed something like that once, yes, when I had the child." . . .

"I screamed . . . You have no idea." (79)

The dialogic reconstruction of the crime's course and motives transforms itself into an invention of those very sources, a channeling of a desire for death interwoven with Chauvin's invention of Anne's own story, and with her invention of the story of her own maternity. The child, who insistently asks "what the scream was about," becomes a textual center of death and desire; "He worries me to death [il me dévore]," says Anne (67). To use *dévorer* here, as the French does, without a specific figurative sense, implies the mortal duality of this relationship. "Sometimes I think I invented you," Anne repeats (76). This is also the last narrative that Anne desires to relate: "My child . . . I didn't have the time to tell you . . ." (115); "Sometimes, I think I must have invented him" (115). This is the undeniable event that Chauvin has repeatedly denied: "You never screamed, never." It is through the repetitive dialogue, constantly punctuated by the demand "Talk to me" (another inversion of *L'Amante anglaise*'s dialogic structure, "Listen to me"), that the reconstruction or narrative account becomes an invention; within this same movement, desire is bound to death, maternity to murder.

Through its binding of the scream, the voice outside discourse, with maternity and death, this text stresses the problem of the relation between discourse and its nondiscursive limits, in specific connection to the feminine. *Moderato* performs at the border of discourse, between articulation and pulsional movement, stressing the split symbolization that is at work in language.

The musical frame of the text, the *repetition* as scene, is central in another way also, since it figures the loss of the word through disarticulation—the cry—and through withholding, in the child's refusal to define "moderato cantabile." In this sense, speech itself becomes a textual figure. The withheld speech of the music lesson is itself echoed in the central scene of the text, the dinner. Not only is this scene framed as central, but it is also the only passage narrated in the conventional diegetic form. Furthermore, it concludes with a curious slippage between past, present indicative, and future tenses: "In spite of himself the man *will retrace* his steps. Again he *sees* the magnolias, the railings, the bay windows in the distance, still lighted . . . On his lips the song *heard* that afternoon, and the name that he *will utter* a little louder this time. He

157

will come . . . sooner or later the man *will pass* by the garden. He *has come*" (111, emphasis added).

In its overt appeal to diegetic coding, however, this passage explodes narrative time. In so doing, it recalls the relay of cries that "[confirms] an already established fact" and anticipates the last dialogic exchange between Anne and Chauvin: " 'One last time,' she begged, 'tell me about it one last time.' Chauvin hesitated . . . then he decided to tell her about it as if it were a memory" (115). The story they have elaborated obsessively, without advancing its narrative movement, is now repeated as if already incorporated into memory.

The collapse of narrative time as emphasized in this dinner scene is linked to the thematics of orality. Description of food casts it simultaneously as cadaver and spectacle. The table thus constitutes the intersection of culinary and mortuary codes, as well as of orality and sociality: "The salmon, chilled in its original form, is served [*arrive,* active voice] . . . It is not proper to talk about it . . . In the kitchen, the women [*des femmes*] . . . smothering a duck in its orange-shrouded coffin" (106). Vacillating between two poles—between the dinner conversation and the devouring of nourishment—the scene of the dinner stresses the conjunction of consumption and speech.

> Slowly the digestion of what was once [ce qui fut: passé simple] a salmon begins. . . . Nothing upset the solemnity of the process. The other waits, snug and warm, in its orange shroud. . . .
> Little by little the chorus of conversation grows louder and, with considerable effort and ingenuity, some sort of society emerges. . . .
> The remains of the salmon are offered again [le saumon repasse sous une forme encore amoindrie]. The women will devour it to the last mouthful. Their bare shoulders have the gloss and solidity of a society founded and built on the certainty of its rights, and they were chosen to fit this society. Their strict education has taught them that they must temper their excesses in the interest of their position. (106–7)

A *society* of hands and mouths is exposed in the form of its coding and regulation: speech and food—moderato cantabile. Within this scene, Anne's refusal to speak, and thereby to enter into conversational exchange, coincides with her refusal of food. In this she is again linked to Chauvin, whose promenade constructs an exterior space. "He doesn't eat. He cannot eat either, his body obsessed by another hunger" (108).

Anne's mouth becomes the central figure of the scene: "Her mouth is desiccated by another hunger that nothing, except perhaps the wine, can satisfy" (109–10). But she cannot consume, because her mouth is already full—full of a name. "Her mouth, filled with wine, encompasses a name she does not speak. All this is accomplished in painful silence" (110–11). This silent Medusa-headed figure ("the blond disorder of her hair" [109]) finds the zone of oral consumption blocked by the unpronounceable word—the lost name. The sign serves merely to designate a border—when it can be neither incorporated, nor expelled. In a literal sense, she eats her own word, chokes on her demand, the calling of the name she fails to pronounce.

This scene ends with the reversal of alimentary order—purgation: "She will go into the child's room, lie down on the floor and to the inviolable rhythm of her child's breathing, she will vomit forth the strange nourishment [nourriture étrangère: literally, *foreign* food] that had been forced upon her . . . This time she will offer an apology. The shadow will not reply [On ne lui répondra pas: no one will answer]" (112). Only after expelling the foreign body of nourishment can Anne speak, and even then, her speech is non-exchangeable. More important, the text here establishes a link between the unspoken word and the oral purge, as if Anne vomits a word, a nonfunctional name—a name proper to no one. For although we may imagine this to be Chauvin's name, it is never determinate in the text. It is, rather, "un nom," a "name," a "no," (French "non," also) the name of a name, nominal capacity dislodged from its referential function: the *mot-demande*, the unspoken and unanswered vocative.

The failure of communication, of oral exchange, that is figured in the dinner scene is reflected and translated in the text's last scenes, where the dialogue becomes an exchange of a "rien."

> "There's no use trying to understand. It's beyond understanding." . . .
> "Does it take a long time, a very long time?"
> "Yes a very long time. But I don't know anything." He lowered his voice: "Like you, I don't know anything. Nothing at all." (116)

This "nothing," as the end of the account, is also related to the centrality of the mouth, as empty, as the site of failure and death: "They lingered in a long embrace [leurs lèvres restèrent l'une sur l'autre posées: here the

French stresses disembodied lips, and says nothing about an embrace],
their lips cold and trembling, so that it could be accomplished, performing the same mortuary rite as their hands had, an instant before" (117).
In this case, the oral exchange of dialogue is literalized in the kiss that
kills desire, that inscribes the border of the exchange in putting to death
the possibility of its consummation.

Vomiting, in this text, also marks dispossession, insatiable demand,
refusal, and generosity. Most of all, it thematizes the problem of orality
and materiality—speech and appetite. As figure, the oral zone remains
on the border of figurability. The focus on orality disclosed in *Moderato*
is translated in *L'Amante* through its emphasis on Claire's nausea at "la
viande en sauce," the use of the mint as a purgative, antidote to the toxic
food. This oral obsession is bound up with the question of investigation
and identification of the woman's body. Anne Desbaresdes rehearses
more and more obsessionally the desire of death that motivates the other
woman's complicity in her murder; Claire Lannes, we are told, has gone
so far as to stuff her ears with wax in order to imitate Marie-Thérèse,
the deaf-mute. In this case, the identification leads to the murder of the
imaginary double. The murder's consequence is a renewed investigation,
at a distance, which implicitly aims at identifying Claire herself: "I'm
trying to find out what sort of a woman Claire Lannes really is, and why
she says she committed this crime. She can't give any reason for having
done it, so I am looking for a reason for her [Je cherche pour elle]" (36).
The investigator himself slips between the two poles of the verb "to look
for," as in: to search for *Claire,* as if she might be found, and to search
on her behalf, in her place.

Clearly, Claire has problems with differentiation; she relates "everything to everything else" in her discourse, and, for her, "all things were
equal"; "I think that if Claire hadn't killed Marie-Thérèse she would
have ended up killing someone else . . . it didn't matter who was at the
end of the tunnel, Marie-Thérèse or me," says her husband (76). The
homophony *mari-Marie* here materializes a peculiar textual indifferentiation; the murder itself reads as a substitute for suicide ("In this case I
think that the murderer killed the other person as if he were killing
himself . . . because they were together in a situation that was too static"
[18]), as the investigator speculates. Claire distinguishes reality from
dreams, and life from death, only with difficulty; she speaks of the policeman from Cahors as if he were still living. This indifferentiation is

even operative on the level of her syntax, if not a condition of it: "Did you hear what I just said," remarks Claire to the interviewer. "I'm talking differently now. I'm not separating my sentences. I just noticed myself [je viens de m'entendre: to hear myself]" (111).

It is as if the act of hearing herself were only occasionally accessible to her. This speech which cannot hear itself is here linked to the disturbance of punctuation and syntax, to the impossibility of ending a phrase, thus marking its border and separation from the next, establishing a relation of linear order, succession, meaning. If the "reason" of grammar, or the syntax of reason is at stake in Claire's discourse, the "logic" of the murder is also unaccountable. The "reason" of the murder is connected with food, as in the nauseating food Marie-Thérèse prepares, and with identification, lack of difference.

Claire's effort to produce differentiation is emblematized in her *cutting*: "And she used to cut things up. Once I remember, she cut up every blanket on her bed into three equal strips" (67). This figure reintroduces the triangle—the possibility of differentiation through the intervention of the law—thereby reproducing the connection between a failure of syntactic cutting, of discursive punctuation, and its relation to reason.

What is important, it seems to me, is the text's focus on the complex articulation of desire and demand, appetite and the law, with the woman's body as the place of the law's inscription. What complicates the figuration of difference established through the cut and the separation is the problem of the word and the cry.

In the "case" of L'Amante anglaise, the horrifying space of indifferentiation from an englobing maternal body is rent by the cutting, a fragmentation of the body, and followed by the inscription of the name. Furthermore, beside the "cut" of this text, it is a word that makes all the difference. Marie-Thérèse is "cut off" from the world of speech, while Claire's speech is the scandal that the law attempts to regulate or reduce. Moreover, it is a word, "forest," that has led Claire to confess her crime (24, 77–78); and it is a word withheld that perpetuates the exchange between Claire and the interviewer: "I've told everything except about the head. If I tell where the head is, I'll have told everything" (86–87).

If Duras' texts are always "au bord de la mer(e)," if Anne Desbaresdes' trajectory, her *aller-retour*, round-trip, on the Boulevard de la Mer defines the circumference of the scene that investigates death, desire, and maternity, then L'Amante anglaise elaborates a fascination with borders in another way. Desire and demand are mutually implicated in the double articulation of consumption and speech, incorporation and expulsion. The privilege of the oral zone, as thematic, figural, and conditioning metaphor of these texts, reflects on the question of discursive communication, articulating issues of discourse in relation to the body and of the word as a sort of "dead" body in discourse.

This "dead" body of the word may be related to the space of orality as the scene of demand's production of desire, and of the propping of language upon the drive. Derrida elaborates upon this process, in "Fors," as a transaction or negotiation between the literal and the figural.[22] Introjection (the process of the ego's constitution by transforming itself on the model of parental images) is derived from incorporation, the oral assimilation of objects into the body. As such, introjection is a "metaphorization" of the literal, physical operation. The mouth, the oral passage, is an intersection: the site where speech first replaces the presence of the object, where representation fills the gap, the void created by the absence of the object. Complications arise at this border site where the differentiation of literal from figural, object from language-speech, itself first arises.

Figuring the problem of the oral border, the zone of exchange where desire and nourishment are imbricated, where the sign becomes nourishment and food becomes a sign, Duras' narratives also interrogate the possibility of a zone of exchange between the metaphoric and metonymic, the literal and the figurative, the voice and writing.

Derrida's exposition of the fantasy of incorporation, as a failure of the metaphorization necessary for introjection, sets it over against the idealizing movement of introjection. The fantasy of incorporation literalizes the metaphor of introjection, introducing an object into the body. However, in this case, the object is devoured, assimilated, in order to stave off the necessity of its introjection. It is vomited back, expelled, or buried "inside," rather than assimilated, in a refusal of the idealizing movement.

This description surely brings to mind Laplanche's theory of propping, in its relation to the oral, and to sexuality as an "alien internal entity." Duras' texts are continually throwing up fragments—a fragmented repetition of a maternal scene, or of the mother's body, or of what Madeleine Borgomano calls the "generative cell," the figurations of the beggar woman, the feminine exchange of The Vice-Consul.[23]

Borgomano sees the beggar woman's exchange of her child, the maternal substitution, as the generating seed or cell of the textual network that constitutes Duras' oeuvre. For her, the textual movement can be related to the mode of dreams and fantasy, since it involves indefinite displacements of characters and figures from text to text. It is displacement based on replacement and exchange of figures that remains a constant function in Duras' texts. According to Borgomano, the estranging, uncanny force of these substitutions lies in both their repeated *translation* of the beggar woman figure and their connection to the desire of their own annihilation.

Translation may indeed be the most appropriate word here, in its etymological connection with death and repetition. Besides its more common senses, translation can also mean: to transplant, to graft in; to remove a person from a position, to remove a body from one grave to another, to remove the seat of a disease from the body; to retransmit a telegraphic message by means of an automatic repeater. Duras' narratives situate themselves in a constant process of translation, perpetually displacing the body that cannot be buried, automatically repeating their signifying mechanisms. But if this is the case, they are perpetual displacements of a text/scene whose original is lost, whose original is, in fact, loss itself.

In connecting these textual repetitions and investigations to the ambivalent figure of the mother, and to propping upon the maternal body, Duras' narratives respond to the hysteric's question—desire or identification?—by emphasizing the undecidable relation of the two. The textual repetitions constitute a metonymic and metaphoric deflection, *dérive*, a drifting off that is inflected both metonymically and metaphorically.

Through their figuration of an hysterical discourse, an exchange mediated through a set of identifications, these texts articulate a particular relation of language to the body. We may connect this complex binding of identification and introjection, which destroys, and incorporation, which neither consumes nor idealizes, with the more general scriptural project that Duras' text embodies. The vicissitudes of the metaphors of self-generation and autotransmission, across Duras' corpus, are characterized by repetition and translation of the figures of desire and death converging upon maternity. Borgomano sees the translation of the figure from one text to another as related to the movement through which generic boundaries are questioned and ruptured in this oeuvre, which "unfolds like a vast book" and still remains fragmented in texts of various generic categories, including those she calls "hybrids." These hybrids, as she indicates, are the texts specifically designated as cross-generic—"script," "ciné-roman," or "texte-théâtre-film," and which constitute implicit interrogations of generic possibility/purity.

As Borgomano points out, in Duras' first novel, *Un barrage contre le Pacifique,* there is already a kind of generic contamination, if only figuratively, since it recounts a film seen by the heroine, Suzanne, in such a way that the act of filming or of watching films is connected to death and mutilation. This effect is characteristic of all Duras' texts—filmic or narrative—which constitute acts of "cannibalization," consuming and re-presenting mutilated fragments of other texts. Textual mutilation and its relation to both consumption and death are linked to the central figure of *L'Amante anglaise,* the writing on the amputated body parts, as well as to the central questions of narrative representation that Duras' texts elaborate.

Through their very self-consumption, continued translation, these narratives figure the inscription of the law on the feminine, on the body, and continue to break the law, the law of the text, of genre, just as they perpetually fail to account for the death/the body at their center. As such, they dramatize the problem of the border, of differentiating inside from outside, the body from its voice, the subject from its discourse. This is the paradox of textual designations such as often appear on Duras' texts, where the generic coding is part of the title: roman, texte-théâtre-film, the subtitle of *India Song.* Once such generic marking designates the text as belonging to a category, while not belonging itself to the text, the mark marks a difference within the writing.

The execution of the law in the texts' generic confusion, in their mixing of genres, parallels the breaking of the textual contract the detective story forges with the reader. The reader's position mimes the textual movement in its critical performance, thereby constructing another zone of exchanges (like the primitive zones of bodily exchange), where indifferentiation both produces and disorganizes the lines and direction of exchange. Because of this disruption in exchange, the reader's position is constituted through a split identification. (Duras' texts foreclose solution, produce neither the evidence, nor the judgment, nor even the dead body; rather, they inscribe death itself, the death of the text.)

If I focus on the issue of translation, as the "last word," so to speak, of this project, it is precisely because translation is that which abolishes the possibility of "having" the "last word," which it displaces as consistently and insistently as it does the "originary" word.

But, just as any translation nonetheless "appeals" to its original for its identity, so Duras' textual discourse "appeals" to the body, to femininity. Similarly, just as in translation, there is no guarantee to this appeal, neither is there any "appeal" to the body by language which is fully satisfied, or conversely, any "appeal" to language by the body. The two are radically heterogeneous. Duras' texts, then, map this heterogeneity, a perpetually active process of "appeal" between the two, a calling, or a recalling, that never attains stasis. It is in this perpetual "calling" of language to the body, of the body to language, that I locate the "feminine" voice of Duras' texts.

Voice, here, might be characterized as that intersection of body and discourse, that excess of body in discourse, the site of an unlocalizable juncture, a doubling of the two. The doubling figured in this term—voice—is analogous to that which grounds the notion of "propping," which characterizes the relationship of body and language.

Within this perpetual translation, the displacement of textual *voice*, we might say, finally, that the reader's position is continually translated as well. As the sites of emission and address are increasingly destabilized by the effects of narrative in the second person in the later works, as in "Savannah Bay is you," the problem of memory and history intensifies. The scenes played out in Duras' most recent work, *Navire Night, Savannah Bay,* "The Seated Man in the Passage," and *L'Homme atlantique,* are translations of the central obsessions that extend back to the earliest work. As its readers, we now share its memory. But this memory always fails; it is faulty, the translation misses the mark, because of its perpetual displacement and reframing.

Just such a troubling refusal or failure of consistency is at work in the verb tenses of these recent works. Most are written in the conditional or future anterior: "You would have," "You will have," "You might have . . ." These are the modes of desire, hypothesis, a future of the past, yet another dispersal in the contradictory rapprochement of memory and anticipation, where we cannot establish ourselves in a consistent temporal position.

Navire Night is emblematic of the destabilizations the recent works perform:

> Your voice, alone.
> The text of voices says the eyes are closed.
> —No image on the text of desire?
> —What image?
> —I don't see what image.
> —Then there's nothing to see.
> —Nothing, no image. . . .
> Blind, advancing.
> On the sea of black ink.
> The Navire Night has just entered its own story. (31–32, my translation, here and following)

The inadequacy of *my* translation (how to translate the hybrid, bilingual name: Navire Night?) reflects the relation of reciprocal inadequation of image, text, and voice figured here. Image, text, and voice continually fail each other, fail to coincide.

Within this narrative that simply orchestrates voices talking about the voices that *have* talked (the exclusively telephonic exchange that constitutes the love affair of the dying woman and the telephone operator), there is a moment when the image of the image emerges. The woman has sent the man some photographs, perhaps of herself.

> —The story stops with the photographs.
> —The Navire Night is arrested on the sea.
> —There is no possible route left. No more itinerary.
> Desire is dead, killed by an image.
> — . . . He can no longer answer the phone.
> From these photographs he would no longer recognize her voice.
> (51–52)

It is precisely the dream of consistency, mutual support in the coincidence of image and voice that is radically in question here. This narrative of the image killing voice, voice failing image, refusing it, is emblematic of the contradictions at work in Duras' text. There is no translation that is not a mistranslation, no frame that doesn't hold off, render absent, as much as it renders present.

Voice and image, body and discourse, deflect each other, continually veer apart in translation effects, and the narrative slips out of frame. In this slippage, we, the readers, move out of frame like the wandering image of a man in *L'Homme atlantique*. This text opens with the following commands:

> You will not look at the camera . . .
> You will forget.
> You will forget.
> That it's you.
> I believe it's possible to do so.
> You will also forget that it's the camera. But above all you'll forget it's you. You . . . (7, my translation, here and following)

The uncanny effects here are multiple: our forgetting is demanded and anticipated for us, but precisely within the moment of our discomfort at the direct address with which we cannot quite coincide. The "you will forget" produces a startling distant echo of as early a production as *Hiroshima mon amour*: "Look how I'm forgetting you!"

L'Homme atlantique is explicitly, and uncannily, the narrative of a film that "will be made," but cast in the mode of failure, as already failed, stressing the impossibility of cinematic *presentation*.

> You have left the frame of the camera.
> You are absent.
> With your departure, your absence has occurred; it has been photographed, just as your presence was . . .
> Only your absence remains, it is henceforth without any density, without any possibility of making a trace.
> You are precisely nowhere. (15)

This moment leaves us in a radical instability, stressing our absence from and *implication* in the text, all at once. As we are translated into "you," and from presence into absence, we are forced to recognize the mobility of the position of address that constructs us as much as it is constructed for us. Consequently, we are interpellated, arrested by a textual voice that addresses us directly, but only to declare our disappearance. It is precisely this noncoincidence of our reading with the address, where we are perpetually re-sutured into the movements of this most highly staged of dialogues, that is significant. We must continually rewrite our position, reposition ourselves in relation to the text, the representation. The splits or doubling disclosed by this enforced mobility of our position may be linked to the problem of the body, as gendered both *in* and *through* representation. Here we are ourselves figured as spectacle and spectator, on the impossible site of the camera in *L'Homme atlantique,* both in the frame and entirely outside it.

We find ourselves split and mobile as spectators, unable to keep the image in frame, unable to find an assurance or support for a consolidated, fixed subjectivity here. As spectators/readers, and particularly as women readers, since we are explicitly addressed as "male" (the "you" is determined as male here; significantly, a male rendered as spectacle), our position is split, incompletely anchored.

Perhaps more important, the *fading* of the reader's position, a figure for the subject's fading, is here conjoined with a gender position that is disclosed as a construction effected by the narrative's form of address. In their asymptotic approach to the limits, the edges, of discourse and image, Duras' texts render all framings unstable, but, simultaneously, disclose the enframing operation by which representation constructs its addressee. Furthermore, these texts rework the problem of construction within a problematic of sexual difference. Their feminine spaces, feminine voices, disclose "femininity" as the noncoincidence of body and discourse, where each must constantly *appeal* to the other, where each leans on the other in the impossibility of any final appeal, any adequate translation.

In *L'Homme atlantique,* as in all Duras' narratives, what is missing is also what is *missed:* the body from discourse, discourse from the body. Because these texts both posit and perform the incommensurability of these terms, as well as their inextricable binding—in a relation of interference as well as interdependence—they constitute a particular appeal to the feminist reader.

To the space coded as "feminine" by a shared collective discourse, this feminine speech maintains its own specific relation, doubled upon that limit. Duras' texts, then, approach and explore the limits of narrative representation itself, which can be called, "improperly" or not, feminine—feminine, that is, within a discursive space and a historical moment that codes sexual difference in this way.

In the same movement, these texts demand of us an interrogation of our own occupation or investment of gender position, that complex and contradictory process by which we accede to subjectivity only in and through codings that are supported by social discursive formations.

They thus invite us to work within the contradiction of body and discourse, since body is socially inscribed but always exceeding discourse and representation, and since discourse, while propped on the body, inevitably outruns it, into the field of social agency.

NOTES

1. Mary Ann Doane, "Women's Stake: Filming the Female Body," 35.

2. See, for example, Geoffrey Hartman, *The Fate of Reading* (Chicago: Univ. of Chicago Press, 1975). In a more recent study, *Mystery and its Fictions* (Baltimore, Md.: Johns Hopkins Univ. Press, 1979), David Grossvogel describes one of the cardinal features of the detective code as related to striptease, the slow, stylized unveiling of the known, shrouded in its discursive veil: "Mystery is, in fact, a patent knowledge over which a veil has been drawn at the first page that cannot extend beyond the last" (15). There is, in this characterization, the suggestion that the story's economy operates analogously to the suspense mechanism essential to fetishism, and that that economy shares with the latter the feature of disavowing the "known," all of which places the narrative code within a particularly "masculine" economy (here, "masculine" is to be understood as a constructed position, the term of a particular form of address).

3. Jacqueline Rose, "The Cinematic Apparatus: Problems in Current Theory," in *The Cinematic Apparatus,* ed. Teresa de Lauretis and Stephen Heath (London: Macmillan, 1980), 181–82.

4. See Mary Lydon, "Translating Duras: 'The Seated Man in the Passage,'" *Contemporary Literature* 24 (1983): 259–75, for a remarkable discussion of what she calls the subversion produced by " 'pure' sexual difference . . . on the level of the signifier" (265). This discussion includes a careful examination of Freud's essay on fantasy as well.

5. Catherine Clément, "De la méconnaissance: Fantasme, scène, texte," *Langages* 31 (1973): 36–52.

6. See Mary Ann Doane, "*Gilda:* Epistemology as Striptease," *Camera Obscura,* no. 11 (1983): 6–27, for one of the most detailed and subtle treatments of this configuration available.

7. Erica Eisinger, "Crime and Detection in the Novels of Marguerite Duras," *Contemporary Literature* 15 (1974): 512.

8. See Sarah Kofman, "The Narcissistic Woman: Freud and Girard," *Diacritics* 10, no. 3 (1980): 36–45. This is a translation of a central chapter of *L'Enigme de la femme* (Paris: Galilée, 1980).

9. See Michel Foucault, *The History of Sexuality, Vol. 1: An Introduc-

tion, trans. Robert Hurley (New York: Random House, 1978), for a discussion of the articulation of pleasure on power through the confession. The power involved here is, he contends, already influenced, if not seduced, by the pleasure it seeks to master. Simultaneously, as power and pleasure are bound together, pleasure is stimulated and intensified in the very act of evading containment, fleeing surveillance. It is at the confrontation of these two forces that their interdependency is forged, power giving in to pleasure just when it is parading its mastery *over* pleasure. (In detective fictions, it is frequently a woman's desire that is, either centrally or peripherally, the object of pursuit which is finally brought under control through a similar mechanism.)

10. Jacques Derrida, "The Law of Genre," *Glyph* 7 (Baltimore, Md.: Johns Hopkins Univ. Press, 1980), 215.

11. Shoshana Felman, "Turning the Screw of Interpretation," *Yale French Studies* 55/56 (1977): 167.

12. Patricia Fedkiw, "Marguerite Duras: Feminine Field of Hysteria," *Enclitic* 6, no. 2 (1982): 81.

13. On the relationship of the detail or fragment to the totality, see Naomi Schor, "Le Détail chez Freud," *Littérature*, no. 37 (1980): 7.

14. Sanford Ames, "Mint Madness: Surfeit and Purge in the Novels of Marguerite Duras," *Sub-stance*, no. 20 (1978): 38.

15. See Marie-Claire Ropars-Wuilleumier, "The Disembodied Voice: *India Song*," *Yale French Studies* 60 (1980): 267. What happens in this segment of *L'Amante anglaise* seems to me coherent with a strategy that Ropars identifies as the metaphorization of signs in Duras' filmic practice. She outlines it in *India Song* as follows: "The fact that the meaning of the name is distinct from its reference is amply stressed by the clash between verbal statement and representation. . . . However, the suspension of reference reflects on the meaning itself: the statement loses its transparency when the enunciative approach, unacknowledged by the visual representation, is referred back to the mere play of signs, taken over by the writing. No meaning can be expressed in itself. Although meaning and reference are necessarily differentiated by analysis, they cannot possibly be dissociated in their actualization."

16. Kaja Silverman, *The Subject of Semiotics* (New York: Oxford Univ. Press, 1983), 219.

17. Marguerite Duras, *La Maladie de la mort* (Paris: Minuit, 1982).

18. Marguerite Duras, *Savannah Bay* (Paris: Minuit, 1983).

19. Marguerite Duras, *L'Homme atlantique* (Paris: Minuit, 1982).

20. Teresa de Lauretis, *Alice Doesn't* (Bloomington: Indiana Univ. Press, 1984), 141.

21. Marguerite Duras, *Moderato Cantabile,* in *Four Novels,* trans. Richard Seaver (New York: Grove Press, 1965), 118.

22. Jacques Derrida, "Fors," introduction to *Cryptonymie: Le Verbier de l'homme aux loups,* ed. Nicholas Abraham and Maria Torok (Paris: Aubier Flammarion, 1976).

23. Madeleine Borgomano, "Histoire de la mendiante indienne," *Poétique,* no. 48 (1981): 489.

Bibliography

Works by Marguerite Duras

L'Amant. Paris: Minuit, 1984.

Abahn, Sabana, David. Paris: Gallimard, 1970.

Agatha. Paris: Minuit, 1981.

L'Amante anglaise. Paris: Gallimard, 1967.

L'Amour. Paris: Gallimard, 1972.

L'Après-midi de Monsieur Andesmas. Paris: Gallimard, 1962.

Un barrage contre le Pacifique. Paris: Gallimard, 1950.

Le Camion, suivi d'Entretien avec Michelle Porte. Paris: Minuit, 1977.

Détruire, dit-elle. Paris: Minuit, 1969.

Dix heures et demie du soir en été. Paris: Gallimard, 1960.

La Douleur. Paris: P.O.L., 1985.

L'Eden cinéma. Paris: Mercure de France, 1977.

L'Eté 80. Paris: Minuit, 1980.

Hiroshima mon amour. Paris: Gallimard, 1960.

L'Homme assis dans le couloir. Paris: Minuit, 1980.

L'Homme atlantique. Paris: Minuit, 1982.

Les Impudents. Paris: Plon, 1943.

India Song: texte-théâtre-film. Paris: Gallimard, 1973.

With Michelle Porte. *Les Lieux de Marguerite Duras*. Paris: Minuit, 1977.

La Maladie de la mort. Paris: Minuit, 1982.

With Joel Farges and François Barat. *Marguerite Duras*. Paris: Albatros, 1979.

Le Marin de Gibraltar. Paris: Gallimard, 1952.

Bibliography

Moderato cantabile. Paris: 10/18, 1958.

Nathalie Granger, suivi de La Femme du Gange. Paris: Gallimard, 1973.

Le Navire Night (suivi de *Césarée, Les Mains negatives, Aurélia Steiner, Aurélia Steiner, Aurélia Steiner*). Paris: Mercure de France, 1979.

Outside: papiers d'un jour. Paris: Albin Michel, 1981.

With Xavière Gauthier. *Les Parleuses*. Paris: Minuit, 1974.

Les petits chevaux de Tarquinia. Paris: Gallimard, 1953.

Le Ravissement de Lol V. Stein. Paris: Gallimard, 1964.

Savannah Bay. Paris: Minuit, 1982.

Le Square. Paris: Gallimard, 1955.

Theatre I, II. Paris: Gallimard, 1965.

Les Viaducs de la Seine-et-Oise. Paris: Gallimard, 1960.

Le Vice-consul. Paris: Gallimard, 1966.

La Vie tranquille. Paris: Gallimard, 1944.

Les Yeux verts, Les Cahiers du cinéma. Paris: Gallimard, 1980.

In English

L'Amante anglaise. Trans. Barbara Bray. London: Hamish Hamilton, 1968.

Destroy, She Said. Trans. Barbara Bray. New York: Grove Press, 1970.

Four Novels. Trans. Richard Seaver. New York: Grove Press, 1965.

Hiroshima mon amour. Trans. Richard Seaver. New York: Grove Press, 1961.

India Song. Trans. Barbara Bray. New York: Grove Press, 1976.

The Little Horses of Tarquinia. Trans. Peter Du Berg. New York: Riverrun, 1980.

The Lover. Trans. Barbara Bray. New York: Pantheon, 1985.

The Malady of Death: Five Novels. New York: Grove Press, 1985.

The Ravishing of Lol V. Stein. Trans. Richard Seaver. New York: Grove Press, 1966.

The Sailor from Gibraltar. Trans. Barbara Bray. New York: Riverrun, 1980.

The Sea Wall. Trans. Herma Briffault. New York: Farrar, Straus and Giroux, 1985.

The Square: Three Plays. Trans. Barbara Bray and Sonia Orwell. London: John Calder, 1967.

The Vice-Consul. Trans. Eileen Ellenbogen. London: Hamish Hamilton, 1968.

The War. Trans. Barbara Bray. New York: Pantheon, 1986.

Whole Days in the Trees and Other Stories. Trans. Anita Barrows. New York: Riverrun, 1984.

Selected Bibliography

Abel, Elizabeth, ed. *Writing and Sexual Difference*. Chicago: Univ. of Chicago Press, 1982.

Abraham, Nicholas, and Maria Torok. *Cryptonymie: Le Verbier de l'homme aux loups*. Paris: Aubier-Flammarion, 1976.

———. "The Shell and the Kernel." *Diacritics* 9, no. 1 (1979): 16-28.

Adams, Parveen. "A Note on the Distinction between Sexual Division and Sexual Differences." *m/f* 3 (1979): 51–57.

Ames, Sanford. "Mint Madness: Surfeit and Purge in the Novels of Marguerite Duras." *Sub-stance,* no. 20 (1978): 37–44.

Andermatt, Verena. "Big Mach." *Enclitic* 4, no. 1 (1980): 24–35.

———. "Rodomontages of *Le Ravissement de Lol V. Stein*." *Yale French Studies* 57 (1979): 23–35.

Austin, John. *How to Do Things with Words*. Cambridge: Harvard Univ. Press, 1962.

Bal, Mieke. *Narratologie*. Paris: Klincksieck, 1977.

Barthes, Roland. *Camera Lucida*. Trans. Richard Howard. New York: Hill and Wang, 1981.

———. *Le Grain de la voix: Entretiens, 1962–80*. Paris: Seuil, 1981.

———. *Image-Music-Text*. Trans. Stephen Heath. New York: Hill and Wang, 1977.

Bashoff, Bruce. "Death and Desire in Marguerite Duras' *Moderato cantabile.*" *MLN* 94 (1979): 720–30.

Baudrillard, Jean. *De la séduction*. Paris: Galilée, 1979.

Baudry, Jean-Louis. "The Apparatus." *Camera Obscura,* no. 1 (1976): 104–26.

———. "The Ideological Effects of the Basic Cinematic Apparatus." *Film Quarterly* 28, no. 2 (1974–75): 39–47.

Belsey, Catherine. *Critical Practice*. London and New York: Methuen, 1980.

Benamou, Michel, and Charles Caramello, eds. *Performance in Post-Modern Culture*. Milwaukee: Center for Twentieth Century Studies, University of Wisconsin, 1977.

Benjamin, Walter. *Charles Baudelaire: A Lyric Poet in the Era of High Capitalism*. Trans. Harry Zohn. London: New Left Books, 1973.

Berg, Elizabeth. "The Third Woman." *Diacritics* 12, no. 2 (1982): 11–20.

Bernheim, Nicole Lise. *Marguerite Duras tourne un film*. Paris: Albatros, 1981.

Bernheimer, Charles, and Claire Kahane. *In Dora's Case*. New York: Columbia Univ. Press, 1984.

Besnard-Coursodon, Micheline. "Significations du métarécit dans *Le Vice-consul*." *French Forum* 3, no. 1 (1978): 72–83.

Bishop, Louis. "The Banquet Scene in *Moderato cantabile*." *Romanic Review* 69 (1978): 222–35.

Borgomano, Madeleine. "L'Histoire de la mendiante indienne." *Poétique*, no. 48 (1981): 479–94.

Bortin, Mary Ellen. "Une voix, Marguerite Duras." M.A. thesis, Cornell Univ., 1977.

Boundary 2 (Winter 1984). Special issue: *On Feminine Writing*.

Brown, Beverley, and Parveen Adams. "The Feminine Body and Feminist Politics." *m/f* 3 (1979): 35–50.

Cameron, Deborah. *Feminism and Linguistic Theory*. New York: St. Martin's, 1985

Chambers, Ross. *Story and Situation*. Minneapolis: Univ. of Minnesota Press, 1984.

Charpentier, Françoise. "Une appropriation de l'écriture: *Territoires du féminin avec Marguerite Duras*." *Littérature*, no. 31 (1978): 117–25.

Chase, Cynthia. "Paragon, Parergon: Baudelaire Translates Rousseau." *Diacritics* 11, no. 2 (1981): 42–51.

Chasseguet-Smirgl, Jacqueline, ed. *Female Sexuality*. Ann Arbor: Univ. of Michigan Press, 1970.

Cixous, Hélène. "Castration or Decapitation?" *Signs* 7 (1981): 41–55.

——. "The Laugh of the Medusa." *Signs* 2 (1976): 39–54.

——. *Portrait de Dora*. Paris: Des Femmes, 1976.

——. *Prénoms de personne*. Paris: Seuil, 1974.

——. *Vivre l'orange*. Paris: Des Femmes, 1979.

Cixous, Hélène, Madeleine Gagnon, and Annie Leclerc. *La Venue à l'écriture*. Paris: 10/18, 1977.

Clément, Catherine. "De la méconnaissance: Fantasme, scène, texte." *Langages* 31 (1973): 37–52.

——. *Lives and Legends of Jacques Lacan*. Trans. Arthur Goldhammer. New York: Columbia Univ. Press, 1983.

Clément, Catherine, and Hélène Cixous. *La Jeune Née*. Paris: 10/18, 1975.

Conley, Verena. *Hélène Cixous: Writing the Feminine*. Lincoln: Univ. of Nebraska Press, 1984.

Copjec, Joan. "Flavit et Dissipati Sunt." *October,* no. 18 (1981): 21–40.

———. *"India Song/Son nom de Venise dans Calcutta désert:* The Compulsion to Repeat." *October,* no. 17 (1981): 37–52.

Coward, Rosalind, and John Ellis. *Language and Materialism.* London: Routledge and Kegan Paul, 1977.

Dallenbach, Lucien. *Le Récit spéculaire.* Paris: Seuil, 1977.

de Lauretis, Teresa. *Alice Doesn't: Feminism, Semiotics, Cinema.* Bloomington: Indiana Univ. Press, 1984.

de Lauretis, Teresa, and Stephen Heath. *The Cinematic Apparatus.* London: Macmillan, 1980.

de Lauretis, Teresa, Andreas Huyssen, and Kathleen Woodward. *The Technological Imagination: Theories and Fictions.* Madison, Wis.: Coda Press, 1980.

Deleuze, Gilles, and Félix Guattari. *L'Anti-Oedipe.* Paris: Minuit, 1975.

Derrida, Jacques. *La Carte postale.* Paris: Flammarion, 1980.

———. "Economimesis." *Diacritics* 11, no. 1 (1981): 3–25.

———. *Epérons: les styles de Nietzsche.* Paris: Flammarion, 1978.

———. "Fors." In *Cryptonymie: Le Verbier de l'homme aux loups,* ed. Nicholas Abraham and Maria Torok. Paris: Aubier-Flammarion, 1976.

———. "The Law of Genre." *Glyph* 7. Baltimore, Md.: Johns Hopkins Univ. Press, 1980.

———. *L'Oreille de l'autre.* Montréal: VLB Editeur, 1982.

———. "Signature, Event, Context." *Glyph* 1. Baltimore, Md.: Johns Hopkins Univ. Press, 1977.

———. *La Vérité en peinture.* Paris: Flammarion, 1978.

Doane, Mary Ann. "Film and the Masquerade: Theorising the Female Spectator." *Screen* 23, no. 3/4 (1982): 74–87.

———. *"Gilda:* Epistemology as Striptease." *Camera Obscura,* no. 11 (1983): 6–27.

———. "Woman's Stake: Filming the Female Body." *October,* no. 17 (1981): 23–36.

Doane, Mary Ann, Patricia Mellencamp, and Linda Williams. *Re-Vision: Essays in Feminist Film Criticism.* Los Angeles: American Film Institute, 1984.

Donzelot, Jacques. *The Policing of Families.* Trans. Robert Hurley. New York: Pantheon, 1979.

Eagleton, Terry. "Ideology, Fiction, Narrative." *Social Text* 1, no. 2 (1979): 62–80.

Eisenstein, Hester, and Alice Jardine, eds. *The Future of Difference.* New York: G. K. Hall, 1980.

Eisinger, Erica. "Crime and Detection in the Novels of Marguerite Duras." *Contemporary Literature* 15 (1974): 503–18.

Fedkiw, Patricia. "Marguerite Duras: Feminine Field of Hysteria." *Enclitic* 6, no. 2 (1982): 78–86.

Felman, Shoshana. *La Folie et la chose littéraire*. Paris: Seuil, 1978.

———. "Turning the Screw of Interpretation." *Yale French Studies* 55/56 (1977): 94–207.

Foster, Hal, ed. *The Anti-Aesthetic: Essays on Post-Modern Culture*. Port Townsend, Wash.: Bay Press, 1983.

Foucault, Michel. *The History of Sexuality, Vol. 1: An Introduction*. Trans. Robert Hurley. New York: Random House, 1978.

Foucault, Michel, and Hélène Cixous. "A propos de Marguerite Duras." *Cahiers Renaud-Barrault*, no. 89 (1975): 8–22.

Freud, Sigmund. *The Standard Edition of the Complete Psychological Works*. 24 vols. Ed. James Strachey. London: Hogarth Press, 1953.

Gallop, Jane. *The Daughter's Seduction*. Ithaca, N.Y.: Cornell Univ. Press, 1982.

Garner, Shirley Nelson, Claire Kahane, and Madelon Sprengnether. *The M(O)ther Tongue: Essays in Feminist Psychoanalytic Interpretation*. Ithaca, N.Y.: Cornell Univ. Press, 1985.

Genette, Gérard. *Figures I*. Paris: Seuil, 1966.

———. *Figures II*. Paris: Seuil, 1969.

Glassman, Debbie. "The Feminine Subject as History Writer in *Hiroshima mon amour*." *Enclitic* 5, no. 1 (1981): 45–54.

Graham, Joseph, ed. *Difference in Translation*. Ithaca, N.Y.: Cornell Univ. Press, 1985.

Grossvogel, David. *Mystery and Its Fictions*. Baltimore, Md.: Johns Hopkins Univ. Press, 1979.

Hanet, Kari. "Does the Camera Lie?" *Screen* 14, no. 3 (1973): 59–66.

Heath, Stephen. "Anata mo." *Screen* 17, no. 4 (1976–77): 49–66.

———. "Difference." *Screen* 19, no. 3 (1978): 50–112.

———. "Narrative Space." *Screen* 17, no. 3 (1976): 68–112.

———. "Notes on Suture." *Screen* 18, no. 4 (1977–78): 48–76.

———. "The Question Oshima." *Wide Angle* 2, no. 1 (1977), 48–57.

———. *Questions of Cinema*. Bloomington: Indiana Univ. Press, 1981.

Husserl-Kapit, Susan. "An Interview with Marguerite Duras." *Signs* 1 (1975): 423–34.

Irigaray, Luce. "Approche d'une grammaire d'énonciation de l'hystérique et de l'obsessionnel." *Langages*, no. 5 (1967): 99–109.

———. *Ce sexe qui n'en est pas un*. Paris: Minuit, 1977.

———. *Speculum de l'autre femme*. Paris: Minuit, 1974.

Jacobus, Mary, ed. *Women Writing and Writing about Women*. London: Crown Helm, 1979.

Jameson, Frederic. *Fables of Aggression: Wyndam Lewis, the Modernist as Fascist*. Berkeley and Los Angeles: Univ. of California Press, 1979.

———. "Imaginary and Symbolic in Lacan: Marxism, Psychoanalytic Criticism, and the Problem of the Subject." *Yale French Studies 55/56* (1977): 338–95.

———. *The Political Unconscious: Narrative as a Socially Symbolic Act*. Ithaca, N.Y.: Cornell Univ. Press, 1981.

Jardine, Alice. "Gynesis." *Diacritics* 12, no. 2 (1982): 54–65.

———. *Gynesis: Configurations of Woman and Modernity*. Ithaca, N.Y.: Cornell Univ. Press, 1985.

———. "Pre-texts for the Transatlantic Feminist." *Yale French Studies* 62 (1981): 220–36.

Kamuf, Peggy. *Fictions of Feminine Desire: Disclosures of Heloise*. Lincoln: Univ. of Nebraska Press, 1982.

———. "Replacing Feminist Criticism." *Diacritics* 12, no. 2 (1982): 44–47.

Kaplan, E. Ann. *Women and Film: Both Sides of the Camera*. London and New York: Methuen, 1983.

Klein, Melanie. *Love, Guilt and Reparation and Other Works, 1921–45*. London: Hogarth Press, 1975.

Kofman, Sarah. *L'Enigme de la femme*. Paris: Galilée, 1980.

Kristeva, Julia. *On Chinese Women*. Trans. Anita Barrows. New York: Urizen Books, 1977.

———. *Desire in Language*. Ed. Leon S. Roudiez. New York: Columbia Univ. Press, 1980.

———. *Histoires d'amour*. Paris: Denoel, 1983.

———. *Polylogue*. Paris: Seuil, 1977.

———. *Powers of Horror: An Essay on Abjection*. Trans. Leon S. Roudiez. New York: Columbia Univ. Press, 1982.

Kuhn, Annette. *Women's Pictures*. London: Routledge and Kegan Paul, 1982.

Kuhn, Annette, and AnnMarie Wople, eds. *Feminism and Materialism: Women and Modes of Production*. London: Routledge and Kegan Paul, 1978.

Lacan, Jacques. *Ecrits: A Selection*. Trans. Alan Sheridan. New York: Norton, 1977.

———. *The Four Fundamental Concepts of Psycho-analysis*. Ed.

Jacques-Alain Miller. Trans. Alan Sheridan. New York: Norton, 1978.

———. *The Language of the Self*. Ed. and trans. Anthony Wilden. Baltimore, Md.: Johns Hopkins Univ. Press, 1968.

———. *Le Séminaire, livre I. Les Ecrits techniques de Freud*. Paris: Seuil, 1975.

Lamy, Suzanne, and André Roy, eds. *Marguerite Duras à Montréal*. Montreal: Spirale, 1981.

Laplanche, Jean. *Life and Death in Psychoanalysis*. Trans. Jeffrey Mehlman. Baltimore, Md.: Johns Hopkins Univ. Press, 1976.

Laplanche, Jean, and J.-B. Pontalis. "Fantasy and the Origins of Sexuality." *International Journal of Psychoanalysis* 49 (1968): 15–23.

———. *The Language of Psychoanalysis*. Trans. Donald Nicholson-Smith. New York: Norton, 1974.

Lydon, Mary. "Translating Duras: 'The Seated Man in the Passage.' " *Contemporary Literature* 24 (1983): 259–75.

Lyon, Elisabeth. "The Cinema of Lol V. Stein." *Camera Obscura*, no. 6 (1980): 9–39.

Lyotard, Jean-François. *Dérive à partir de Marx et Freud*. Paris: 10/18, 1972.

———. *Des dispositifs pulsionnels*. Paris: 10/18, 1973.

———. "Fiscourse, digure: The Utopia Behind the Scenes of the Phantasy." *Theater Journal* 35, no. 3 (1983): 333–58.

———. *L'Economie libidinale*. Paris: Minuit, 1974.

———. "For a Pseudo-Theory." *Yale French Studies* 52 (1975): 115–28.

———. "One of the Things at Stake in Women's Struggles." *Sub-stance*, no. 20 (1978): 9–17.

MacCabe, Colin. "Theory and Film: Principles of Realism and Pleasure." *Screen* 17, no. 3 (1976): 7–27.

———, ed. *The Talking Cure*. New York: St. Martin's, 1981.

McConnell-Ginet, Sally, Ruth Barker, and Nelly Furman. *Women and Language in Literature and Society*. New York: Praeger, 1980.

MacKinnon, Catherine A. "Feminism, Marxism, Method and the State: An Agenda for Theory." *Signs* 7 (1982): 515–44.

Marini, Marcelle. *Territoires du féminin avec Marguerite Duras*. Paris: Minuit, 1977.

Mawkward, Christiane. "Structures du silence/du délire." *Poétique*, no. 25 (1978): 314–24.

Miller, D. A. "The Novel and the Police." *Glyph* 8. Baltimore, Md.: Johns Hopkins Univ. Press, 1980.

Miller, Nancy. "The Text's Heroine: A Feminist Critic and Her Fictions." *Diacritics* 12, no. 2 (1982): 48–53.

Mitchell, Juliet, and Jacqueline Rose, eds. and trans. *Feminine Sexuality: Jacques Lacan and the École Freudienne.* New York: Norton, 1982.

Montrelay, Michèle. "Inquiry into Femininity." *Semiotext(e)* 4, no. 1 (1981): 228–35.

———. *L'Ombre et le nom.* Paris: Minuit, 1977.

Mulvey, Laura. "Visual Pleasure and Narrative Cinema." *Screen* 16, no. 3 (1975): 6–18.

Murphy, Carole J. *Exile and Alienation in the Novels of Marguerite Duras.* Lexington, Ky.: French Forum, 1983.

Nichols, Bill. *Ideology and the Image.* Bloomington: Indiana Univ. Press, 1981.

Oudart, Jean. "Sur *Son nom de Venise dans Calcutta désert.*" *Cahiers du Cinéma,* no. 268–69 (1976): 75–77.

Pajaczkowska, Claire. "Introduction to Kristeva." *m/f* 5/6 (1981): 149–57.

Rainer, Yvonne. "Looking Myself in the Mouth." *October,* no. 17 (1981): 65–76.

Ricardou, Jean. *Nouveaux problèmes du roman.* Paris: Seuil, 1978.

———. *Pour une théorie du Nouveau Roman.* Paris: Minuit, 1971.

Riffaterre, Michael. *Semiotics of Poetry.* Bloomington: Indiana Univ. Press, 1978.

Rifflet-Lemaire, Anika. *Jacques Lacan.* Trans. David Macey. London: Routledge and Kegan Paul, 1977.

Robert, Marthe. *Roman des origines et origine du roman.* Paris: Grasset, 1972.

Ropars-Wuilleumier, Marie-Claire. "The Disembodied Voice: *India Song.*" Yale French Studies 60 (1980): 241–68.

Safouan, Moustafa. *La Sexualité féminine.* Paris: Seuil, 1976.

Schneiderman, Stuart. *Jacques Lacan: Death of an Intellectual Hero.* Cambridge: Harvard Univ. Press, 1983.

———, ed. *Returning to Freud.* New Haven: Yale Univ. Press, 1980.

Schor, Naomi. "Le Détail chez Freud." *Littérature,* no. 37 (1980): 3–14.

Sibony, Daniel. "Hamlet: A Writing Effect." *Yale French Studies* 55/56 (1977): 53–93.

Silverman, Kaja. *The Subject of Semiotics.* New York: Oxford Univ. Press, 1983.

Smith, Joseph, and William Kerrigan, eds. *Taking Chances: Derrida, Psychoanalysis and Literature.* Baltimore, Md.: Johns Hopkins Univ. Press, 1984.

Todorov, Tzvetan. *Poétique de la prose.* Paris: Seuil, 1971.

Vance, Carole, ed. *Pleasure and Danger.* London: Routledge and Kegan Paul, 1984.

Van Herik, Judith. *Freud on Femininity and Faith.* Berkeley and Los Angeles: Univ. of California Press, 1982.

Vircondelet, Alain. *Marguerite Duras.* Paris: Séghers, 1972.

Williams, Linda. "*Hiroshima* and *Marienbad*—Metaphor and Metonymy." *Screen* 17, no. 1 (1976): 34–40.

Index

183

Index

Feminism (*cont.*)
  der, 11–31; and film theory, 135–37, 139–40, 152–53, 164
La Femme du Gange, 1, 3, 67, 88
Fetishism, 59, 141
Figure, figuration: Duras as, 2–8; and disfiguration, 39–40, 53–60, 90–94, 139–47; railway system as, 46–48; of *fort-da* game, 48–50, 131; place names as, 51–52, 79–80; synecdoche, 52; fantasy as, 54–56; Lol V. Stein as, 90, 93, 121, 126; mother as, 93–94, 96, 114–15, 140; figurability, 99–100, 160–61; of writing, 103–4, 125–26, 147–51; film as, 109, 155; Medusa, 103, 117, 139; beggar woman as, 103–4, 117, 162–63; Vice-Consul as, 109–12; ball scene as, 110; mirror as, 112–14, 126; Anne-Marie Stretter as, 118; master figure, 118–19, 162–63; and ground, 119; triangle, 121–22; letter as, 125–26; woman as figure of law, 134–42, 155–57; and sexual difference, 136, 152–53; inscription of death, 137–62; fragmented body as, 145–47; and hysteria, 146–47, 163; voice as, 155–57; and literal, 161–64; of reader, 167–69
Forrester, Viviane, 88, 110–11
Fort-da game: in Lacan, 39, 48–49; in Derrida, 50; in Freud, 48–50; in *The Vice-Consul,* 110, 117–18, 131. *See also* Repetition compulsion
Foucault, Michel, 63, 169–70n
Fragment: fragmented body, 64, 145–47; textual, 113–14; in *L'Amante anglaise,* 143–47; and totality, 144–47, 170n; and detail, 146–47, 170n
Framing: as a textual issue, 12, 123; in *The Ravishing of Lol V. Stein,* 78; and narration, 104–9, 120–21, 123, 143–46, 153–56, 168; in sentence, 122; cinematic, 127–32, 152–55, 158, 164–68; and fantasy, 139–41. *See also* Gaze; Suture effect; Syntax

Gallop, Jane: "Writing and Sexual Difference," 16; *The Daughter's Seduction,* 119–20, 142

Gaze: desire to see, 35–36, 142; in *Hiroshima mon amour,* 40–42, 45, 55–57; as part object, 45–46, 55–56, 76–77, 91, 108–9, 120–21, 129, 138–39; in *The Ravishing of Lol V. Stein,* 74–78; in *The Vice-Consul,* 101–3, 108–9; cinematic, 130–31, 152–55, 164–68; and voice, 130–31; reader's, 154
Gender: of reader, 9, 132, 134–35, 138–42, 150–55, 164–69; constructed in representation, 11–31, 134–42, 150–55, 163–69; position, 116–17, 134–35, 138–39. *See also* Sexual difference; Reader
Genre: generic label, 1; generic boundaries, 12, 134–35, 137–44, 155–56, 161–64, 168–69; "law of," 144
Grammar, of fantasy structure, 44–45, 138–40. *See also* Syntax

Heath, Stephen: "Difference," 21–22; *Questions of Cinema,* 40, 47, 57, 88–89, 136, 140, 154
Hiroshima mon amour, 1, 24–25, 33–61, 145, 167
History: and sexual difference, 14, 21–22, 165–69; and representation, 23–25, 165–69; as referent in *Hiroshima mon amour,* 33–36, 52–55, 57–61; woman as subject of, 52–53, 115; as referent in *Aurélia Steiner,* 85
L'Homme assis dans le couloir ("The Seated Man in the Passage"), 7, 8, 138, 141, 165
L'Homme atlantique, 1, 128, 141, 151, 154, 165, 167–68
Hysteria: and sexual difference, 14–15, 25–30; hysterical discourse, 25–30, 146–50, 163–64; hysterical symptoms, 26–30, 33–34, 60–61, 100, 163; as textual figure, 28, 137–39, 146–50, 160–62, 163–64; and fantasy, 33–34; and identification, 33–34, 60–61, 96–97, 138–39, 160–62, 163–64; and memory, 46–47; and mourning, 60–61; and phobia, 99–100. *See also* Identification; Mourning

Sharon Willis received her Ph.D. from Cornell University and is currently on the faculty of the Department of Foreign Languages at the University of Rochester. *Marguerite Duras: Writing on the Body* is her first book.